MW00622292

"IMPOSSIBLE" MARRIAGES REDEEMED

They Didn't End the Story in the Middle

EDITED BY
LEILA MILLER

Copyright © 2020 by Leila Miller

All rights reserved. No part of this publication may be reproduced, distributed, or transmitted in any form or by any means, including photocopying, recording, or other electronic or mechanical methods, without the prior written permission of the publisher, except in the case of brief quotations embodied in critical reviews and certain other noncommercial uses permitted by copyright law.

Scripture quotations are taken from the Catholic Edition of the Revised Standard Version of the Bible (RSV), © 1965 and 1966 by the Division of Christian Education of the National Council of the Churches of Christ in the United States of America. Used by permission. All rights reserved.

Cover design by Andrew Centrella.

Cover photo by Beth Pack.

LCB Publishing
4427 E. Blanche Drive
Phoenix, AZ 85032
Leila@LeilaMiller.net

Ordering Information: Quantity sales. Special discounts are available on quantity purchases of 10 or more copies. For details, contact the publisher at the email above.

"Impossible" Marriages Redeemed/Leila Miller—1st ed.

ISBN 978-0-9979893-2-8

To LeeAnne Abel

One of the most beautiful creations of God is marriage and family. The blessing God gave to marriage remained even after the original sin of Adam and Eve, the progenitors of humankind. They were married directly by God, while they were still in paradise before the Fall. Since the Fall, Satan started his attacks on this paradisiacal institution. As we know, the final battle between Christ and Satan will be over marriage and family. We are witnessing in our days the beginning of this battle. The present book, *"Impossible" Marriages Redeemed*, edited by Leila Miller, proclaims and demonstrates convincingly and movingly the truths that conjugal crises can be healed and that the cross of difficult or, humanly spoken, "impossible" marriages bears many spiritual fruits in the eyes of God and eternity. I trust that this book will bring light and spiritual strength to wounded marriages and families, and may they in a special manner be protected by the Holy Family: by Jesus, Mary, and Joseph.

+ Athanasius Schneider, Auxiliary Bishop of Saint Mary in Astana

CONTENTS

HOW THIS BOOK CAME TO BE

When I published *Primal Loss: The Now-Adult Children of Divorce Speak* in 2017, the pain that poured forth from the pages was overwhelming and even unbearable. While compiling the testimonies of the 70 contributors, I knew I'd need to introduce some light and hope at the end of the book. As I said in the *Primal Loss* introduction:

> I understand that this book may weigh heavily on the spirit, so please don't leave until after you have read Chapter Ten, where you will find beautiful stories of marital redemption —seemingly hopeless marriages brought back from the brink of divorce.

Many readers told me that Chapter Ten ("Stories of Hope") was their favorite chapter, and a priest friend said more than once, "I could really use a whole book of those stories to share with parishioners in struggling marriages." With feedback like that, I had my marching orders, and what you have before you is the natural follow-up to *Primal Loss*.

FOREWORD

By Philip F. Lawler

Journalist, founder of Catholic World News service, author of *The Smoke of Satan, Lost Shepherd,* and *The Faithful Departed.*

This is a book full of heroes.

What is a hero, if not someone who makes sacrifices for another? In this book we have the testimony of people who have sacrificed their comfort and their pride to save their marriages, for the sake of their spouses and their children.

Most of the people who contributed to this book don't think of themselves as heroes, I'm sure. They may still be struggling from the lingering influence of neighbors and relatives and friends and even pastors who advised them to look out for themselves, to escape an unhappy situation. They may think of themselves merely as survivors. If so, I'm here to contradict them. They're heroes. At a time when marriages break down routinely, we need such heroes, as witnesses and models.

That need may become more acute, if the stories in this book are any indication. Notice how many contributors cite the ruinous influence of pornography on their marriages. Alcohol abuse has always been a danger to the marital union, but easy access to porn is something new; today the breakdown of a marriage may be just a few mouse-clicks away. Notice, too, how many contributors (and/or their spouses) are themselves the children of divorced parents. That problem, too, suggests a geometric increase in marital problems in coming years.

As a group, the contributors are religious, in most cases practicing

Catholics. So they have an advantage in their struggle with marital upheavals: a recognition that the marital union is something more than an ordinary partnership. Still it is remarkable that despite being regular members of a parish, they did not receive adequate help from the Church when their marriages were in crisis.

Why is it that, in so many cases, the first time that a troubled couple talks seriously with the pastor is when they begin to discuss divorce? Something must have gone wrong long before that, and the Church should have mobilized to defend the union. We need to find ways to spot marital trouble earlier, to encourage married couples to seek help before a manageable problem becomes a crisis. Catholics should be routinely talking about their marriages in sacramental confession and in spiritual direction. (Of course that assumes that they are going to confession regularly, since the sacrament is, among other things, an indispensable aid to marriage.)

While if it's sad that the Church does not offer married couples adequate help, it's downright scandalous that often the "help" that is offered is the toxic acceptance of divorce. Out of a misguided sympathy for an unhappy spouse, priests and parishioners leap to the conclusion that the situation cannot be salvaged. But it can!

Far better advice, for someone unhappy in marriage, would be something like this: "You took a vow to be faithful 'for better or worse.' Right now it looks worse. Your vow still binds you." Or this: "This is an opportunity to draw closer to Jesus Christ. Right now your marriage is your cross to bear. Can you ask for His help, to imitate Him?"

When a marriage seems to have broken down, the options can seem like a binary, on/off choice: to end it or to slog on joylessly. Not so. There is a third and better option: to dig down, solve the problems, and renew the loving relationship on a deeper, stronger foundation. One perceptive contributor put it in a nutshell:

> People often comment, "How do you go back to a marriage
> that is so broken?" My answer is, "You don't."

To repair a damaged marriage may require enormous quantities of patience, forbearance, and forgiveness. It will require an acknowledgment of wrongs, a confession of sins, a commitment to repentance and reform. To make matters more difficult still, sometimes a spouse who has been grievously wronged must, to save the union, reach out lovingly to the one who has done the wrong, and who may well reject the attempt at reconciliation.

Yes, the bid to save a marriage can mean time on the cross. Some of the stories that follow are heartbreaking; the situations sound intolerable; one can easily see how lesser people would have called it quits. But not these heroes.

Particularly poignant is the testimony of the "standers," who have chosen to honor their marriage vows even after their spouses have abandoned them and perhaps even remarried. The "standers" remain "single" even when society— and quite likely the diocesan marriage tribunal—would tell them that they, too, are free to remarry. In *Familiaris Consortio* (20), St. John Paul II remarks that the Church must "recognize the value of the witness of those spouses who, even when abandoned by their partner, with the strength of faith and of Christian hope have not entered a new union." Have you heard anything like that message recently from the pulpit in your parish? From your diocese? From the Vatican?

Still while the "standers" are the easiest heroes to identify, the happier stories here involve the people who persevered in their marriages—through the suffering, through the false hopes and false starts, through the mortification—and finally emerged with a stronger union, fortified by mutual understanding and forgiveness, by sacrifice and especially by prayer.

Some of these inspiring success stories will never be known, except to the spouses themselves, to a few of their close friends and their confessors—and to the privileged people who read this book. For obvious and healthy reasons, people who have survived a marital crisis are not ordinarily anxious to publicize their past troubles. We readers should be grateful to the contributors who have bared their souls, and to Leila Miller for collecting their testimony.

Once or twice as I read these stories, I wondered whether the anonymous author might be someone I know. If so, that person could only rise in my estimation. I say that these authors are my heroes, but I can pay them a greater compliment. They remind me of Jesus Christ. Because they have found a way to love someone who has become unlovable. And that's what the Lord has done with me.

INTRODUCTION

Catholics are against divorce in theory, but not in practice.

A few weeks ago, a horrified friend sent me the following message after being involved in a contentious Facebook discussion among seemingly faithful Catholic women:

> I canNOT believe how many married women get venomous and flip their lid when you merely suggest that someone's marriage has hope for reconciliation!

Sadly, I was not a bit surprised, as being viscerally against saving marriage has become the default position in many Catholic circles, especially among Catholic women's groups online. Even among our clergy and counselors, there is a near-universal "divorce, annul, and move on" mindset. One woman told me a story that is frighteningly common:

> Over the years, I consulted with up to six different priests while going through a tough time in our marriage. Each one said I had grounds for an annulment, and that he would help me through the process. The last time I consulted a priest was about 15 years ago, and this one said the same thing. I told him I did not want a divorce or an annulment, but rather to stay married and find meaning in my situation. He said that in his experience of witnessing marriages in an ongoing crisis like mine, healing was impossible. He said I

would pay an enormous price....In the 15 years since, much has changed and even improved. Our marriage is not perfect, but we have found happiness and peace. I am so glad my instincts were to stay and not leave. Giving over my tears and anguish as a kind of gift also gave my suffering meaning. That valley, though, was one tough haul —and I got little to no help from the Church. Maybe I should have looked elsewhere within the Church for encouragement, but by the time I consulted with that sixth priest, I just didn't want to hear any more 'give up, and get on with your life' advice.

This pervasive "divorce and move on" mindset makes it hard for us to imagine that there was a time—namely, the entire span of Christian history until a few decades ago—when the following sentiment by Pope Leo XIII was fully operative (emphasis mine):

When, indeed, matters have come to such a pitch that it seems impossible for [spouses] to live together any longer, then the Church allows them to live apart, and strives at the same time to soften the evils of this separation by such remedies and helps as are suited to their condition; *yet she never ceases to endeavor to bring about a reconciliation, and never despairs of doing so.* (*Arcanum*, Feb. 1880)

Never ceases. *Never* despairs.
  Never.

It sounds like a fairy tale now, yet this all-but-forgotten disposition is still a Christian imperative. In fact, the diligent and unending work to *restore* broken marriages—not end them!—is still the official teaching of the Catholic Church.

"But, what about abuse?"

Even though the vast majority of divorces do not proceed from high conflict marriages,[1] the question of abuse is brought up immediately in any discussion of divorce (much like the "but what about rape or incest?" question in the abortion debate), effectively derailing the conversation. As with abortion, however, we must never allow the

8

"hard cases" to be used as the mute button on any discussion of divorce. Rather, we must go straight to the Church's directives in this area, and insist that they be followed.

According to canon law, in cases of unrepentant adultery, "grave mental or physical danger," or unlivable situations, physical separation of spouses is allowed with the bishop's permission,[2] but: "*In all cases, when the cause for the separation ceases, conjugal living must be restored...*" (cf. canons 1151-1155, emphases mine). Even should circumstances require continued separation, the marriage bond remains.

In addition, although civil divorce may be "tolerated" by the Church if it's the "only possible way of ensuring certain legal rights" for an innocent spouse,[3] such a decree does not make one "unmarried"—and Catholics must never adopt the dangerous mindset that it does.[4] Sacramental marriages are indissoluble and can be ended only by the death of one of the spouses, and even valid natural marriages (marriages in which one or both spouses are unbaptized) are designed by God to be permanent.

Unfortunately, even when a couple's issues are not about abuse, but entail more of a general misery, deep discontent, and/or non-stop bickering, our interaction with suffering friends or family members who want out of a bad marriage usually goes like this:

We rally with all of our sympathy and then, because we have no real tools to help them, we tell them it's okay to divorce. We never mention that divorce is a sin[5] (because we have been conditioned to believe that only civil remarriage without annulment is a sin[6]), and we assure them that "your marriage probably isn't valid anyway."[7] All of this is reinforced by usually well-meaning but poorly trained priests, as well as by misguided therapists and counselors.

The two wide exit ramps of no-fault divorce (automatic) and annulment (almost always granted) are a near-guarantee that no couple truly suffering will stay to fight through the darkness. Why should they? The potential for relief and happiness dangled in front of them is so tempting that it's practically irresistible, much like the woman tempted to freedom through the death of her unborn child ("it's not a baby anyway"). Each of us—and really it takes just one voice—can either help to kill the life of the marriage, ripping the "one-flesh" apart, or we can help to save it,[8] sparing souls, families, and generations.

Nothing is impossible with God.

We Christians know that with God all things are possible, and we know that the greater good and ultimate redemption come only and always through the cross. And, to be able to embrace our cross and follow the Lord, we need to have hope. According to the *Catechism of the Catholic Church*, hope "keeps man from discouragement; it sustains him during times of abandonment; it opens up his heart in expectation of eternal beatitude" (1818).

Whereas the devil and the world shout, "Throw off that cross! You shouldn't have to suffer! You deserve to feel fulfilled, have romance, and be appreciated!" the Lord whispers, "Stay faithful, stay true. Love even the unlovable and the unfaithful unto death, as I have loved you. Imitate my quiet, unfailing love, and even my humiliation, and carry your cross to the end—where your redemption and glory await."[9]

Our crosses, and particularly our crosses in our state of life, are our ladders to heaven. All marriages are cruciform, and the weight of what we are promising is unknown to us on our wedding day. Consider these stunning words from the Church's *Exhortation Before Marriage*,[10] which, until recent years, was read to every couple at the altar (emphases mine):

> This union, then, is most serious, because it will bind you together for life in a relationship so close and so intimate, that it will profoundly influence your whole future. That future, with its hopes and disappointments, its successes and its failures, its pleasures and its pains, its joys and its sorrows, *is hidden from your eyes*. You know that these elements are mingled in every life, and are to be expected in your own. And so *not knowing what is before you*, you take each other for better or for worse, for richer or for poorer, in sickness and in health, until death.

We do not know what awaits us, but we promise to love and be faithful anyway, no matter what, until death.

Within the pages of this book, you will find stories of these words lived out. You will feel the weight of nearly unbearable crosses just as surely as you will rejoice in the hope of redemption. Over all the clamoring for "moving on" and "starting over," you'll hear the real experiences of ordinary people who found their way by honoring the vows they made before God and witnesses.

I pray that those of you in struggling or seemingly hopeless marriages find in these stories the inspiration to stay true to your sacred promises—*even if your spouse does not*—and I pray that the rest of us, whether lay, clergy, or counselor, never have a hand in encouraging the destruction of a marriage, the elimination of a home, and the dismantling of a child's family.[11]

If we Christians are not a people of redemption, then we are nothing at all. May these stories remind us of who we are, and of what a great and mighty God we serve.

HOW TO READ THIS BOOK

The vast majority of the stories in this book are anonymous. Most are recounted by the spouses themselves or by the grateful children of once-disastrous unions, while two or three are told by other close family members. Each contribution has been assigned a chronological number that has been bracketed at the end of the story. Unlike the format of *Primal Loss: The Now-Adult Children of Divorce Speak*, the numbers in this book are for reference purposes only; they do not connect to any demographical data.

The first section of this book contains 50 stories of redemption—the details of marriages that went through the wringer and survived. Some of those marriages turned blissful, some merely content, but all were redeemed.

I want to add an important note here. You will surely notice that the vast majority of contributors are female. This same phenomenon occurred in *Primal Loss*, and you mustn't read anything more into that fact than this: Women, due to our more verbal and relational nature, are much more likely than men to respond to and execute a request to tell a personal, emotional relationship story. In no way should we take this imbalance to mean that men are more often the "bad guys" in marital break-up. In fact, today, women are much more likely to file for divorce than men, a statistic that is largely explained by the pervasive and corrosive influence of feminist ideology, which grossly misunderstands and/or deliberately rejects sexual complementarity and the meaning and order of marriage—all of which is a story (or a book) for another day. Please read the stories knowing that for every woman writing her story, there is a man who has his own difficult tale that never made it from his heart to the page.

The second, smaller section of the book contains 15 stories of "standers"—those wives or husbands who have chosen to stand for their marriage vows despite complete abandonment by their spouses. Even the Church seems to have forgotten these few courageous souls, who are often patted on the head, scolded, or even deemed emotionally unhealthy for not "moving on" to find that shiny new romance themselves. The profound sacrifice of these lonely but faithful souls makes the rest of us uncomfortable,[1] yet we need to honor them as heroic witnesses for matrimony. As St. John Paul II said in *Familiaris Consortio* (83): "[T]heir example of fidelity and Christian consistency takes on particular value as a witness before the world and the Church." These faithful spouses know well what Christ is asking, and it's no less than a share of His saving cross, that, while rough-hewn and heavy, is made light with His grace, and with the knowledge that the cross alone leads to glory and salvation—and to union with our True Spouse.

As you read, please consider each story as a stone in David's slingshot, aimed and fired at the forehead of the Goliath divorce culture within society and our own Church.

SECTION ONE

THE REDEEMED

Two days after what had been the most joy-filled day of my life—the First Holy Communion and Confirmation of my twin sons—I learned that my husband had been having an affair with a co-worker.

I was sitting on the floor, changing a diaper, when his phone vibrated on the couch next to my head. I looked over as the screen lit up with heart-eye emojis. I picked up the phone, entered the password, and opened the text message as a sense of dread filled the deepest recesses of my soul.

What followed is a blur of tears and terrible language. He denied it for a couple of hours, and, foolishly, I almost believed him. I called my best friend who encouraged me to check the phone records, and there it was in black and white—proof of a six-month-long affair. I ranted and raged and eventually poured holy water on his head. Through God's grace, we met with our priest that day, and the battle for my soul began.

That fateful day in May began my descent into darkness. I started smoking again and drinking heavily, numbing my pain in flavored beer, cigarettes, and Netflix binges. I looked everywhere—except at God.

Until one day in December 2017.

The day started off as they all did. I awoke, stiff and groggy, to the sound of my alarm at 5:30 a.m. My head was pounding...a six pack of beer will do that to a girl. The sounds of *Grey's Anatomy* emanating from my phone, combined with the booze, had lulled me to sleep the night before, allowing me to numb the pain yet again. I trudged to the kitchen through my dark and gloriously quiet house, threw back a couple of Tylenol, chugged a glass of water, and made coffee—ready to start my day.

I showered, dressed, and was out the door for work before anyone else was up.

As the day continued, the headache didn't go away, and my body aches worsened. Around 2:00 p.m., it was clear that the cause of my malaise was not just a terrible hangover, but likely the flu. My temperature climbed, and I decided it was time to leave.

By the time I arrived home and placed a thermometer under my tongue, I was sitting at a nice, warm 102.5 degrees. I collapsed straight into bed.

On this particular day my physical condition was certainly a reflection of my soul.

For seven months, I had been battling my inner demons with everything except what I truly needed: my Lord. Instead of turning to Him, I masked the pain, the sorrow, and the grief with alcohol, cigarettes, and *Grey's Anatomy*.

Yet, despite my best efforts to ignore God, there had been beautiful moments of grace during this time. The Lord blessed me with an incredible job in His Church; I had the opportunity to walk with two beautiful souls on their journeys into the Faith; I never stopped attending Mass; I never spoke ill of God or Jesus. But the sadness, the despair, and the anger were slowly chipping away at my soul. The light of Christ was becoming dimmer and dimmer.

During the days, I was a normal and functioning mom, wife, and worker in God's vineyard. But at night, the darkness overcame me. At night, I believed all the lies the evil one whispered in my ear. That nobody loved me, that I couldn't do anything right, that I was a bad mom, a bad wife, and a bad daughter. When the sadness didn't win, the anger did. Anger at everyone—my husband, my children, myself, and God. At night, the darkness won.

That night, though—that particular December night—the darkness didn't win.

I awoke as the sun was setting. The fever caused an uncontrollable shiver and no matter how many blankets I was under, the shaking wouldn't stop. My body fiercely ached, both from the influenza and from the withdrawals. I tossed and I turned, but relief and comfort escaped me.

Then the whispers started. The terrible whispers from the evil one, confirming all the negative thoughts that plagued my heart. Had I not been unable to move, I would have been running for the booze.

The tears started slowly, but it didn't take long for them to turn into full-fledged whole body sobs. I don't remember forming any words in my mind, but in my desperation, I heard the following words leave my lips:

"Oh, God. I can't do this anymore. Help me. Save me. I cannot do this without You."

From the very depths of my broken soul, I cried out to heaven, to Him. I continued, whispered words mingled with tears, begging Him to heal my heart. Though I did not recognize it that evening, my anguished, quiet cry was an echo of our sweet Savior's last words on the Cross:

"My God, my God, why have You forsaken Me?"

I can't do this, Lord.

For months, I had been running from the cross and from suffering, doing everything I could to avoid it. That night as I cried out to the Lord, I finally stopped running away and began ever so slowly and tentatively to embrace it. The same Lord, both Divine and human, had faced the very same betrayal, anguish, and anger I faced. Yet, He didn't let the darkness win, and I couldn't either.

For months, my soul had been dying on the cross, refusing to look toward heaven, refusing to embrace the suffering. I refused to forgive —unlike my sweet Jesus, who forgave those men who pounded the very nails into His hands and feet.

My crucifixion, a crucifixion of my own making, lasted an agonizingly long time. But without the sufferings of the cross, there can be no rising from the dead, a glorious resurrection.

At last the tears and the words ceased, and He spoke. The words were perfect. They were filled with a tender love, but spoken with the firmness I needed to hear.

"My beloved daughter, it is time. This pity party of yours is over. We have work to do."

As I let the words He spoke sink in, and as the tears staining my cheeks began to dry, a new and unfamiliar feeling entered my heart. It took several moments before I recognized it.

Peace.

An unmistakable and truly indescribable peace began to spread. The resurrection of my soul had begun. The stone was rolled away, and the light pierced the darkness that was my tomb.

This peace was such a stark contrast to the anxiety, grief, pain, and suffering that had been my constant companion in recent months! It was quite jarring to my sensibilities. For the first time in a *long* time, I found that I was no longer afraid.

My Father, the One who I thought had abandoned and forgotten me, lavished grace upon grace that night. Not only did He grace me with peace, but also with the strength to stop drinking completely, and with the courage to face the source of all my pain. This night was the beginning of my journey to surrender. It was the beginning of a new life in Him.

Around midnight, I literally rolled out of bed. The house was still quiet. I walked straight into the kitchen and pulled all the alcohol out of my refrigerator and cupboards. Slowly and methodically, I opened each bottle and began pouring the contents down the sink. Thanks solely to the grace of God, I haven't had even a taste of alcohol since.

My journey to the center of His most Sacred Heart began that night. It is through His grace that I was able to face the role I had in my husband's betrayal. For years, I had systematically destroyed his masculinity, viscerally cutting his heart and soul with heartless, disrespectful words. He could do nothing right in my mind, and I had no problem sharing each and every one of his faults with him on a daily basis. I believed every single lie the devil whispered in my ear about my husband, and I essentially wrapped the broken pieces of this man in a package with a shiny red bow and gave him to a woman who made him feel like the king of the world.

Yes, my husband had free will and is responsible for his choices, but my choices and my behavior sent him on his way.

Never once did divorce enter my mind, not even when I discovered he had resumed the affair one year after my initial discovery. He never physically harmed me or the kids, and I was in this marriage for life. The mere *thought* of dividing our family was more painful than the discovery of the infidelity, twice.

Mama Mary's hand was all over the second discovery—after all, she purifies all things and brings light to the darkness. The second affair lasted for nine months and utterly destroyed my husband. He shared that he had been praying for months for help to end the affair. He was tired of living a double life, but he was scared. Mama came through, and it was through her that this cross was made light; she held me so close to her heart during this time.

In fact, it was only three weeks after my discovery that God infused a supernatural love into my heart for my sweet husband, and I was able to give myself to him completely, intimately.

Through therapy, honesty, and most of all through the grace of God, our marriage has survived and thrived. My own profound spiritual transformation has me on my knees in gratitude for the *gift* of this cross. For it is through the cross that I found Him, His radical love, and His unending mercy. I pray daily for my husband's deeper conversion, and I have complete faith that someday he will truly know the depth of our Lord's love for him. [1]

The day my husband and I were married, we were headed for divorce. Not because it was what we wanted, but because we didn't know how to avoid it. Although we were married in the Church and had the graces of a sacramental union, the odds were stacked against us. His parents had a bitter divorce, which led my husband to porn addiction and dysfunction. My parents did not divorce, but they were poor examples of what communication and forgiveness should look like.

My husband and I had agreed on a traditional family life, where I would stay home to raise the children. We were both cradle Catholics, raised our children in the Faith, and never missed Mass. Looking from the outside, we seemed to have it all together, as we were blessed with healthy children and financial success. Yet from the inside, it was a living hell.

It took only a couple of years for my husband to become bored with family life. I was solely responsible for the childcare, housework, cooking, and shopping. No matter how hard I worked, he never seemed to be happy; he was easily angered and verbally abusive. He would refuse to help me and would criticize and insult me. I felt used and resented my husband. He had the time and interest to advance his career, but he didn't care about my feelings or improving our marriage. I quickly learned that I couldn't depend on him for emotional, physical, or spiritual support. We grew apart.

I put all my time and attention into the house and kids. He came and went as he pleased, as if he were a tenant. When he was home, we would fight, and he became physically abusive to me and to the older kids. It was around this time that I discovered his addictions, mainly porn and alcohol. I had little sympathy and gave up hope for the marriage. I didn't fight back or yell—I simply shut down. I didn't care about my husband or anything he said to me. Feeling trapped, I had resigned myself to the fact that this was my life. I had no control over it and couldn't change it. Divorce would only make things worse for the kids. I hated him, and I saw his death as the only way out. Why did God give me this cross? I did not understand the purpose or meaning.

I continued to pray for changes in my husband and my marriage. After 13 years of marriage, he finally agreed to counseling (on the advice of our parish priest), and I began reading books on marriage and Alcoholics Anonymous (AA) for families. Over the next three years, we went through separation, a domestic violence arrest, Department of Family Services visits, and orders of protection. It seemed like the more I prayed and offered suffering, the more difficult things became. Maybe God wanted me to get a divorce—an idea I couldn't ever have imagined before now.

Then, something amazing happened.

It was a little thing, but it made a big difference. I changed my prayer request. Instead of telling God what changes I wanted in my marriage, I asked God what He wanted me to do. His reply was to love and serve my family. At first, I was offended. This is what I'd been doing for 16 years, or so I thought. Then the scales fell from my eyes. I was instantly allowed to see how my response to my husband was damaging the family. I was cold, judgmental, and unforgiving. I had been so caught up in my own lack of happiness and fulfillment that I could not see my husband's pain. Through my spiritual pride, I had allowed the devil to convince me that my husband did not deserve my forgiveness. And that was the example I gave to my children. I was willing to offer years of abuse, loneliness, and disappointment to God, but I couldn't manage to be kind to my husband.

So, I started putting the counseling and books to use. I only thought of the things my husband did well, was good at, and I verbally thanked him and told him that I appreciated it. Surprisingly, he reacted by increasing time and work with me and the kids around the house. We began to do fun things we liked as a family again. My heart softened, and I knew it was only by God's grace that I was able to see my sin. I apologized for years of unforgiveness and anger toward him, because I had experienced forgiveness and mercy from God. I gave him the dignity to make his own choices—even wrong ones—and to be the head of our family.

Submitting to God's will enabled me to submit to my husband. Our suffering was redemptive! When I stepped out of the way, God was able to work on my husband's healing and conversion. That was never my job. I discovered that the best thing for my marriage and children was to love my husband unconditionally and to support him.

Because of images fried in the brain, porn is still a struggle for my husband (it's the beast of our era, designed to bring our men down). But I don't focus on his sin anymore. The change in our relationship started when I asked him for forgiveness for my own actions: the years of unforgiveness, judgment, contempt, and resentment that had hardened my heart and led to a lack of compassion and withdrawal of any love and affection. My humbling of myself was, of course, quite a surprise to him, and he forgave me. It was *such a relief* that I no longer had the responsibility of being my husband's prosecutor, judge, and executioner. I was able to focus on my vocation of wife and mother.

Becoming more loving, gentle, and supportive really diffused and de-escalated the anger and violence in our marriage. His experience of being loved unconditionally for the first time greatly limited his desire/need for porn. Although we are still living with the effects, we are *not* at each other's throats all the time with accusations and threats. We are more trusting; we are quicker to talk and resolve issues rather than let them fester.

After 24 years of marriage, we want to be with each other now—date nights, walks together, even grocery shopping. We hold hands and kiss throughout the day, even in front of the kids. When we discuss issues now, we stay on topic, and it's not clouded with fears and manipulations. Once he was free from worrying about me leaving him, he could concentrate on being a good husband and father. We truly became a team, for the first time in our marriage. Today, we act as one, while being able to respect and admire our differences, especially as male and female.

Now I can offer to God my faithfulness to my vocation, and my response to my husband and children—which is love. [2]

My husband and I were high school sweethearts. Few people have known me longer than he has. We married young and started our family right away, both of us devout Catholics who were eager to learn about and grow in our faith. Our marriage was perfect. I had a perfect husband. I was the perfect wife.

Then, late one night—ten years into our marriage, when our seventh child was about six weeks old and I was struggling with postpartum depression—my husband confessed to me that he was addicted to pornography.

He had been introduced to pornography as a child. I won't go into the complexities of his story, except to say that his addiction started early on, even before he knew me.

My husband describes the use of porn as an almost "out-of-body" experience. I've asked him, "Is it like when you're stressed to the point of feeling like you're going to explode, and suddenly you realize you ate the entire bag of cookies when you only meant to have one?" He said that, yes, it is sort of like that. He's emphasized that he does not consider himself blameless, as he is very much aware of his sinfulness. However, he's also emphasized that he has never looked at pornography because I am lacking in some way.

My husband hadn't planned to tell me, ever. He had been making excuses to himself for years: *It's not that bad because I'm not actually cheating. Everyone does it. It's not really a mortal sin if addiction is involved.*

I don't know where we would be right now if a devout friend of his hadn't confessed his own addiction and described the effect it had on his marriage. It was then that my husband snapped to his senses and realized the weight of his sin.

At the time of his confession, I considered myself lucky. I did not stumble upon a secret internet cache or find a locked file cabinet full of magazines; he told me without any prior suspicion on my part. Then why did I feel like I was falling apart?

During our nightly prayers with the kids, I could barely get through "forgive us our trespasses as we forgive those who trespass against us" without crying. I didn't want to get out of bed in the mornings. I didn't want to eat. I found myself obsessed with what kind of girls he was looking at. Were they taller than I was? Were they blonder? Did they have whiter teeth than I did? On the flip side, I was horribly bitter. No girl on the internet knows how my husband likes his coffee. I fold his socks. I clean his house. I raise his children. I would feel my blood boiling whenever I thought about it.

I knew I could not get through this betrayal alone, and so I sought help online. I thought, surely there is a Catholic forum out there for Catholic wives with porn-addicted husbands. I was right; there are many. Unfortunately, they contain very little support for a wife who wants to stand by her husband despite his addiction. What I found were women who had kicked their husbands out, taken the kids to their mother's house, presented their husbands with divorce papers, etc. When a woman did speak up to ask how she could repair her damaged marriage, she was lambasted: "Leave him!" "You're too good for him." "Why would you stay with someone like that?" "You're hurting your children by staying." I was aghast and felt more alone than ever.

In addition to all of this, I started to question the validity of our marriage. Did the fact that he had this addiction at the time of our vows invalidate his vow? Were we really married in the eyes of the Church? I lost sleep over this fear.

However, I remembered an agreement my husband and I had made during our engagement. I (a child of divorce) and he (whose parents came dangerously close to what would have been a very messy divorce) both agreed that divorce would not be an option, no matter what. We agreed to humble ourselves and seek counseling if needed, either as individuals or as a couple. I decided to take him at his word and ask for counseling. At the time, we were both in contact with a fantastic priest who had agreed to hear our general confessions (going over the sins of our entire lives) and say prayers of deliverance over us. With those solid steps being taken, my husband questioned our need for couples counseling, but he agreed to do it if I wanted.

As it happened, the power of the sacrament of confession was enough. I saw my counselor twice—once before my general confession, and once after—and realized that the priest had hit at the root of our problems within a few hours, whereas the counselor was recommending many months of therapy. I absolutely do not discount therapy, but, in our case, heartfelt confessions with a loving priest was the first step on our path to healing.

We never went to couples therapy. Instead, we did our general confessions, increased our individual and family prayer, spent more time in the Adoration chapel both individually and together, and made each other our priority.

My husband, who would be happy to spend his weekend on the couch, took me hiking, went for walks with me in historic districts with cobblestone sidewalks and quaint coffee shops, and woke up early to cook me breakfast.

For my part, I realized that while my children were indescribably important, I had to put my husband first. Often he had felt shunned when I poured all of my energy into parenting and had nothing left for him in the evening, when I could barely handle a ten-minute conversation before nodding off. I worked on my priorities, started sticking to a more structured daily schedule, and made sure to have time for him every day, no matter what. Sometimes that meant staying up after midnight when he had to work late, and I didn't care.

It was like we had reverted back to the dating period of our relationship, and I suddenly understood the advice to "never stop dating your spouse." I remembered all the things I loved about him, and both of us still strive to make the other happy.

The addiction lingers. As a former smoker, I understand the way an addiction can come creeping back. Sometimes I smell cigarette smoke and, instead of cringing, I feel a sense of relief. Other times, a craving will come out of nowhere, and with frightening intensity. My husband's addiction works in much the same way. He fights temptations with his rosary and frequent reception of the sacraments, but sometimes the addiction wins the battle. He sometimes feels defeated and wonders if he, like the slaves out of Egypt, will be "wandering in the desert" for the rest of his life, not finding relief until death.

Yes, we have a cross in our marriage, but after his revelation and my forgiveness, my husband was no longer carrying it alone. I carried it with him, and we both had a new sense of purpose, something new to fight for. It's hard to describe, but there was a refreshing feeling that came with the forgiveness. With my own parents' divorce always hanging over me, I often feared that I would one day snap and leave my family. Yet, when a perfect opportunity to do so presented itself, I hunkered down. *I was utterly relieved that my gut instinct was to mend the marriage, not to leave it.* When I start to feel insecure and fear abandonment, my husband teases me gently by saying, "I can't leave you; you know too much." Our marriage was good before his admission, but the fact that we had to fight for each other made us grow even stronger in our faith and love. [3]

My wife and I have been married for almost 25 years. We have been to hell and back.

Leila, through your book [*Primal Loss*] and its aftermath, you and others talk a lot about how bad divorce is—and it's bad. But I want to talk about how my wife and I got through a terrible patch in our marriage. And it is this: we relied on God and His Church.

I did once slap my wife, and that's when she immediately booted me out. I did not punch her, and it wasn't a forceful slap. But it horrified my kids, and to this day I am deeply ashamed of it. It happened at the beginning of my recovery in Alcoholics Anonymous (AA), and it marked the lowest point of my life—and there have been some really low ones.

Interestingly, a Catholic counselor was talking about this kind of thing today on the radio. He talked about how authentic love can include one spouse demanding that an out-of-control spouse live up to his or her dignity by not inflicting abuse, and that holding the spouse accountable can include physical separation, letting the offending spouse feel the pain of the consequences of his or her actions (I see this in AA all the time). Thankfully, the counselor certainly did not advocate or suggest divorce, and he absolutely held out the prospect that a marriage can recover.

It took some time for my wife and me to recover, and for her to trust me. I do not believe that my wife and I are alone in having been through this, and I want people to know that the power of Christ can and does overcome these terrible situations.

This is crucial: Her booting me out but *not* divorcing me, and her doing only so much as was necessary for her (and the kids') psychological and physical comfort and safety, marked a *major* turning point—not only in our marriage, but in my own salvation. It brought me face-to-face with things that needed to go.

At the time, I prayed to God to get me out of what I thought was the most misery I could be in—but every path I envisioned apart from my wife was a path to hell, even if it would mean some temporary relief here on earth.

When I was living out of the house, I kept going to confession, and I think we even went to Mass together. We prayed. She let me inside for showers and meals (but not overnight), and sometimes I slept at friends' homes, or at my older brother's place, or in the car. But she never kicked me to the curb, which would have been the conventional wisdom. Let's face it; there is a feminist brainwashing that has seeped into the mentality of even the most Catholic of women, but my wife knew the sacredness of her vow, and she never entertained the idea of divorce, which is why my marriage—and my children's family—is whole and intact today.

Getting through a difficult marriage is not a contest of seeing how tough one can be. It is a test of faith (literally) and the opportunity to rely on and trust in God, to let Him bring you out of slavery and through the desert. So, does He listen? Yeah. Can God's answers suck? Well, for a while, yeah. Does He know what He is doing? Yes. Does He abandon His people? No.

We came back from vacation tonight singing classics at the top of our lungs. We were laughing. If you had known us ten years ago, you would have said, "No way." But to you I say, "Jesus looked at them and said to them, 'With men this is impossible, but with God all things are possible'" (Mt. 19:26).

Had either of us (or really, had I) looked elsewhere other than God and His Church for answers, I think I'd be a stumbling drunk, and our home would be a disaster. And I believe very firmly that it is our Catholic convictions, specifically, that got us through some horrible stuff. It does not hurt, of course, that we have both surrounded ourselves with good people along the way. They, too, have carried us, sometimes in small ways, sometimes in big ones. God works through His people.

Tomorrow marks the 25th Pentecost Sunday since that Pentecost Sunday on which I was confirmed. Thank God for Pentecost. Thank God for the sacraments, including the sacrament of matrimony. [4]

My husband and I were married in 1965. We were already having trouble within five years, partly because I was young and selfish, and partly—mostly—because I had slackened in my practice of the Faith.

Before we were married, our shared Catholic faith and the sacraments were of paramount importance to both of us, and I can honestly say that I dated him because of his deep faith. Early on in our dating, he told me that marriage was the way we were going to help each other get to heaven—and I knew that's where I wanted to go ;). He also told me the most romantic line I ever heard: "I love you most of all when I follow behind you after Holy Communion." After we were engaged, we would meet every day for the noon Mass instead of taking a lunch break. After our marriage, I was a daily communicant up to the birth of my first child, when a move made daily Mass impossible.

After six years of marriage, my husband left me and our two daughters for another woman. He did come back a few weeks later, but his stay lasted only two weeks—long enough for me to get pregnant. Thanks be to God, in Texas at that time one couldn't divorce a pregnant wife!

It's important to note that during our first separation, I was a 24-year-old woman with two children in the 1970s—the beginning of the sexual revolution—and I didn't want to spend the rest of my life alone. I went to see the priest who had married us, a good friend of our family, to ask about grounds for an annulment. Fortunately for me, he told me I had no grounds, because on the day of our wedding: we freely chose marriage; we intended to marry for life; we intended to be faithful; and we intended to have children.

There it was. If I wanted to "re-marry," I would have to do so outside of the Church. And, thanks be to God for my Catholic education (and my mother's prayers), I knew that meant I could not get to heaven—which I still desired despite my laxity. So, I resolved that I would not pursue another relationship.

Our third daughter was born in early 1972, and my father passed away the next month. Those two events aren't connected, but they are part of the reason that I returned to a more fervent practice of my Catholic faith. The death of my father brought my sister and her family back into my life. With my sister's example and guidance I began reading *good* Catholic literature and periodicals. We joined orthodox groups like CUF (Catholics United for the Faith) and CREDO (Catholics for the Restoration in Education of Doctrinal Orthodoxy). But most importantly, I began attending daily Mass and going to confession regularly. My children and I began praying the nightly rosary, and we had our home consecrated to the Sacred Heart.

After my sister and I made an all-night vigil before the Blessed Sacrament, my husband returned to our family, 18 months after he had left us. We made another all-night vigil in thanksgiving.

My husband and I had two more children while we lived in Texas. In 1978, I was professed in the Secular Franciscan Order (again because of my sister's example), and the next day we moved to a different state.

Babies six and seven were born in that beautiful southern state, a place we all loved and called home. However, in 1984 my husband left again for another woman. No-fault divorce meant that there was nothing I could do to stop the divorce, which became final on our 20th anniversary. Our children ranged in age from 16 years old to 18 months.

My husband gave me sole custody of the children, and the financial settlement was good enough that I didn't have to go to work. In fact, at the time he left, I prayed before our little altar; I told Our Lord that since the children had lost their father, they could not lose their mother to a job. I promised Him I would be the best mother I could be, and that I would trust Him—the King and Head of our family—to take care of my children. Which He did, through my husband. I never had to get a job.

One day, my husband announced that he was going to marry again. If the children and I stayed in our city, he would have visitation, sometimes in his home. I reasoned that this could cause great harm and confusion, because either the children would lose their respect/ love for their father (which the 4th Commandment obliges them to have), or, in their love for their father, they would come to accept that divorce and remarriage aren't so bad.

So, I moved to the East Coast where my sisters and mother were now living. The tight-knit Catholic community there offered the example of good fathers for my children and support for me. We were far enough away that it would be financially impossible for my husband to have the children visit him, but he was welcome to visit us here. I knew that he loved the children, and that his not being able to see them would eventually make him realize what he had lost.

I always understood that my husband—who had spent his high school and two years of college in seminary and who was everything I described in the first part of this story—was Catholic in the deepest part of himself. I knew that *someday* he would return to the Faith, even if only on his deathbed. His conversion was our nightly intention during the family rosary.

I want to explain what got me through this second separation and the civil divorce. It was not easy, but this time I didn't fall apart. I decided that instead of medication or doctors, I would make a daily holy hour before the Blessed Sacrament. My husband had sought help from a psychologist and asked me to see him, too, which I did. That experience validated my decision to take more of a spiritual route; I have found that, although there are certainly some helpful and sound therapists and counselors, most *do not* encourage fidelity to the marriage vows. Sadly, even priests are very quick to suggest annulment. I don't believe that priests are acting with malice when they do, but such suggestions make it exponentially easier for a spouse to stop trying.

In 1987, I spoke again to the priest who married us, the same one who told me I didn't have grounds for an annulment. Somehow, *now* he told me that I did have grounds![1] However, I thank God that at this time I had the great privilege of having Servant of God Father John Hardon, SJ as my spiritual director. I called Father Hardon and asked him whether I was right in my thinking, that "the graces of the sacrament work; we are helping one another get to heaven even when we are apart. The suffering which we endure we can offer for souls—especially for our husband and children." Father Hardon told me that was exactly right. He recounted that he had been in Rome with Pope Saint John Paul II the week before, and that the pope had pushed off his desk a stack of annulment applications from the U.S., saying, "Enough!"

After years of prayer, hope, and my commitment to fidelity, in the summer of 1988 my husband called to ask if I would take him back. I said "yes," and we began the process of trying to reconcile. We renewed our vows in 1989, and he made the very courageous and humble decision to move here—to a community that knew our history.

Thanks be to God, we are still happily married. My husband is a respected attorney in our community and a Eucharistic Minister in our parish. Our seven children are all married to wonderful Catholic spouses, most of whom were or are daily communicants themselves. We now have the blessing of 32 grandchildren.

Much has changed in the culture since my separations and divorce, especially the female spirit. Carrie Gress explains it well in her book, *The Anti-Mary Exposed*. Rescuing a marriage requires a lot of dying to self, and that's difficult for most modern women who have been told via the feminist movement that they need power and control. But for those women who are living their Catholic faith, it is possible to endure the very real tragedy of separation and divorce—and to strive for a reconciliation with their spouses. And even more than just *enduring* the separation, it's possible to find joy and be grateful while carrying the cross given to us by a loving God, whose will is always perfect and always good.

I'm certain that it was daily Mass and daily rosary—and the Sacred Heart enthronement—that kept our family together. I also believe that my children have such wonderful spouses because they prayed and sacrificed for their father and received him into their lives with love and mercy. God is very good.

To those women now sent to me for advice, I stress the main reason for the hope that sustained me and that fueled my fidelity:

The sacrament of matrimony makes husband and wife "one" in God's eyes. When the abandoned spouse offers the sufferings of desertion/rejection in union with the Holy Sacrifice of the Mass, those sufferings, *now super-naturalized*, are a source of grace and a promise of the future happiness of heaven. Those graces will one day be shared by the prodigal spouse when he or she returns to the Faith. The spouses help one another get to heaven through the sacrament of matrimony, even when they are not living together, and even if they are divorced. Getting each other to heaven is the goal.

So, when a suffering woman calls me for advice, I tell her: Go to Mass as often as possible. Pray the rosary. Have Masses offered for your husband. Make holy hours. Consecrate your home to the Sacred Heart. Remember that the graces of the sacrament help you get to heaven, and keep before your mind the words of St. Paul in 1 Corinthians concerning love—that love bears *all* things, believes *all* things, hopes *all* things, endures *all* things. That love never dies.

Of course, there are no guarantees that the marriage itself will be repaired, but since the goal of marriage is the salvation of each other's soul, in that we can pray to be successful. My husband and I know that we are better people because of our great suffering, and we can honestly say that the cross was a blessing and a grace. To Him be the glory forever and for all ages. [5]

"All badness is spoiled goodness. A bad apple is a good apple that became rotten. Because evil has no capital of its own, it is a parasite that feeds on goodness." — Archbishop Fulton Sheen

I love my husband.

Our marriage started on solid footing: three years of courting, an ecclesiastical engagement blessing, and a beautiful Catholic wedding witnessed by four priests, family, and friends. We traveled to Rome and received the *sposi novelli* blessing from Pope Saint John Paul II, followed Church teaching, were consecrated to Our Lady, and were an active couple in our parish. We held each other close and clung to our faith. In a word, we thought we were bulletproof, or, to be honest, *I* thought we were.

You see, Satan only needs a small crack to enter into the fortress. For us, this came the day we had a child born prematurely. It was a small crack, but it nonetheless breached the fortified walls of our marriage. How, you ask? In the form of exhaustion.

With a child struggling for life in a Neonatal Intensive Care Unit (NICU), I spent endless days, which turned into months, at his bedside. I prayed, sang, and watched our baby struggle to breathe and live. My days began at Holy Mass, while my spouse went to the NICU early each morning for the night shift's report and for some time with our child before reporting to work. A little later in the day, I would go to our son's side and stay until evening. My parents watched our older children and aided us in holding our life together.

We prayed for a miracle for our child, and we received one. After 139 days, we came home with a baby who had a feeding tube and required continuous oxygen. We were left alone now, with no owner's manual and no more nurses. It was up to us to pull up the drawbridge and find rest and reprieve in our fortified home; however, the crack began to grow.

We were spent, physically and mentally. Friendships were put on hold and homeschooling was paused. My job was to manage our son's daily routine and deal with the steady line of therapists coming in and out of our fortress, while my husband managed the increasing mound of bills and the maintenance of our home and family. Unfortunately, this maintenance was happening on the physical and material levels only. Neither of us could see the need for mental and spiritual help.

Attending Holy Mass daily was now impossible, and attending Sunday Mass together as a family was a fanciful dream, not a reality. Our family prayer life stopped. It didn't happen all at once, but, subtly, the crack in our marriage grew, and the devil quietly entered.

My dear husband was the public face of our family; he did the shopping and tried to have evenings out with our older children so they had a bit of normalcy. Meanwhile, I was the private face of the family; I gave all my time, devotion, and care to our special needs child. Our bedroom looked like a hospital room—it was sterile, as it had to be for the sake of our child. I needed to be up at all hours of the night for feedings, which added to my overwhelming fatigue and exasperation. I was most likely suffering from PTSD. Our days ended with my husband putting the older children to bed and then sleeping in another room so as not to be disturbed by the night feedings and the endless beeping of the oxygen monitors.

One day these invisible cracks became a gap large enough for my husband to fall into, unknowingly; I would have never imagined that the wall of our fortress would begin to crumble. On an outing with our older son, my husband saw a co-worker and her child at a local restaurant. The children played as the adults talked, and this simple encounter was the start of an intense emotional affair. She was in an unhappy marriage, and my spouse needed someone to talk to.

The size of the breach grew, and the trajectory of his fall was marked by continuous text messages, phone calls at all hours of the night, and frequent getaway lunches (witnessed by friends). My spouse's faith became lukewarm, and this was palpable and visible during Holy Mass, where I believe Our Lady was opening my eyes to this unfolding calamity. Being attentive to all the needs of a medically fragile child drains both parents, ending real communication; had Mother Mary not helped me be aware, I might have stayed blind to what was going on in my husband's new life.

Knowing we were on the brink of a separation, I selectively brought a few key people into our circle of prayer and friendship. I firmly believed that we had entered into our marriage covenant with God at the center—and divorce was not an option. The children were aware that something was wrong, and we began to pray again as a family, starting with the Novena to Mary, Undoer of Knots. I shared my pain with two priests who knew us well, with a married couple who were friends to us both (and who would not gossip or judge), with my mother, and with my husband's brother and his wife. Each of these trusted people wanted our marriage to survive and prosper. They did not sit and watch; instead, they joined us in prayer and listened to the Holy Spirit guide them as they helped us rebuild our fortress.

Priest #1: He immediately came to our home and blessed it. This just happened to be on our wedding anniversary; unfortunately, my husband was away on business. He listened to my story, heard my confession, and for the first time since our baby was born, I felt peace in our home. He gave me counsel and hope, he shared stories of couples who overcame the same cross we were carrying, and he reminded me that it was a cross we both needed to carry together, even if I was tasked at present with carrying most of it.

Priest #2: He gave me firm counsel over the phone and assured me of his prayers and sacrifices. He said that if my husband chose to continue to live that way, he needed to move out and have a time of separation to think. I was so worried that my husband might harm himself. This priest committed to pray that my husband would choose, instead, to sin no more and love his family.

Married couple: These two were amazing. The husband was the ear my own husband needed, listening more than he talked, offering support for our marriage without judging. The wife prayed and sacrificed. She listened to me and gave me a soft place to land in my anger and resentment. When my husband and I needed to be alone to talk, they watched our children—a sacrifice which required them to learn to take care of our special needs child, too.

My mother: She prayed unceasingly, she sacrificed, and she came and watched the older children while I broke down.

My husband's brother and his wife: They immediately came and stood in the gap, supporting both of us. They got in touch with Greg and Julie Alexander of The Alexander House Apostolate,[2] and we began to meet with them. I had known of this incredible marriage resource, but I'd never imagined we would need it. My husband was still full of bitterness and shame when we first started working with them, and I was an emotional wreck. But by the second session, my husband could see that I didn't want a divorce—I wanted my husband back, and I wanted healing. Deep down, he wanted that, too.

If there was one pivotal moment for the turnaround in my husband, it was the night we went to see the movie *War Room*. "She" was actually texting him during the movie, and when the lead actor had dinner with the other woman on-screen, it was at that moment that my husband decided: no more texting or calling her. It was as if he could finally see all the pain of the breach.

The steps we took to seal the breach were many. Practical, ongoing, specific things that are too numerous to mention here, but that kept moving us forward in healing to where we are today.

Looking back, it's hard to know how this crisis could have been prevented, as our exhaustion took everything out of us. But, if you are a family living with a special needs child, I encourage you not to let family prayer go by the wayside, to make time every day for your spouse, to look for the little cracks forming in your fortress, and to carry your cross together. Satan likes to get a trophy. Do not let him.

Now, each night, we gather to pray a family rosary, something we've been doing for over three years. If my husband is away on business, he joins with us on the phone and leads the last decade. The family rosary is powerful, and it is a healing balm and a sturdy sword! This year we celebrate 20 years of marriage, and I praise God every day for the gift of our strong and fortified family. [6]

Let me begin by saying that I have been married to my high school sweetheart for 34 years, and that most people with our history would have given up plenty of times. We are so incredibly happy now in our marriage.

We started dating at age 16 and married at 24. The first year was hell. I had abandonment issues, and we both had childhood abuse issues. I hid my pain in overachieving, almost to the point of OCD. My husband dealt with his pain by drinking. We always had a strong chemistry and love for each other.

It was just the two of us for the first three years, and we fought. Usually our fights were me freaking out because he, a good-looking man who had women hitting on him, was going out on the town (to the bars) without me. Then we had our first baby. My mother died when I was newly pregnant, so my daughter was such a blessing to me. I wanted to be such a good mother, and I poured my life into her. Sixteen and a half months later came number two, a baby boy. Even though my husband's income was not great, I quit work. I washed diapers out by hand and used the WIC program, and we got by. Our third child, a daughter, was born 27 months after our second.

I had three children in 3.5 years, via C-section, and an old-fashioned husband who thought that parenting was for the mom only. With my own parents dead and a husband who did not help, I didn't have the support I needed. Yet, to earn some extra money, I began a daycare business that, of course, was too much for me! But at 31 years old and "headstrong," I pushed on. My husband's drinking continued every night after work, and he often missed dinner and came home at midnight or later. I was a nervous wreck. I felt abandoned and angry that the kids and I weren't enough for him.

Throughout our marriage up until this point, I had explored divorce, praying that God would show me His will. He always showed me to work on myself, find my significance in Him, and act lovingly toward my husband in spite of my feelings. And, He showed me to pray.

I also began counseling and read tons of Christian self-help books, which slowly unraveled the dysfunction. I began attending Al-Anon.

Slowly, as I healed from my own issues and learned to "act" and not "react," along with other relationship tools, things began to improve. Our fourth baby came five years after our third.

Slowly but surely, things have come around, and we are happy. We have four beautiful adult children and three grandchildren—with two more on the way. [7]

"For I know the plans I have for you, says the Lord, plans for welfare and not for evil, to give you a future and a hope." —Jeremiah 29:11

Click, click, click...the rosary slid through my fingers...the first Sorrowful Mystery, the Agony in the Garden....My mind went to Jesus, suffering alone, abandoned by all of His friends and knowing the Cross that lay ahead. I approached Him and leaned against His shoulder. I was always consoled by meditating on the sufferings of Jesus. His sufferings and mine, entwined.

"Our Father, who art in heaven, hallowed be Thy name..."

I love you, Lord.

"Thy Kingdom come, Thy will be done, on earth as it is in heaven..."

Jesus, I trust in you. I accept this cross. Help me to accept it again tomorrow.

"Give us this day our daily bread; and forgive us our trespasses..."

I'm sorry for having offended you.

"As we forgive those who trespass against us..."

I forgive my husband. Help me to keep forgiving.

"And lead us not into temptation..."

There but for the grace of God, go I.

"But deliver us from evil..."

I beg you to protect our family, Lord.

"Amen."

"Hail Mary, full of grace, the Lord is with thee. Blessed art thou amongst women, and blessed is the fruit of thy womb, Jesus..."

Jesus, I love you.

"Holy Mary, Mother of God, pray for us sinners, now and at the hour of our death. Amen."

Mary, my Mother, keep me close.

Winding through the decades, tears began to fall as I contemplated my life and the life of the Lord...my sorrows along with His sorrows. I wept. I wept from the lingering pain of a broken heart, but I also wept in gratitude for all God had done to bring me back to the Catholic Church and into a personal relationship with Jesus. As usual, I ended my nightly rosary with a small measure of consolation and a supernatural hope that all would be well no matter what lay ahead. Drying my tears, I tucked my rosary beneath my pillow and fell asleep.

More than a year earlier, I had discovered that my husband was having an affair. Devastated, I had tried everything to save my marriage, but nothing had worked—marital and individual counseling, repeated forgiveness, living apart for a year, stepping up my efforts to be a "better wife." None of it had changed anything. He said he wanted to be married and be a father to our two young children, but he had continued leading a double life: attending a Protestant service with us on Sundays (we were fallen-away Catholics) and "working on our marriage," all while exchanging love letters and enjoying a relationship with another woman behind my back.

After repeated betrayals and broken promises, our marriage counselor determined that his three-year affair was part of a sex addiction. Having begun viewing pornography in childhood, my husband's porn addiction had escalated to infidelity, and, due to the compulsive nature of the affair, his attempts to end it were repeatedly unsuccessful. The marriage counseling that I had hoped would help us restore trust would not be helpful as long as his addiction was active. "You don't have a husband as long as he's an addict," our therapist told me privately. "His fidelity is to the addiction. Until he gets sober, marriage counseling is a waste of your time. Sex addiction is as difficult to beat as a heroine addiction. His only hope," she continued, "is rehab or a 90/90."[3]

I had left our therapist's office devastated again. I felt totally alone. Even our marriage counselor had sent us away. The close friends at church who had told me to divorce him over a year earlier had long since dropped me as a friend. My in-laws irrationally blamed me for his affair. I had virtually no emotional support system, and now I faced the frightening reality that my husband might be totally unfixable and unreachable. God, too, seemed very far away.

Raised in Catholic families, my husband and I had been married in the Church thirteen years prior. We'd had a "Church wedding" primarily for sentimental reasons rather than devotion to our Faith.

Despite my years of Catholic schooling, my understanding of the Faith was almost nonexistent. I did not understand that marriage is a vocation, I had no personal relationship with Jesus or Mary, and I had no understanding of the Real Presence of Jesus in the Eucharist. I had never stepped into an Adoration chapel or prayed a rosary, and it had been more than 20 years since my last confession. At the initial discovery of my husband's affair, we had for years been regularly attending a Protestant church as a family, and we had no desire or intention to return to the Catholic Church.

While tempted to despair after learning of my husband's sex addiction and continued affair, I was so emotionally exhausted that I just resolved to take it a day at a time, without getting my hopes up but also not giving up altogether. He did agree to go to a Sexaholics Anonymous (SA) meeting and said he would consider trying a 90/90. SA meetings were offered daily in our city, but it would be difficult for my husband to attend one every day. He would have to fit the meetings into his hectic workday and travel all over town, at different hours, to accommodate this recovery work. Not only would he need to adjust his workday life, but he would also have to give up his long-term affair partner.

Having been lied to so many times, I was suffering from post-traumatic stress disorder and was experiencing anxiety on a daily basis. Attending weekly S-Anon meetings helped me cope, as I learned to keep the focus on myself and stop trying to control or investigate my husband.

However, the deep sense of loneliness remained with me. At some level, I believed the lie that I was not worth loving. Without the security of my marriage, I felt undesirable, unlovable, and disoriented.

By the grace of God, shortly after we began sex addiction recovery work, I stumbled upon and began reading the collected works of St. Teresa of Avila. Despite 12 years of Catholic schooling, I had never read any writings of the saints, nor any Catholic theology. Reading just the first few chapters of St. Teresa's writings opened the door to a torrent of graces. The feeling of loneliness and sadness began to lift a little. Tears fell as I read the words of this Spanish saint from the 1500s, and I felt quite literally as though I had a real friend, someone who understood me and cared about me.

Soon thereafter, I felt a desire to pray the rosary. Growing up, none of my family or friends prayed the rosary, and in all my years at Catholic school, I'd never been taught how. However, I had kept a rosary that I had received at my First Communion. I purchased a book on how to pray the rosary and taught myself. I joined the Confraternity of the Most Holy Rosary and promised to pray the rosary daily for all of the intentions of those in the confraternity. In turn, they prayed for my intentions.

Before long, I began to desire to learn more about the Catholic Church. For the next several weeks, I spent my evenings alone in my bedroom soaking up everything I could about Catholic theology. To my surprise, I was discovering beauty and truth in the Catholic faith that I had casually discarded. My excitement grew to such an extent that I was only secondarily aware that my husband, now living back home but sleeping on the couch, was actually making positive changes. He had been attending daily SA meetings, had found a sponsor, was meeting weekly with a therapist, and had begun meeting a Christian accountability partner every Sunday after our church service.

We were still attending a Protestant church, but I was quickly growing in my desire to return to the Catholic Church. I told my husband that I wanted to attend Mass, and he agreed to accompany me to the Saturday vigil Masses while we continued to attend the Protestant services on Sundays.

In the meantime, I prayed that God would lead me to a holy priest for confession, which he soon did, and I gratefully made my first confession in over 20 years. By now, I had some sense that many of the moral views I had held were wrong, including my support of legal abortion, same-sex "marriage," and the use of contraception. I had also been attracted to New Age healing arts such as Reiki, and to Buddhist forms of meditation.

I was slowly learning how far from God I had been, and I saw with wonder that, while I had been for so long intently focusing on my husband's sin, I was, ironically, just as lost as he.

Within about two months of praying my daily rosaries, my husband, incredibly, told me that he, too, wanted to pray the rosary, and he asked me to teach him! Soon thereafter, he felt called back to Mass; we stopped attending the Protestant service and began exclusively attending Sunday Mass as a family instead.

By now, my husband had completed his 90/90 and was continuing to attend SA meetings daily. I was beginning to notice real change. For example, for years he had been a heavy drinker. In the recent past, he would drink up to a bottle and a half of wine a night. Now, the heavy drinking had stopped, and I no longer felt desperate to hide alcohol. His marijuana use, which typically cost us hundreds of dollars a month, was lessening.

Several months passed. He had been working a solid recovery program, even beginning to sponsor other men. One night he called me on his way back from a meeting. "I need to tell you something." He sounded excited. "What is it?" I asked. "I'm in love with you," is what I heard him say. "You're in love with me?" I asked. I was happy to hear that! "No," he said. "Well, yes, but what I said was, I'm in love with the Eucharist."

I was confused. "You're in love with the Eucharist?" I asked.

"I can't explain it," he said, "but I have a desire to attend daily Mass, so tomorrow I'm going to attend the 6:30 a.m. Mass instead of attending my morning SA meeting."

Something about his intensity and excitement struck me. For the first time, I felt a flutter of real hope. God was working in my husband.

The next morning, and for years afterwards, my husband would drive 20 minutes across town to attend 6:30 daily Mass before work. He found a holy priest and met with him weekly for spiritual direction. He frequented the sacrament of confession often and spent time in Adoration. We began to pray the rosary together in our bedroom, kneeling across from each other on either side of our bed. Soon thereafter, we consecrated ourselves to Jesus through Mary on the Feast of Our Lady of Mt. Carmel. Eventually, we would transition to praying the rosary together as a family each night.

Slowly, I began to trust my husband enough to risk emotional and physical intimacy again. During this period, we also learned about Theology of the Body, and the truth of the Church's teaching on chastity suddenly struck us in a way that can only be described as life-changing.

With the help of two priests who gave us individual spiritual direction, we discerned God's call to be open to life. We had begun using Natural Family Planning when we returned to the Church, but taking the step to try to conceive more children seemed risky. What if my husband cheated again? Was it really wise to have more children? Our history would make me second-guess everything. But there were also compelling reasons to trust the Lord and abandon my fears. I had seen God's hand and heard His voice interiorly pointing me to trust Him and keep hoping for a fully restored marriage. He seemed to be promising a miracle.

My relationship with the Lord continued to deepen as I began a daily practice of mental prayer, meditating on the Gospel each morning. My heart was broken and I had many fears, all of which I laid at the feet of the Lord. During prayer, Jesus healed me of a number of traumatic memories related to the betrayal—but most importantly, through prayer, He dispelled the lie that I was not worthy of love. Jesus showed me that He had truly been with me through every sorrow, every difficult moment that I had endured, and that He would continue to be with me regardless of what my husband did. I might never be able to fully trust my husband, but I knew that I could fully trust the Lord and that He loved me with an incomparable, infinite love.

My husband, also, was coming to know how deeply He was loved by God through his recovery work and his sacramental life. Soon, he was freed from all of his addictions—to alcohol, marijuana, cigarettes, porn, and sex. The abundant graces we received eventually compelled us to say "yes" to more children.

We have now been in recovery for seven years and back in the Catholic Church for nearly that long. We have six children, four living and two with the Lord. We often marvel at the goodness and mercy of God. We understand that we did not merit any of the graces we have received, and we continue to ask the Lord for His mercy in our lives.

Just recently, I realized that "Discovery Day"—the day that I found out my husband was being unfaithful—was the Feast of Our Lady of Sorrows. For three years in a row after that, on that exact feast day, I would learn of a new and terribly painful aspect of my husband's past infidelities. The continued discoveries on that day, hardly coincidental, have been transformed by the grace of God from a source of sorrow into a sign of God's love for me. With the eyes of faith, I know that my Blessed Mother interceded to help me see what needed to be revealed, not only about my husband's transgressions, but also about my own deep wounds and the lies that were keeping me bound in my own sin.

Just as she accompanied Christ through His Passion, my Mother accompanied me during my trials. She aided me by comforting me and carrying me straight to Jesus—the Divine Physician, Wonderful Counselor, and Mighty Savior. In His infinite mercy, God used my husband's infidelity and my ensuing heartache to dispel lies about my identity, to bind up my life-long wounds, and to woo my heart. Ultimately, these sufferings, though deeply painful, have been a source of blessing and a channel of mercy, setting me on the path to union with the One who loves me with an everlasting love. [8]

Fifteen years into our marriage, my husband was unfaithful. I found out from the other woman's husband, who told it to me straight, via Facebook Messenger. I thanked the guy and thought to myself, "What the heck should I do now? How am I supposed to feel?" So I went straight to anger, as it seemed the most appropriate option.

Once my husband knew that I found out, he was instantly sorry. He took himself off to a friend's place and spent a couple of nights alone, getting drunk.

The few people I told gave mixed responses about what I should do. I was never going to leave my husband, but some suggested that I should.

It was very clear that people felt they were supporting me by calling my husband names and suggesting that I deserved better. I note that those who advise are often quick to suggest intolerance and unforgiveness, which can result in many people leaving their spouses. I live in an area where over 50% of people have divorced, and this may be on account of the community's lack of knowledge; folks have no idea how to support someone appropriately in this circumstance.

As an analogy, it reminds me of when I started smoking again some years ago. A prominent woman in our area commented on the fact that I had started smoking again, and she was disgusted. I made all the usual excuses, one of which was that my husband smoked, and so it was always a temptation. She suggested I tell my husband that if he didn't stop smoking, I would leave him. It made me wonder: If prominent (or any) members of our society are suggesting we make such life-altering decisions on minor issues, what hope has anyone got of enduring the major difficulties that marriage presents? (By the way, I have since quit smoking, thankfully; my husband continues to smoke.)

Of all the advice I received, my sister gave me the best support by highlighting all the wonderful elements my husband brought to our family, including the fact that he was a great father to our four children.

Back to the story of the affair. My husband being away from our home after the discovery of his affair was not acceptable, and I had to put a stop to it. I thought, who did he think he was to go off and drown his sorrows, when I was left to mind our children alone? Surely,

I should've been the one getting drunk somewhere! So, I told him to get his sorry ass back home and face the consequences.

We spent an evening talking. Our relationship had been fine; there was no reason why he should have needed to find "love" elsewhere. We were the best of friends, too.

He said he felt I was "too Catholic." That I needed to calm down and not be so "obsessed" about God all the time. I told him that wasn't an option—God was first for me. If my being less Catholic was his requirement for making things right, then he would have to leave me, but I was not going to leave him. That conversation led to what seems like a miraculous transformation. He accepted what I said, and he stayed! He not only puts up with my conversations about God and the universe, he even gets involved if the mood is right, and he supports me in my faith! Sometimes he graces me with time to speak to him about God when it's evident he is really not in the humour of hearing it. I guess sometimes that's what love is: being an ear to your spouse when, in truth, the subject matter doesn't always interest you.

We've been married for 21 years, and our marriage is stronger now than ever before. God moved in our situation and brought us closer to each other and closer to Himself. [9]

Being a poorly catechized Catholic from a divorced family set me on a path to deep sin. I got civilly married at 18, left him at 22, and subsequently lived as a New York party animal: nonstop drinking, barrooms, clubs, and men. I got my college degree, but I barely remember my 20s.

In my early 30s, I had a child out of wedlock. My boyfriend and I were both heavy drinkers, and when he refused to quit drinking and was not safe for our son, I told him to leave. I never saw him again, and he passed away five years later. I continued to live sinfully, which led to more brokenness and pain.

One day as I walked past my front door, I caught sight of the crucifix I had on the wall. I can't put into words what came over me, but when I looked at Christ on that cross, I fell to my knees and started sobbing uncontrollably, repeating, "I'm sorry! I'm so sorry!!" It was as if I could feel how every one of my sins hurt Him, and I promised Him that I would never disrespect my body again. I was 33, and I lived chastely for five years, though not attending Mass.

At 38, I broke my promise of chastity and began a relationship with the man who would become my husband. We each brought a child into our civil marriage, and, even in the best of circumstances, these situations are *always* hard. My way of dealing with my problems was pot smoking and wine. *Lots* of wine. Alcohol is a gift for people who respect it, but sadly, I did not. I was a binge drinker, and, had there not been those periodic reprieves, our relationship would not have survived. I was a functioning alcoholic, but even that starts to get difficult as we age. We would go from peace to chaos in a vicious, awful cycle.

My husband's daughter was young, confused, and deeply wounded; her own mother had abandoned her, and she viewed me and my son as a threat. I did what I could to make her happy, but there was some cruelty to my young son, which is where I drew the line (she was 15; he was seven). In his instinct to protect his daughter, my husband would lie to cover up for her. We went to Catholic counseling, and despite the advice, he would not stop.

This is the problem we have created in society. Kids deserve both their natural parents and a family. These smacked-together families are riddled with problems, and someone always feels slighted. How could they not?

I ended up leaving and moving back to New York. He came back and forth several times, but even as his daughter became an adult, she came first for him. We still loved each other, but things seemed beyond repair. It was at this point that he had an affair with his former wife (out-of-state), which I did not find out about until over a year later. We got back together a couple of years after that, but I had not stopped drinking. It was going to take something drastic to save me and to fix this massive mess we had created.

One night, I was sitting on my couch while my husband slept, and the movie, *The Craft*, came on. I had watched it in my bar days, when my friends and I got into very dark things: the New Age movement, chakras, tarot cards, astrology, etc. We relished in the fact that many people thought we were witches. Little did I know this was demonic stuff, and I believe I picked up many demons during this period of my life. Combined with all the other mortal sins I was committing, it was a recipe for disaster. Unsettling and seemingly coincidental things would happen, and we even ended up going to the local Carmelite monastery in our town to talk to a priest about it. He warned us that these happenings were likely not from God, but from the devil. We didn't understand what he was talking about (I'd never learned about the preternatural vs. the supernatural, and I thought all spiritual things were from God).

That night watching *The Craft*, I was still feeling resentful over wrongs that had been committed against me by others. I remembered the "powers" I believed I had possessed (willing things to happen, having small amounts of secret knowledge about people), and I thought: *I could exact willed revenge on these people.* And suddenly, it was as if two roads opened before me, clear as day. I could choose good or I could choose evil, and I did not know where this thought came from.

With the movie on pause, I picked up my phone. Under a YouTube video I had already watched, there was a preloaded video called "There is a Hell and I Am in It" on the *Sensus Fidelium* channel. I watched it and was scared out of my mind. I just sat there stunned. This was all real, and I knew it.

I watched the next video as well, then got up and went out to the trunk of my car, feverishly searching for the rosary beads my mother had given me about 20 years earlier. Amongst the hundreds of things that I had lost or thrown away over the years, they were *still* there!

I started praying the rosary that night, with the help of an app. It was the week before Holy Week, and on the third night, while meditating on Christ's Passion, I saw all of my sins. I began to cry, telling Him how sorry I was. I could not stop. Suddenly, my breathing changed, and what happened next is impossible to put into words, but I will try.

It was as if I was in His light. Something came over me that I cannot explain. But *everything* changed, and it was as if something (Someone) entered my soul. I was in such a state of peace, one that only someone who'd experienced it could understand. I could not talk for almost three days, other than to utter short answers. I had no physical pain, no anxiety, no anger, no resentment, no worry. This was a peace I'd never known.

The TV shows I watched religiously—tawdry, nonsense shows about money, alcohol, and drama—GONE. The music I listened to, my language, my bad habits—GONE, instantaneously. The F-word, the Lord's name, and every other curse you could imagine—*I was the worst offender of all*—it was GONE. Not only could I *not* curse, I could not be in the presence of anyone who did. Alcohol? My ever-present desire for alcohol was GONE! I have not had a drink in two years.

Obviously, my husband noticed this change. He started getting irritated—"What is going on with you?? Why aren't you talking?" (I usually never shut up!) I knew I had to explain it to him, but how do you explain God to someone? I finally told him, "I've been wrong about everything, *everything* in life. It's all about love, Ryan." I'd been enraptured by Divine Love that night.

When I finally stopped exerting my will over my husband—because these things tend to snowball and become a power struggle—and when I finally began to pray, that is when the conversion of the relationship happened. I also devoured everything I could about the Faith. I had *Sensus Fidelium* videos playing in a loop. Scripture jumped off the page at me, crystal clear….How? It *had* to be something divinely graced to me.

Now came the *really* hard part. I'm craving holiness but living in sin. I had a previous and current invalid marriage. With great discomfort, I eventually explained to my "husband" that, although I loved him, we could no longer have sexual relations until we married in the eyes of God. I belonged to Christ now, the situation had to be made right, and that was that. Long story short, he agreed to live as brother and sister until we could be married. And, he wanted to convert! I sometimes think my husband is the real testimony of God's grace through this all.

We went back to church. I couldn't bear the nearby modern parishes, so we sought out an FSSP (Priestly Fraternity of St. Peter) parish about an hour away. Our first Mass was a high Mass that we stumbled into, and it left our mouths hanging open. When the schola began, our hair stood on end, and we had goosebumps. The four of us all just looked at each other in shock; I personally had never experienced something so beautiful in all of my life. My desire for the Eucharist was tangible, and it made me cry. *All of those years that I wasted!* I could only think of the words of St. Augustine: "Late have I loved You…."

We faithfully attended Mass, awaiting our full communion, and we were finally welcomed into the Church in April of the following year—our *real* wedding day.

Our children are now also full, practicing Catholics. If anyone had told me five years ago that we would all be fervent Catholics, working our jobs together, faithfully attending Mass together, spending time *happily* together—I would've never believed it. This is the grace of God.

Heaven, hell, *eternity*—these realities have been lost in this sad and confused generation. I should know; I was amongst the lost. But now I have a peace I'd never known and a marriage that is quiet, solid, and precious. That's our great God's power when we surrender to Him. He is always there, and He is waiting for you, too. Ask with a sincere heart. He will answer. [10]

My husband and I, both Protestants at the time, were married for 23 years when my beloved sister died unexpectedly after a brief illness at the age of 49. I did not handle things well. I was stunned, exhausted, and bitter. I had been fighting with my husband for weeks prior, and—although I am very ashamed of this and it hurts to talk about—two days after my sister died, I snapped. I packed a bag and announced I was leaving my husband. He returned my fury with his own, and at the very time I should have been a help to my poor parents, I was making it all about me. It was easier to be mad at my husband than it was to grieve my sister.

I took a job through a temp agency and got my own apartment. I was promptly fired for making too many mistakes (because I was too rattled to concentrate on anything!). I moved back in with my husband after this, but soon got a job that I liked. Things in my marriage went from bad to worse.

I was too busy to work on my marriage, and I was too busy to help my parents grieve their eldest daughter. But I was not too busy to get interested in a male co-worker. Because my marriage had been stumbling for a long time, both my own grief and my interest in this man served as catalysts for me to cut ties with my husband. Several of the Christian women at work were divorced (they had bought the lie that God doesn't hate divorce), and most of my friends were on second marriages—so I got a lot of encouragement to divorce and move on!

That is when I told my husband that I wanted a divorce. He was tired of fighting me, and I assumed he had given up; however, right before I saw a lawyer, he begged me to reconsider. I had a date that night, so I blew him off as if it were nothing. After that, he did give up and soon found the woman he would quickly marry. I realized—too late—that I was not interested in being with this new man, or any other man for that matter.

I cannot begin to tell you the pain I suffered. The woman my husband married was an extremely beautiful woman. Blonde hair, long legs, nuclear breasts—you know the type. She was almost perfect, and certainly perfectly suited for him in terms of interests, hobbies, goals, etc.

While he was out of my life and busy making a new life with her, I was diagnosed with neuropathy. I ended up moving to a different town to attend a small university majoring in social work (a tedious degree that is nothing more than a political agenda, but that's another story).

I was a Christian in a new town, and the daunting question of where to attend church loomed over me. My late sister had been an Episcopalian and, before she died, we had discussed the Communion of Saints. This was a hard concept for me, a lifelong member of a small, non-denominational church with Pentecostal undertones. At any rate, she put a bee in my bonnet, and now I began to read up on the matter.

During my research, I stumbled across some Catholic blogs. When I was young, I had been told that Catholics did not pray to Christ—they prayed to the pope who in turn would pass on the messages to Christ. I knew this was bad theology, so I had never even entertained the idea that Catholics might be Christians.

I was 47 years old, and I had *no* idea what Catholics believed. If I had ever met a Catholic, I sure didn't know it, because no one talked about Catholicism even if that person was Catholic! But my study of the Communion of Saints led to reading many, many Catholic things, and before I knew it, I began to attend Catholic Mass.

In the meantime, I was coming unglued psychologically and emotionally. I went to therapy to deal with the divorce, but it wasn't working. One day, the therapist told me that he could tell I was in no better shape than when I first started. He recommended that he start treating me as a woman who was not divorced but rather whose husband had died.

Everything changed for me at that point, because it was true. My marriage had died—and I had profound regret and grief over this. I didn't need to "get on with life," I needed to mourn. And while I mourned, I relied more and more on the teachings of the Catholic Church.

The matter of annulments made me squirm. For the life of me, I could not find any reason why my marriage could ever be annulled. I rarely talked with my "ex"-husband unless it was a matter concerning our grown daughter, but I needed to know: Did he think our marriage had grounds for an annulment? Via email, I sent him an article on the topic. I asked him to read it and tell me if he thought there were grounds, even though we were not Catholic.

The article offended him. He even came to see me, to talk about it. He said that although he had given up on organized religion and certainly did not believe the things Catholics believed, he found the article insulting. He told me that he knew in his heart there was no reason for an annulment, and that his motives for marrying me were pure, true, and honorable. He took me through the list of impediments in the article and was able to dispel each reason for annulment in our case.

"Why are you getting involved with something like the Catholic Church?" he asked. Instead of giving him an answer, I asked him if I could pray a rosary. He had never heard the rosary prayed before, but he consented to my odd request. And so I prayed, "Hail Mary, full of grace...." While I prayed all the prayers of the rosary, I silently asked Jesus, Mary, and Joseph to heal this broken marriage. When I had finished, he was not impressed, but he was respectful.

We spent another hour or so together, and he occasionally would ask me a question about the Catholic faith, but I had the feeling that he was generally not interested. He left, and I found myself blushing in embarrassment. Why on *earth* had I prayed a rosary with him there? What was I thinking?

We started talking more frequently after this, however. He was unhappy in his second marriage, and I was continuing to study the Catholic faith. I eventually graduated with my degree in social work, and by the time I had returned to our hometown, my husband had divorced his new wife. I moved in with my parents—my mother was sick, and Dad and I began the long process of losing her. I was busy in graduate school now as well, but I continued to see my husband. It looked like there was hope for our relationship.

Only, there was no hope. One day, my husband told me he was getting back together with his second wife, and he was sorry if he led me on. I was devastated. That night I prayed, only this time I made a vow to God. I told God that I would never, ever speak to this man again unless a) it related to our daughter, or b) he joined the Catholic Church. And then I laughed. It was a safe bet that this was never going to happen. It was a cheesy vow, but I meant it.

Days turned into weeks, and weeks turned into months. I told no one about this rather unloving vow, and I simply told my parents that I had decided not to get involved with my husband again; they stopped commenting on his sudden absence. I studied at school, and I studied the *Catechism*. I was unable to attend RCIA[4] due to my schedule, but by now I knew that I wanted to join the Church. Next year, I told myself. Next year.

I got through the fall and a long winter, and then finally spring arrived. One night, out of the blue, my husband called. Our daughter had lost her job and was moving to a different city, and he wanted to consult me on this matter. He informed me that things had not worked out in his relationship with this woman, but that he was going to be okay. He tried to chat for awhile, but I cut him off.

And then, remembering my vow, I marched to my computer and sent him an email telling him that I did not want any contact with him at all. We had nothing more to say to each other. He could email me with any information about our daughter, but we were to limit it to that.

A few days later my cell phone rang. It was my husband. I was tired, and I wearily answered, prepared to tell him sternly to email me with any concerns. But before I could say anything, he stopped me.

"Sarah, I know you said not to call you. I know that, and I am not trying to invade your boundaries, but something has happened, and I need to tell you."

I listened in silence. He told me that on the following Thursday, he was going to make his first confession. He had been attending RCIA, and on Saturday he was entering the Catholic Church. He said he had no right to ask, but since I was the one who had introduced him to the Church, he wanted to know if I would attend the Easter Vigil service. "It just seems fitting and proper for you to be there, even though I would understand if you did not want to attend," he said. I told him I would let him know and hung up.

I was shocked and stunned. I had no idea that he had been attending RCIA! And oh, the irony! *He* was going to enter the Church before *me!*

It took a while for the shock to wear off, but eventually it did. And then came the *joy!* I attended that Easter Vigil. And we haven't been apart since.

I was unable to attend RCIA classes that next year, because my mother was so unwell. But since I had studied so much and for so long, it was decided that I could enter the Church that year. Sadly, my mother passed away two weeks before my confirmation.

I wasn't immediately ready to "remarry" my husband (civilly). I knew that in the eyes of God, we had never been unmarried, but the marriage had been stressful and unhealthy in many ways, and I knew we needed to change. Finally, on what was our 33rd anniversary, we stood with our priest at the altar. It was a quiet ceremony, a weekday, with only our daughter and one other friend in attendance. It was after the 8:00 a.m. Mass, and there were a few elderly people in the back who had stayed to pray a rosary. While they softly murmured, *Hail Mary, full of grace...*, we repeated our sacred vows.

Marriage *is* sacred. And I cannot begin to express the gratitude I feel for Christ, the Church, for *all* that makes His Church holy.

This was a broken marriage that has been healed and restored. I have a good marriage now. We *did* change. And we know that giving up solves nothing.

I wish I could say that my story inspires others—it does not, mainly because I never tell anyone. My health is not great, and these days I live a "hidden life," without much interaction with the world. If my story in this book can help others, that would be wonderful. However, I realize that a couple whose marriage is in trouble can't just join the Catholic Church and—*poof!*—problems solved. It doesn't work that way. And yet—it kind of did for us. Christ didn't wave some magic wand and heal our marriage. But He *did* pour His grace on us. And that was the beginning of the healing. It was the beginning of what my husband and I consider a miracle.

He turned my mourning into dancing! [11]

Where do I begin? After 13 years of marriage and five kids, I found out that what I knew about my marriage was a lie. One day my husband told me he was not feeling "in love" anymore, and he started asking for a divorce. I was blindsided and devastated, and for months I tried to fix it in any way I could. His declaration was right before Christmastime; after the holidays, I made an appointment with a priest and a marriage counselor.

When we met with the priest, he told us about the love languages, and that love is a decision. As I looked over at my husband, I saw the face of a stranger. He was different—in a bad way. It was my first taste of what he had become.

At the counseling appointment, I was alone. The counselor had expected both of us, but, for almost a year, my husband was unwilling to attend these meetings. At one of the first sessions, the counselor told me he felt there was either another woman or a porn addiction. Little did I know at the time, this would prove to be true.

I spent months being uncomfortable in my own house, and I was so scared of the future that I became sick and lost 35 pounds. The only place I could find comfort was in Eucharistic Adoration, although as a convert to the Catholic faith, I didn't totally understand. But after encouragement from friends, I would go at any time of day, at those moments when I just needed to be with God.

After months of my husband talking about leaving, one day I came home to find his stuff gone. He said he was living with friends...but who knew? Life was miserable as my children cried for their father to be in their lives, and he chose his own path. Things got so bad that I finally felt I had to file for divorce—to protect my children and so that we didn't lose everything we knew.

On Good Friday, I picked up my legal paperwork in tears, but I stashed it, still hoping that I wouldn't have to give it to him. This whole time God was leading my path, as I found more and more clues of how bad it had gotten. I saw an email about a credit card hitting a limit, a credit card I didn't know we had. I was curious, so, in the wee hours of the night before Easter, I looked into it further. And there it was, hitting me square in the face: vacations, weekend stays, and expensive dinners that I knew nothing about. I called the vacation company, was able to find out the parties involved, and my heart dropped. How could I have missed this?

On Easter evening, I called the woman. I left a message telling her that *I knew*, and that what she was doing was wrong, and hurtful to my children. I got a call back from my husband, and he was very angry. It was that night that I served him with the divorce papers, and the process began.

On Divine Mercy Sunday, after Mass, some friends of ours called him out for his actions. They used tough love to let him know the hard truths of what he was doing. This challenge to his sins was not well received, but he heard every word in his heart.

What I hadn't realized then was the importance of Divine Mercy in our lives. Many Sundays, we skated into Mass at the last minute, and we were only able to sit up front—right in front of the picture of Divine Mercy. We kept sitting there because the kids behaved better there, and I read those words, "Jesus, I trust in you," over and over.

I hadn't stopped leaning on God. In fact, I spent time at the Adoration chapel, my kids and I often went to daily Mass, and we said the rosary every night. I tried any prayers I could to help us. My faith was growing strong, and God just kept asking me to trust that He had a plan.

I tried to make the divorce process happen as slowly as I could endure. I could not accept that a relationship that had started almost 20 years before, with God telling me, "this is not the type of guy you date, this is the guy you marry," would end this way. This couldn't be His plan, for five boys to end up with a sometimes-father. My best friend Clara dropped everything to move in with me, to help support me in this time of need. Unavoidably, my husband and I approached mediation that August.

I had attended a women's event shortly before, where my friends and I decided to start a novena asking the intercession of St. Thérèse, the Little Flower. The presenter that day had gone through a similar experience, and she offered prayers and support for me.

Mediation happened. All I had was my desire to reconcile, and he said no. When they saw that I was shattered by this, the attorneys met in a different room. After their meeting (where my lawyer got new information from my husband's lawyer), the attorney and the mediator came in and told me that he was lying to me. They told me that he was, in fact, living with another woman, and that I should just move on. There it was—my worst nightmare.

I couldn't go home because it hurt too bad. I went to Adoration; the chapel was packed, but I found someone I knew and dove into the pew space next to her. She hugged me as I cried. After I got home, I started to realize that maybe this really was happening.

The next week was different, and I had a newfound confidence. I didn't think I had anything else to lose, so I told him off. The following day, my husband suddenly cared about talking to me, showing me something he'd bought, like he always used to. I was so confused. Clara and I were ready to leave on a girls' weekend, when that Friday morning I got a text from my husband: "Make a list of what you need from your husband, and I will figure out if I can give it to you." Wow —this was a game-changer, and what did it mean?

We spent a lot of that weekend on that phone, and it was then that my husband told me that the other woman wasn't the first person he had cheated with—she was the fourth. His unfaithfulness began out of a pornography addiction that had been there all these years. I had no idea.

I called off the divorce, he moved back in, and we tried to fix what we had broken and heal all the hurt, which sometimes seemed too much to bear. We had to learn to communicate and understand each other, the very things we had never known how to do before.

At one point, he felt like he had made a bad choice to come back home, and I began walking on eggshells, doing whatever I could to please him. After a few months, my friends told me I needed to take care of myself more, and so I did. My husband continued to be unhappy, and eventually met with his attorney again (unbeknownst to me). Thankfully, his attorney was a family man who led a ministry for helping marriages, and he refused to re-file divorce paperwork. Frustrated, my husband found another attorney who would do the work. A week later that attorney lost his job, but left the work for another.

During this providential delay, my husband spent a lot of time asking God for clarity, to show him the way to peace in his life. In response, God showed him his family, and made it known that he needed to stay. So, one day, he called me from another business trip and told me he had done something. My heart sank as he admitted that he had filed for divorce again, but then he told me that he no longer wanted that; he wanted to make our marriage work. He was going to tear up the papers when they got there, he said, and he was all in and not looking back. He told me he loved me, and now he knew that for sure.

That was six years ago, and, since then, we have worked every day to have a better marriage. We have come to realize the amazing things that Divine Mercy has done in our life. We both have Adoration hours, and mine happens to be Fridays at 3:00 p.m.—the Hour of Mercy; God chose that for me. We have spoken to teens about the weeds we have encountered in life, and we are both catechists at our parish. God willing, we will continue to grow and to help others redeem their marriages. [12]

––––––––––––––––––––––––––––––

Several years ago, I nearly bankrupted the family. I've always kept the checkbook and paid the bills, and my husband trusted me. I didn't manage things well, however. I ran our credit card up to the limit, I started missing payments on bills, and checks were bouncing all over the place. I hid my overspending, and I even lied to him at times about our finances. In my mismanagement, I even caused the utilities at the house to be shut off.

My husband started getting creditor calls at work, and that was his first clue that anything was wrong. When it finally all came crashing down, it was bad. After realizing I'd been dishonest with him for years, and on a large scale, he couldn't trust me and hated being around me. At that point, I believe he was only ever around me because of the kids.

My husband became prone to outbursts of rage, and he eventually crossed the line into taking it out on the kids, even approaching a level of serious abuse toward the children a couple of times. I finally had to tell him that he was rightfully allowed to be angry with me, but if he was going to physically or emotionally abuse the kids because of his anger with me, then he needed to go to his mother's house and sort himself out. I also told him that if that was all there was left in our marriage—if rage and verbal abuse was all he had left to give—there was no point in continuing. I never denied that his anger and even hatred toward me was justified, but he had to learn to keep it away from the kids.

The most painful thing for him, I think, was that he didn't actually hate me, even if, for a while, he hated being around me. He still loved me and didn't want a broken family, but he couldn't figure out how to reconcile that with my long and profound betrayal. I mean, honestly, I cringe now at the level and pervasiveness of dishonesty it took for me to maintain the illusion.

My husband was eventually able to rein it in enough to stop taking it out on the kids. (If he hadn't, this story would be very different.) Our redemption took years. Years of me being completely transparent about everything I did; years of having him not trust me at all on almost every topic; years of taking his verbal barbs and his venting of anger and hurt and mistrust (only protesting when he truly crossed the line into cruelty); years of forgiving him for all of that, as he was forgiving me for my sins. It took a long time, but we eventually got past it.

Yes, I still cringe inwardly whenever I have to discuss anything financial with him, because money issues upset him like nothing else. I'm still tempted to hide difficulty and see what I can get away with so that I don't have to talk to him about it—but I don't do that. I force myself to be honest with him, even though I know I risk the opening of old wounds.

I spent a lot of years gagging on humiliation and shame at what I had caused, compounded by the fact that he just didn't seem to be able to let it go. But after a few years, my husband appreciated that I was trying, and he began to trust me again. He saw that I talked to him about every financial decision, even if it was just about groceries. He came out of his fog of anger and understood how much pride I swallowed to keep our marriage intact, a marriage that still had love within it.

My greatest horror is the thought of putting my kids through a divorce. I lived through my own parents' "amicable" divorce—which really meant that my mother destroyed our family and my dad accepted that he couldn't stop her. I was willing to endure a lot to save my kids from that, as long as they were safe. And I earned everything I got.

I've said many times that my husband acted almost like I had cheated on him—because the level of lying, hiding, and deceit was very similar to infidelity—and that must have been something like what he felt. We are proof that a marriage *can* get past some horrible stuff and come out the other side stronger, happier, healthier, and more honest. We recently celebrated our 20th anniversary. [13]

For the first ten years of our marriage, we lived for ourselves, not knowing how to be married. We lived separate lives under the same roof, passing as strangers. About a year before I discovered my husband's infidelities, I craved intimacy and answered the call to weekly Adoration of the Blessed Sacrament. Little did I know that I was being strengthened and prepared for a battle against forces that were trying to destroy my marriage.

On that dreaded evening when I uncovered the lies, I wanted to leave, I wanted revenge, I wanted him to die—but I could not deny my own actions that pushed him out of our marriage. I take full responsibility for guarding myself against vulnerability and protecting myself, to the detriment of our relationship, all those years.

I knew in my heart that my husband had lost his way, as I myself have done (in other ways) so many times. I knew that if I left him, I would lose him forever to the very thing—an evil thing!—that was trying to break us. If I had separated from him, I would have grown more cold and more angry, and I didn't need any help with that. I needed to stay and fight.

How could I, a sinner who flees to the confessional and who is forgiven every time, not forgive my husband? And yet, I begged God to let me die. I pleaded for an end. I would not forgive. I just wanted out...but I could not and did not leave. I was reminded time and again of God's merciful love for me. The more I dug in my heels to whip him with his sin, the more I saw my own sins in our marriage and my own broken relationship with God.

My husband and I woke up every morning after that dreaded evening and battled our sins, pain, years of neglect, and anger—face to face, every day, and together. Being vulnerable to my husband who had just hurt me was the hardest thing I have ever done, but vulnerability was what was needed to move forward. I thought that the excruciating bombardment of thoughts and suspicions were never going to leave me. I didn't think I would ever be able to trust my husband again. But we have moved forward, by the absolute grace of God. That terrible time seems like a distant memory to me.

In the aftermath of the affairs, my husband quit his job, we were dragged through a lawsuit (connected to the infidelity), we relocated to another state with a new job, and we are absolutely thriving! Can you believe it? I can't either. Only by the grace of God can we be living this abundantly. I don't mean in material things, but simply in the joy in our life, which exceeds whatever joy we'd experienced earlier in our marriage. I can't wait for my husband to come home every day, and most days I go to him, just to be with him.

Through all the trauma, the Lord sent me a "Simon of Cyrene" to help me carry the crushing burden of that cross. I would not have been able to do it without her. Not knowing what to expect on the other end of the line, she answered the phone every single time I called, for a solid year. Most of the time it wasn't pretty: either I was a sobbing mess and couldn't talk, or I was a raging monster. At times I would be so angry, desperately wanting control over the situation, that I became little more than a ranting basketcase. My friend rightfully had to put my anger in its place and remind me of my vows. I can't even imagine where I would've been mentally had she not been there as my cheerleader in one of the hardest crises I've ever experienced.

In the depths of that hell, and under the burden of that cross, was precisely where I fell in love with my husband all over again—a deeper love than ever before. A love I never thought was possible for us. We are years past the crisis now, and I wake up still caught off guard that we are together and that we are living this beautiful life. It's the simple things that we do now, things we never did before, that I will not take for granted. Things that would never have come about except for the cross.

I want so badly to tell my story of redemption and forgiveness, to be transparent with the world that it is possible to repair your marriage if you stay true to your vows and remain focused on Christ—no matter how badly you or your spouse have sinned. I hate that it took all of this for us to be where we are now, but what we have now was worth the trial and the pain. I wouldn't trade my life for anything. [14]

When divorce isn't an option, all other options become more realistic. When divorce isn't sought after, healing is.

After 20 years of his lies, infidelity, and pornography addiction, my husband and I were in a tough spot. God had revealed these horrible truths to me, sins that my husband had keep hidden for years. Through prayer, patience, and listening to the promptings of the Holy Spirit, I was able to be brave and hear what God was telling me about my husband's secret life. With 11 children and one on the way, we had few options. Divorce wasn't one of them. I wanted to run the other way, but God showed me a better way. We could not afford expensive counseling, but I knew God wanted for my husband to be healed, and for our marriage not only to survive but to thrive!

The Bible says in John 10:10, "The thief comes only to steal and kill and destroy; I came that they may have life, and have it abundantly." My husband and I sought help where and when we could. We both humbled ourselves to receive discounted counseling, we joined mostly free support groups, and we prayed, both together and separately. He committed to sobriety, and I committed to forgiveness. We both knew that our children's futures depended heavily on how we handled (or mishandled) this situation. I cried more tears than I ever thought possible (and for years I cried; sometimes I still cry). My husband listened, wasn't defensive, and took responsibility for his actions.

Separately, we found the root of our own issues, and, separately, we worked on those issues with Jesus as our Divine Guide. Together, we invited God into our marriage and accepted the hard work that lay ahead for a couple seeking true oneness. We flushed out the toxins from our marriage and began again in what we call "Marriage #2." We are several years out from "disclosure day," and I'm forever grateful that we stuck it out. Our older children are aware of the issues we had and are very happy that we did what we could to keep our family together.

The cross leaves scars, and those first 20 years of verbal and emotional abuse caused a pretty large case of PTSD in me that will likely always be there on some level. But our situation has taught me that, although things can be at their absolute darkest, there's always a way to make it work. Our marriage truly is thriving now. We have since welcomed two more babies, and we have one grandchild with another on the way! God has truly blessed and multiplied our efforts to resist what seemed like the "easy" way—divorce. [15]

"You're what?" was my marriage proposal. Eighteen and pregnant after dating a young man for a year. As Catholic kids with concerned parents, we married in haste to the joy of his parents and the disappointment of mine. He was a spoiled kid adopted by older parents, and they were happy to have him (hopefully) now pointed in a positive and life-affirming direction. As one of the younger children in a large family broken by divorce, I was left to my own devices in my teen years, on my own in many ways. My husband's parents spoiled me and showered me with the love and attention I craved. Neither of us were in any way ready to be responsible adults, but I still took the marital commitment very seriously.

My mom's worried statement a week before the wedding—"You don't have to marry him; I hope you know that!"—made me think seriously. I know she was technically correct, but I had gone into this relationship sexually, with eyes wide open, and I knew my own sense of responsibility. I had made the decision to have sex and knew what I was doing.

Despite the devastation of my parents' divorce, I had devoted my youth and teen years to living with integrity, and, as best I understood, with honor. I was chaste, hung out with only extremely moral girls, and concentrated on my schoolwork. In my family, though, I was the object of derision for choosing to live this way. I was ridiculed for not having sex early or doing drugs. I was so horribly alone and lonely that when a wealthy and wild young man (who was secretly very smart and, in fact, rather shy) asked me out, I jumped at the chance to let him take me away with his endless funds and a fancy car.

With support from his family, we began our married life. My pregnancy went along as we worked in a factory, saving money for a home, while we lived with his parents. Life moved so fast, and my young husband was in no way ready.

We welcomed our baby girl as 18- and 19-year-old parents, and within nine months, we were separated. I moved back with my parents until we reconciled a few months later, deciding to keep trying. Before long, my husband suffered the tragic death of his only brother, followed soon after by the death of his father. The trauma of the deaths and the forced responsibilities of a family affected his still-maturing brain and sent him into a spiral of manic-depression.

A pattern of negative behaviors emerged, and I—with nothing but a will to stay committed—hung on for a ride that continued for years. I developed into a cycle of depression and anxiety that kept me floundering and in a state of stress as we struggled to stay afloat while he went to college and I worked to support us.

Our mode of interaction with one another was not healthy and should have been attended to with greater care, had we only understood. My husband grew increasingly abusive and resentful, and I just dug in my heels and worked harder to care for him and his ailing mother.

The day came when I was ready to walk away. I was far from God and miserable, so miserable I felt as if I would have a nervous breakdown if I didn't leave him. Instead, I turned to the faith community and found the power of God there. I had a dramatic encounter with Jesus Christ, and it changed me. I saw my husband now with *unconditional love* and God spoke to my heart. It was as if He said, "I am asking you to do some hard things, and it is to My glory if you stay and fight for greater love."

I was so in love with Jesus that I said, "Oh Jesus, I will do whatever You ask of me."

Life got hard, very hard. I became pregnant, almost miraculously, after seven years of no pregnancy, but I became mysteriously very ill. My husband was resentful that I was ill, and he neglected us as the pregnancy went along. After our next daughter was born, he abandoned us for a time, only to return a short while later to pick up where we left off.

He began a pattern of infidelity that coincided with his cycles of depression. During these difficult years, I cared for his ill mother and our home while fighting lupus and having more children. My world became very separate from his, yet I trusted God. I knew that divorce was not what God ever wants for families.

My husband and I became separated for several years, while I continued in faithfulness, chaste and committed. During this time, I struggled with the idea of divorce. I was active in my community, and men found me attractive. Yet, it was as if Jesus had become my Spouse. He preserved me in so many ways, and I was able to serve and care for people in my church and community.

In my weakness and pain, Jesus taught me to be a source of strength for others, and I led support and study groups for women with hard marriages. I had a solid spiritual companion in my best childhood friend who prayed with me and counseled me wisely. With that prayer and love, I was able to resist the toxicity of negative peer pressure and the regular advances of men who promised me the kind of love and care my husband wouldn't or couldn't give me.

I only had eyes for Jesus at that time, and I gave my husband over to Him daily—and sometimes hourly—as he continued to live apart from his family. His adultery became a scandal in my community, and I was pressured from all directions to divorce. I did not. I knew instinctively and from my own experience the future my children would have if I did—unprotected, faithless, and broken.

I discovered powerful spiritual truths about marriage—even marriage to a partner who did not share in the marital contract anymore. That power enabled and established a supernatural protection that preserved my children and actually provided a lifeline to my husband who was now drowning in his own sin and brokenness.

Depending utterly on God, and feeling at one point that God said "enough," I told my husband that his unfaithfulness had done such great harm that our separation would need to be permanent. At the time, I was working in a high profile job, my boss had sworn his love for me and my husband had found out. I rejected my boss despite my incredible loneliness and desire to be loved by a man, because all I saw was my husband's adulterous spirit in this man, too.

It was a wake-up call to my husband, who, through God's enlightenment, could see his own sinful actions displayed through this other man. Literally, in a driving rainstorm with thunder crashing and the rain pouring down, he kneeled in the mud and water and lifted up his hands to the sky and gave himself over to Christ. The battle wasn't over yet, but he had finally yielded to the only One who could heal him.

That was over 20 years ago, and we have been married now for 40 years. My husband sought help for his destructive patterns of behavior, and the counseling has been transformative for him in many ways. My own time in counseling has confirmed that Christ indeed preserved me by providing me with healthy responses to sin.

My husband is forever grateful for the power of grace and mercy, and that it wasn't too late for him to be reconciled to his family. We still live in a fallen world, and we have not achieved perfection (our children and I still can become wary when we see his dark mood emerging as it does cyclically), but he is learning to respond differently and each time gets better. Our joy in a preserved home, where family gathers and the grandchildren have begun to fill, is overflowing.

Our children are happily married and believe in the power of love because they saw it. They know they are anomalies (and witnesses!) among their friends, and they've expressed their gratefulness to me for laying down my life for their sake and the sake of their father.

Marriage *is* my vocation; as a Christian, this requires that I indeed pick up my cross and follow Jesus. I can tell you without reserve: He is mighty to save, redeem, and restore, but we must say "yes" in obedience and never count the cost to ourselves. We are to daily walk with Him and allow the Holy Spirit to work in us, through our humility and sacrificial love. You will know you are doing all things in Him when He visits His joy upon you during the dark times in a way that is fierce, strong, and contagious.

If you struggle in your marriage, seek out those who know God and know the real power of sacrificial love—a love borne of suffering. They will be your allies and cheerleaders as you run your race for the crown of life. Your vocation is your path to holiness, and the cross is your ladder to heaven. Let Christ's love transform your marriage and your world. [16]

From her:

When I got married, it was with the notion that if things didn't work out, we could always get divorced. Divorce was my back-up plan.

I already had one child out of wedlock from another man, and I was living with my current boyfriend (future husband), so marriage seemed like the next logical step. I did love him, and I knew that he was a good man, but that was about all that I did know; I certainly didn't understand marriage.

Growing up, I had witnessed my mother threatening divorce on my father anytime they argued. They never did divorce, but it had an effect on me and carried over into my own marriage. Naturally, any time we would argue or disagree about something, I would throw out the word "DIVORCE!" and use it in a threatening manner to get my way. My new husband would cave every time, because he didn't want a divorce. But, he also didn't know how to deal with an unstable wife or marriage, so he turned to drinking heavily.

At the start of our marriage, we were both working in the restaurant business and were full-time students. In order to avoid daycare or sitters, we worked opposite shifts and took classes on alternating days so that we could take care of our children ourselves. This made our lives hectic and stressful, and we stayed up late to spend time together.

My husband lost his job due to drinking while I was on maternity leave from having our first child together. I was so angry, but I went back to work the very next day, and thankfully he was able to get another job immediately.

We fought often. Of course, my threats of divorce continued. I got a call one night from his new employer that he was passed out in his car in the parking garage. He was drinking on the job again. I was over it, and I began to confide in a co-worker (I'll call him Bob) that I was ready to end my marriage and move on. Bob was an older, religious man who began to mentor me.

Divorced himself, Bob was now very much opposed to divorce; he told me of his own regrets and how he wished he had done things differently. He gave me the book, *Love is a Choice*, and he gave my husband a book about being the man you were made to be. Bob also explained to me that I had great power over my husband, and that my words could either build him into the man I wanted him to be, or they could tear him down and defeat him—also sabotaging myself and my marriage in the process.

Bob invited me to a non-denominational church with him. At the time, my husband and I were not practicing our Catholic faith. Despite having gone to Catholic school as a child, I didn't realize there were any differences between Catholics and Protestants, let alone significant ones! When I mentioned my intentions to attend the non-denominational church with Bob, my husband put his foot down for the first time in our marriage and told me he was vehemently opposed.

He had given in to my wants and demands when it came to everything else, but this time he looked at me and said, "Not this. Not our faith."

I was honestly intrigued as to why my husband suddenly had a backbone. He told me I should at least learn about what Catholics believe versus Protestants, and he told me he wanted us to start going to Mass again. I agreed.

We started an in-home bible study with Bob, where we took turns presenting and debating all the issues between Catholicism and Protestantism. This went on for two years, and others attended from time to time, both Catholics and Protestants. Every Sunday, we would meet for two hours after Mass, and, as time went on, I went through a real conversion/reversion to the Catholic faith.

In an almost simultaneous fashion, my health was deteriorating. I had always been a healthy young woman, but I was experiencing debilitating pain in my right side. I couldn't run (a hobby I cherish), and I would stay in bed all day in order to be able to function at work that night; sometimes, I would leave work early. Several visits to the emergency room, a functional medical doctor, specialists, chiropractors, and others turned up zero answers as to why I was struck down by this infirmity.

I knew all along that it was somehow all connected. My marriage was still in turmoil, I was begging God to let me in and to come into my heart forever, my health was hanging on by a thread, and I had no idea what the future held for any of it. I pressed on and leaned in. I started attending RCIA classes in order to receive my confirmation that I had missed out on (due to a move) in high school. I continued looking for answers to the physical pain, as well.

Finally, after two years, a urologist found the problem: a kink in my ureter from a vein and an artery criss-crossing and blocking the flow from my kidney to my bladder. He told me it was a birth defect that, strangely, didn't give me any symptoms or problems for the first 27 years of my life. I believe that in my weaknesses, I began to realize my need for others, including my husband. I leaned on him and relied on him to love me and take care of me in ways I had refused prior to being sick. Before this, I had always considered myself a strong and independent woman who didn't need anyone else. Now I was seeing that allowing myself to be vulnerable and allowing my husband to take care of me was not a bad thing.

There was a moment that changed my marriage, and it was the moment I decided that I wasn't going to get divorced. I wasn't going anywhere; I needed my husband. I had threatened divorce out of fear that that's what he wanted because I was so difficult to love. My husband was at a low point due to "falling off the wagon" again, and we were standing in the kitchen together. Instead of my usual negativity, my nasty words meant to tear him down, and my threats of divorce, I just looked at him and told him that I was going to stand by him and see him through this. I was going to love him forever and be his wife. His face changed, and his behaviors followed suit.

Our marriage changed. It was like my husband now had the confidence he needed to lead our family and to be the man that he and I both wanted him to be. I was able to let go and let him take care of me and our children. I decided to trust him, to love him, and to build him up instead of tear him down.

It was precisely when I decided that divorce was not an option that my perspective changed.

We recently celebrated 13 years, and our marriage is so much better than anything I could have imagined or designed on my own. I am convinced that if I hadn't changed my attitude from one with a back-up plan of divorce to one of perseverance and commitment to making it work, we would not be married today.

From him:

Reading my wife's words brings to mind a lot of memories and feelings, both good and bad. Looking back on the people we were and the choices we were making only confirms for me the power of marital union itself. On a practical level, it truly can be called a miracle that we made it through it all. It is my feeling that most, if not all, married couples could probably say the same thing. When I use the word miracle, I do not mean it in the way that is normally used in our secular world, but rather through the lens of our faith: Miracles are supernatural works of God, either directly or through the prayers and intercessions of saints—and our marriage would not still *be* if that wasn't true.

When I put my foot down about our faith, it was because of my faith that I was able to do so. It truly was the first time (and still one of the only times!) I've said "NO" to my wife. I felt a change in her that day. She did not want me always to acquiesce. She wanted me to lead. I was not ready for it, and I ducked my responsibility in many ways—including by drinking. I felt the change in myself the day that she said emphatically that she wasn't ever going to leave me.

It took a year of not drinking for me to get to the root cause of my problem. More than a drinking problem, I had an honesty problem. I avoided conflict with my wife at all costs, and the costs were many. My emotional maturity level was at an all-time low. Because I was not always honest with her about how I felt or what I wanted/needed, the feeling that resulted was a sense of entitlement to do whatever I wanted.

When my wife said "I'm not going anywhere," I felt more strength in myself and my marriage than I ever had to that point. It was because of her faith that she could say that—I certainly wasn't giving her many reasons to.

Since that time, almost 11 years ago, we've had many highs and lows, but the difference now is that we know we are together because God intended for us to be. We say "I'm sorry" sooner, we honestly work on honesty (more from me and less from her, ha!), and we actively look for ways to make our marriage better and to meet each other's needs. You can't tie a knot too tight, and I know we are both pulling as hard as we can. [17]

I was in love. He was good-looking, had gorgeous legs, was Catholic, and attended Mass every Sunday that the baseball team was in town. He was one of eight kids, and he was the relief pitcher for the southern college we both attended. I lived at home, and he was from the Midwest. We didn't really date, but we hung out at all the same places.

Summer came and instead of going back home he stayed in town, worked, and played ball. I made it a point to be at every home game. I knew he was the kind of guy I wanted to marry. He was getting a degree in education and loved kids—a hard-working, manly man. I think, for him, I was just always around and always available, and I had a little money to spend from my part-time job. We would go two weeks without seeing each other, but when he called, I would drop everything to be with him.

Things got more serious between us over the next couple of years. He went away to be a graduate assistant baseball coach in a beach town, and I thought it was all over; he told me baseball was his life and he didn't have time for a girlfriend. But whenever he was driving back home to his family, he would pass through and see me.

Before long, I found out I was pregnant. I didn't tell him, or anyone, for months. I was six months along before I told him. After many long nights, tears, and discussions, we decided to get married. I was afraid he would feel trapped, but he was the one who really wanted to get married. Of course I did too, but I wanted him to want to because he loved me, not because of the baby. He convinced me that was the case, so we married in the Catholic parish I attended with my family. My whole family and his came to the wedding, along with a few family friends. I was happier than I had ever been in my life.

We lived with my parents for about eight months and then moved into an apartment on campus where we both were finishing up our studies. I was in nursing school, and he was getting his Masters in Education. Life was hard; no money, studying, raising a baby, and he was traveling with the team.

Fast forward 15 years, and now we had four daughters, ages 15, 12, 9, and 3. He was a high school teacher and baseball coach and refereed college basketball. Soon he was offered a full-time officiating job and traveled as a referee for the NBA. I was working nights in the NICU and sleeping very little. Tired all the time, I started to let myself go—physically, spiritually, emotionally.

The signs were everywhere, but I didn't want to see them. He could be assigned a game in any city and had to be there the night before the game. He could be gone 20+ nights per month. When he was home, he would be physically there, but, more and more, not mentally there. He would get back in town after being on the road for five or six nights, and first thing the next morning he would work out at the gym, then be on the phone with another referee I'd hardly ever heard of. He always had his phone on silent and locked. When he was out of town I would call, but he was always unavailable, saying he'd call me back later.

There were other things. For example, it seemed my husband always had to go to the airport to get his tickets, instead of just calling the airline. He would volunteer to take one of our daughters to school or dance lessons, but he would be gone much longer than expected. And one night, our 12-year-old had to go to the after-hours clinic for IV fluids, possibly needing hospital admission; despite this, my husband still left to go to an out-of-town game that had been "added."

In my heart, I knew something was wrong. I was an exhausted, out-of-shape mother of four, and he was hanging around world-famous athletes in every city. All that glamour and no accountability. I would question him, and he always had the same answer: "No! Never! I would never do anything!"

But then one day, my husband left his phone at home when he took our daughter to school. My gut said to look, and I saw the same out-of-state number several times. Then I listened to a voicemail from a girl he was going to meet in a city where he was supposed to be going to golf for the weekend with another referee.

My world as I knew it crashed, and my heart broke into a thousand pieces. When he got home, I confronted him. He lied initially, but eventually told me he had met her in a bar three months earlier in another state. I begged him for as much information as he would give me. He said she was much younger, that she went to his games with him, and that they spent days together while he was on the road—which of course shattered me even more. I could not stop crying. We fought, and I felt like I was standing on a floor that would just drop out from under me. My head was spinning. I felt like nothing in life was real. What was truth...what was a lie? We talked, yelled, screamed, and I cried and cried. It was a day of unimaginable suffering.

Finally, around midnight, I grabbed my keys. I had on nothing but an old t-shirt, baggy gym shorts, and flip-flops, but I couldn't stand to be in the same house with him anymore. I had no idea where I was going. I couldn't tell anyone in my family, and I had no close friends to discuss this with. I felt like such a failure, and I was drowning in sorrow.

After driving around for several hours, the only conclusion I had arrived at was that I couldn't go back home that night. The decision I made next changed the rest of my life. I suddenly remembered a couple of girls in the NICU mentioning a new Perpetual Adoration chapel at a parish I used to attend. If it were indeed a perpetual chapel, it would be open 24 hours, night and day, *right then*. I felt like, after hours of hearing a phone ring on a lifeline, someone had finally picked up!

I raced to the church and found a small porch light on. Hurrying to the door, I knocked until someone answered. As soon as I walked in, I saw the married couple who babysat our first child when I was in nursing school. I felt like I had just found Mary and Joseph. I knelt down and cried before the Blessed Sacrament, and the woman came over and hugged me like I envision Mary would do. She let me cry into her shoulder, and I told her my husband was having an affair. I have never felt so much comfort and relief in my entire life. I stayed for several hours, talking and crying, and when we all finally left, the sun was coming up. I heard a songbird in a cherry blossom tree, and I had a glimmer of hope.

Throughout the next few months, I had pain like I had never known. I felt like I couldn't breathe, like I had bricks on my chest. I wish I could say that it was all solved as soon as that affair was over, but the road had just begun. Eight years later, he had another affair. His brother told me to leave him, that I was stupid to stay. His sister-in-law told me to have an affair myself, that I would feel better. My brother's wife, however, told me, "Don't let his sin cause you to sin." Those words stuck with me throughout the ensuing years.

For months, years, we prayed, fought, and went to counseling. We ended up in Retrouvaille.[5] He said he didn't want a divorce, but he just wasn't 100% into our marriage, either.

From the couple in Adoration, we had found out about Cursillo, and my husband said that something about that weekend really "hit home" for him. I started listening to EWTN radio constantly and digging deep to learn my faith. My husband and I signed up for the sacrificial hour of 4:00 a.m. for weekly Adoration. It was hard, and often I thought of changing hours, but we never have because 4:00 a.m. was the hour I first arrived at the chapel all those years ago. We have been going now for 22 years.

Forgiving and letting go of the pain and hurt took many years, but our marriage is better than ever. We pray our rosary together nearly every night and attend daily Mass as much as possible. My husband is now a captain in Fraternus, a mens'-only spiritual formation group, and has become the spiritual leader in our family. We recently celebrated 37 years of marriage, three of our four daughters are married, and we have twelve grandchildren. We all sit together for Mass every Sunday.

I am convinced that multiple factors contributed to the saving of our marriage. Both of us being Catholic, both coming from intact families, our commitment to our children and ultimately to each other—all were primary factors. On the supernatural level, it was understanding our covenant relationship in our sacramental marriage, and the reception of the graces that started that very first night that I walked into the Perpetual Adoration chapel. In those first years after the initial affair, we never went to Adoration together. I went most of the time, and, if he was in town, he took the hour. After the second affair, we started going to Adoration together. Graces upon graces have come to us through being together in Adoration and prayer. I thank God for what

He has given us. [18]

The Beginning...
  Marie:
Our story begins when Joe and I met during college. We worked together and became friends before dating; we dated for 4 ½ years before marrying in 1991. Joe is a Catholic convert (converted during our courtship) and from a divorced home. I am a cradle Catholic from an intact family with parents married over 55 years. Our dating and first years of marriage were very good. We considered ourselves best friends; we practiced our faith, and looked forward to welcoming children. We were both working professionals and had many friends and a supportive family.

  Joe:
Marie and I met in college. We started out as friends. I had been hurt before in past relationships, so I wasn't looking for a wife while I was in college. Trust was a big issue for me. It took a great deal of effort to trust women and to allow someone to really get close to me.

I was a child of divorce and I have no siblings. My mom divorced my father when I was about five years old. She raised me as a single parent for the next five years, until she met my stepfather. She was married to him from the time I was ten until they divorced when I was 18. My stepfather had alcohol and drug issues, but he was a caring and loving man when he was sober. My mother was always there for me; I trusted her, and we shared a lot. As is common with children of divorce, I was an emotional support for her. She depended on me. I felt that I needed to behave well for her, as I didn't want to create any more problems for her. She trusted me and gave me a lot of freedoms based on our relationship and my behavior. Even though my mom was the only person with whom I shared my emotions, I still kept a lot to myself—I did not want not to disturb the family any more than the divorce already had.

Marie and I dated for roughly five years. Although I did love her, I had commitment issues based on an inability to trust. When I was deciding to marry her, I put together a list of what I needed from our relationship, realizing that no one is perfect. She met all the criteria. She was my best friend, beautiful, and caring towards others and me. I believed that I could trust her and that she wouldn't hurt me. The two issues that I felt were unresolved were her anger and controlling behavior.

I asked her to marry me. During our yearlong engagement, I asked God to take away those issues if she was the right person for me to marry. I relied on God to help Marie work through her anger and control issues. Our entire engagement period was wonderful, and there was rarely a time when I felt controlled or had anger directed at me; I felt at peace.

The Early Years...

Marie:

Looking back now, I can see where things changed for me after our first child was born in 1993.

My vision of Joe and myself became altered. I had this list of expectations in my head of what I wanted Joe to be as a father and a spouse. I also became very concerned about how we looked to the outside world, which was related to my childhood issues. The peace I had somehow turned into a frenzy of what I thought our life should look like. In addition, I falsely assumed that Joe was on the same page as me regarding our goals, home life, and future. I stopped asking for his input, and I began making family decisions alone. From my view, since Joe was not vocal enough about his opinions, I was free to charge ahead with my agenda. He seemed "checked out" to me, but I assumed this is just Joe, and, after all, I was a strong, intelligent woman who made great decisions.

Joe:

Those who know me know that I'm a man of few words. I will offer my opinion when asked, and if I have something to say, I will usually say it once and then let it go. If I feel it's an important issue, I will voice my thoughts again, but if I'm not listened to, I will drop it. I do take responsibility for the times during the early part of our marriage when I often didn't push issues or speak my mind. I didn't want to "rock the boat," and therefore Marie would think that we were always in agreement with her plan.

I noticed some changes in our relationship after our first child was born. It seemed that Marie had a plan for our life. She had expectations of what we should be doing and where we needed to go. I'm not sure if this was driven by our friends or by her, personally. At the time, I didn't have an issue with that plan, because she was a planner and I was the provider for our family.

But eventually, I noticed that when there were decisions that needed to be made, Marie would do what she wanted and not listen to me. Sometimes what I said or wanted to happen would match up with what she wanted and implemented, but other times it would not. This was in all aspects of our life, but most specifically with regard to religion. It seemed that I never did enough in the religion department. I was a very spiritual person—we went to church and had a good prayer life—but that wasn't enough. She wanted more, and she pushed me to be more involved with the church, which wasn't my desire. I felt that she wanted me to be someone that I wasn't. If there were decisions regarding our children, it seemed that she would ask me—but then do what she wanted. I didn't feel that my opinions or thoughts were respected regarding the relationship. I allowed Marie to forge ahead with her plan for our marriage as I stayed in the background.

The Later Years...

Marie:

Life continued this way for the next 15 years, through miscarriages, the birth of our second child, career changes, and a move to a different state. We functioned as co-parents and roommates mainly. We still practiced our faith, raised the children together, and socialized normally with friends. What was missing was the passion and intimate connection we once had.

Joe:

At this point I wasn't happy. It was more of a friendship than a marriage. We had lost the intimacy and passion that we'd had before our first child. Additionally, there was the anger and controlling behavior that Marie now exhibited more frequently. As my voice continued not to be heard, I said less and allowed her to drive the relationship. She hurt me by not listening to me and trusting in what I had to say. I would go over in my head all the time the fact that I had placed our relationship in God's hand from the beginning. Why did the relationship change? Why would God give me this relationship? I really couldn't understand why this was happening. I thought, "Is this the way it's going to be for our entire life?" This made me sad.

Basically, I figured that if this was the way it was going to be, then I would continue to be unhappy and just live with it. I didn't think anything would change, and I had given up on what I thought my marriage would or could be.

The "I'm Done" Conversation...

Marie:

Finally, 19 years into our marriage, I asked Joe what was wrong. I really had to push for him to share, but when he finally did, he said he was done. He meant done with the marriage and his life with me. I was devastated. My world collapsed, and yet I was oddly relieved! I felt something wasn't right, too. So, I went into "fix it" mode, not "give up" mode. It was over the next three years of marriage counseling and talking that I learned the true state of my husband's mentality. He did not love me anymore, and he could not see how things would ever change. He wanted out of the marriage.

This began a deep spiritual journey of inner healing for me. I attended weekends both for family-tree healing and for personal healing. I spoke with priests and looked into the Church's teaching on marriage and family. Divorce was not an option for me. I enlisted close family and friends to pray for us. During this time, through God's tremendous mercy, I was healed in numerous ways. The most significant healing was the "new eyes" that God gave me. When I used to see Joe, I had a litany of expectations attached to him. God removed that, and He allowed me to see Joe as He sees him! It was honestly the most beautiful gift. I was now seeing my precious husband as this beautiful man and as the gift that God gave me. It was a miracle that I needed, especially because I had no idea what the next few years would bring.

Joe:

When we had that conversation in our bedroom where Marie asked me what was wrong, I was not willing to say it was over. Marie kept pushing me for what was wrong, and for what I was thinking. I finally told her that I was done with the relationship. I had actually been done with the relationship several years before, but I continued on autopilot, just trying to get through and pass my time, hoping that God would take me away from this situation. I had no feelings for her. I didn't care about the kids, our life, the financial impacts, or anything else. I was dead in the relationship. There was a sense of relief in sharing how I truly felt, but I didn't think anything could fix our relationship. I didn't believe in divorce, but at the same time, I didn't see any other options. I wanted out of the marriage and away from being miserable. I kept thinking to myself that I would rather be alone than be married.

Marie began to work on herself. She talked with priests, counselors, and close family members. I didn't care. I felt whatever work she was doing, she was doing for herself. I did attend counseling sessions, but I refused to change my mind or heart. I couldn't believe that she did this to me. I felt I had been a loving and caring husband to her and our kids. I stayed in the emotions that had been compounded over the years and was hurting badly. I felt I couldn't trust her based on how I was treated. I was angry that I wasn't listened to or respected for my opinions, and I was also angry at myself for not being more vocal earlier in our marriage. I shut off all emotions towards her, and that didn't change, regardless of the work that she was now doing to change things.

Marie:

I observed that Joe remained distant from me but appeared happy for my personal changes. He did not move out or initiate divorce, so I thought we would be okay. I learned that was not the case when, about four years later, we sold our home and Joe announced that he did not want to move to our next house with the children and me. Eventually, he did move with us, and that is when I discovered that he was having an affair.

No one is ever prepared for this news. I was ill-equipped for the intense physical, emotional, and mental anguish. I know that Jesus was with me during that time, and He sustained me; I was so grateful for my recent interior healing.

I learned Joe was a year into this affair with a co-worker, and I asked every question I could think of, assessing if Joe would make an effort to save our marriage and family. He was willing to try again, and agreed to go back into counseling. But despite more marriage counseling and a Retrouvaille weekend, he was in and out of the affair for the next two years. We separated legally for 18 months, as I couldn't tolerate this betrayal. We both decided we didn't want a divorce, but didn't know how or when Joe would change his mind and stop living this double life. It was a difficult time. I saw Joe suffering and my love for him increased daily. God's grace was astounding, as I was able to forgive Joe. During this time, we consulted two priests who gave good advice about sticking with our marriage. One priest prayed over Joe for healing. I knew our children were watching us, and that our decision would affect them for life.

Joe:

Nothing had changed through the transition period with Marie working on herself. I continued to be self-absorbed with how I was feeling. I was thinking that to make the transition easier, we would sell the house and make finances more streamlined, though I didn't share my plans with Marie. I realized that I was being very selfish, wanting out of the relationship and only being concerned with myself. I was concerned about my relationships with my daughters, but I was looking for a way out of the marriage.

The affair wasn't something that I had planned. I had always put hedges around our marriage to avoid other women getting too close, but now I didn't care. It wasn't my intention to have an affair. But when I lowered those hedges and didn't protect our marriage, I allowed this to happen. When Marie found out about the affair the first time, it was devastating. I didn't realize the pain and anguish that I placed on my wife, and it rocked her to her core. I felt bad about what had happened, but still wasn't committed to the marriage. Marie asked if I still wanted to continue the affair or the marriage. I said the marriage, and agreed to attend several counseling sessions. I stopped the affair, but unfortunately it crept back into my life during this time. I was very stubborn in how I felt, and I wasn't willing to trust that Marie wouldn't hurt me again.

The Resolution...

Marie:

It wasn't until Joe took a job out of town and we attended a secular treatment/counseling center that the affair ended. This secular center, The Meadows, respected our Catholic faith and that we didn't want a divorce. They kept divorce *off* the table, unlike some Catholic counselors who kept divorce as an option! Joe dealt with his childhood issues, and he began earnestly trying to repair our marriage. He experienced his own healing and was able to return to our married life and family. It has been several years since we began living together again, and it is nothing short of a miracle. I am so grateful for all the prayers and God's intervention in our marriage. The marriage we have now is the one I have always wanted. I am married to my best friend and the man that God chose for me. God is and always was the third person in our marriage, and we are humbled by His love for us.

Joe:

The time away from each other was good for me. It allowed me to completely separate from the affair partner and give me space to truly evaluate my marriage. There were several impactful moments for me on my journey back to my marriage.

The first was attending a week-long counseling/treatment center where we worked as a couple, learning about how we were as children and how it affects us as adults. Through those sessions, I learned that my trust and love issues were not with Marie but with God. I needed to let God love me for who I am and to trust in Him that He would take care of everything. At the end of the sessions, the counselor asked me if I could commit to my marriage—but I was still hesitant and couldn't commit.

The second event was how I was being treated by my immediate family. I was amazed that Marie was so patient and kind with me when I'd put her through so much pain. She was encouraging and loving. She treated me differently with no expectations. She listened to me. She took my suggestions. She respected me and what I had to say. Additionally, my daughters were loving and kind to me. They loved me no matter what I did in the past, and they were open and available to talk. My relationship with them grew stronger through this experience. Lastly, Marie's family continued to love me and support our marriage. I thought there was no way they could do it based on what I did. Because of my betrayal, I never thought these relationships would be repaired.

The third event was my personal relationship with God. I learned to let God love me and to trust Him. This wasn't easy. I never felt worthy of His love. I was always quick to tell others how much God loved them, but never believed it for myself. Once I "let go and let God," my attitudes and life changed. I was at peace with my past, and I knew God had forgiven me by removing the guilt that I had carried throughout my marriage. Once I allowed God to love me, then the trust in Him came to me. If God loved me so much, then He would take care of anything that I was worried about or couldn't handle. The more I gave to God the more I trusted Him and the more at peace I felt.

Ultimately, it came down to putting God in charge and not giving up on my marriage and family. Trusting in God that He would take care of the past hurts and strengthen the current relationships, and realizing that our marriage is a sacrament that should be worked through and not discarded. I do ask for forgiveness from Marie whenever she's having a difficult time as many of those hurts take a long time to heal. I also ask forgiveness from my daughters just to make sure they are still good with me. I'm truly grateful for how things worked out and feel blessed to be married to such a beautiful, spirit-filled woman.

Marie:

My simple advice to others in a similar situation is: Don't lose hope, and trust in God's timing.

Joe:

My advice to others, especially men, is three-fold…

Don't have an affair. It's one of the most damaging things that you can do in any relationship. If you're thinking about having an affair or are in one—stop it. Address the core issues of what is happening in your relationship, and work on those areas. The affair will not fix your issues, but only create more distrust and more problems for you.

Speak up and speak your mind. Don't hold back on how you truly feel. If your spouse is not hearing you, or if she is not willing to listen, get a professional third party to mediate those conversations. When you talk to your wife, be kind, respectful, and loving, and don't be afraid to share how you feel. My own situation would never have happened if I had been more vocal in the beginning of our relationship.

Trust in God. God doesn't want you to get divorced. He worked miracles in both my life and Marie's. He completely changed my heart when there was no way I thought He could do it. He gave me perspective when everything was closed off. God is the only reason that I'm still in my marriage, and He's the only reason I'm loving Marie more than when we first were married. God completely healed both of us, and we are stronger than ever in our relationship.

Marie and Joe:

Together, we continue to pray for married couples and those struggling, because this vocation is not easy, and we need to help one another. [19]

My parents seemed an unlikely pair from the beginning. Dad was a middle child from a large, poor, Catholic family, and Mom was the youngest of three from an anti-Catholic, well-to-do Protestant family. He was her paper boy growing up, and when he pumped her gas one spring afternoon years later, she asked him if he was the same boy from back then. He affirmed her suspicions, and he later told a friend that if she came through again, he would ask her out. She did, he did, and 13 months later they were married.

Their marriage was challenging from the start. Mom later confided that she was quick to marry to escape her controlling, ill-tempered father. Dad was still in college and working 40 hours a week to support his new family. Within two months, Mom was expecting their first child. She wanted to please her new husband, but his hot temper and aggressive and unrefined social behavior made living with him difficult. She would try new recipes, and he would shove his plate across the table proclaiming, "I won't eat this sh*t." She struggled with deep insecurity and paranoia. She had dreams of a cute little house with a white picket fence. His dream was to have a farm where he could support his family and work alongside his children. He wanted 14 children. After three challenging pregnancies, she was done giving children to an unsympathetic man who insisted she was a hypochondriac.

As the years went on, Mom perfected the silent treatment, passive-aggressive retaliation, and harboring resentment. Although Dad never struck her, he pulled sinks from walls, broke his hand from hitting a table out of frustration, and lashed out with angry words. She would lock herself in the bathroom to escape his wrath.

To "shut him up," Mom gave in to Dad's desire for a farm, and so began 25 years of broken promises, massive debt, and unending stress. She harbored a deep resentment and acted out by hoarding and by spending sprees that brought collection agencies to their door. She felt justified in her behavior because he had put her through such heartache.

He worked long hours at two jobs—the farm full-time, plus another part-time job to make ends meet. Both of them outrageously stubborn, they continued to fight through each day—fighting with each other and fighting through the challenges they faced.

Their interests were so different (for example, Mom loved music, but Dad couldn't carry a tune in a bucket) that most of the time they went their separate ways. Mom was a Catholic convert, but I have very few memories of us attending Mass together as a family. They each went to the Mass that fit them, and we kids usually went with Dad. Their divergent lives really bothered me growing up, and I was always afraid they would get a divorce; I even remember asking my dad about it. Though they fought a lot and had horrible communication skills, the idea of my family splitting apart was so much worse. Even with their rotten relationship, Dad's bad temper, and Mom's mental illness, we always knew we were loved. They communicated how much we meant to them, and we truly knew it, in spite of the dysfunction in their marriage.

In all my years growing up, I recall one sweet moment between my parents as they held hands at a relative's funeral. That image made such an impact on me! It is burned into my brain as a source of comfort and security that they really did love each other.

After we kids grew up, things continued on their unhealthy path—and so many times, we were caught in the middle. They would pit us against the other parent, each vying for our approval. Because we had grown up with this bad behavior, we recognized it and did our best to remain neutral. But truthfully, I often thought, "If they end up divorced, it will be uglier than if they stay together. I cannot imagine trying to split holidays with these two!"

Then, about 35 years into their marriage, things came to a climax with Mom's mental illness. She told us that the police were following her. She told her grandchildren that people were watching her house, and she was always suspicious of everyone. Her insecurity was illogical, confusing, and even mind-boggling, but by far the worst was her claim that my dad was having an affair and that he was hoarding money to sneak away with his mistress—accusations that were completely untrue.

My dad was deeply imperfect but had never been unfaithful, and he was completely appalled that she would accuse him of adultery. He tried to talk to her, reason with her, explain to her, all to no avail. She even went so far as to go to his workplace and tell his boss that he was having an affair with a co-worker.

Also at this time, she began having crazy outbursts of anger. My normally reserved mother was spewing profanity, accusing us of saying and doing things that never happened. It was so hard on all of us, but my father, of course, was hit the hardest by the accusations of unfaithfulness.

For several years, Dad continued to try to reason with Mom. He would call me crying, not sure what to do and not wanting to slander his wife by talking to anyone about the illogical and unpredictable behavior that left him in tears and speechless. Dad, a very controlling and fact-based person, was now in a situation that he could not control —he could not strong-arm her into sanity.

Mom threatened divorce. He vowed it would never happen. Marriage is forever.

Then something clicked.

Dad, who was up till now a selfish man, realized that the only way to deal with his wife in a productive way was to love her more tenderly than he ever had. Instead of criticizing all the things she didn't get done, he started doing them himself. They began going to Mass together, he tenderly walking beside her to Communion, supporting her unsteady gait. He'd fix her a special meal or pick up her favorite snack on his way home—Dad was finally learning that marriage is not only about commitment, but also about self-sacrifice.

As he grew in gentleness, her bouts of anger and unpredictable behavior grew less frequent. She rarely accuses him anymore, and they are moving forward together, their relationship now better than it has ever been. We are finally witnessing a partnership and companionship we have never seen before. While not perfect, they grow closer each day.

Recently, Dad said, "I love your mother more now than I ever have."

This year, surrounded by their children, grandchildren, and friends, they will celebrate 50 years of marriage. Let's be honest, I know my parents had a rough marriage. I witnessed it, I lived it, and I was a part of the dysfunction for many years (even learning from them what I would never do in my own marriage). But all of that fades when I contemplate their witness to marital fidelity, commitment, and, ultimately, dying to self. Their witness is now evident in the legacy of their children, each married over 20 years and counting. [20]

I was married for the second time when I began having an affair. In my typical way, I was always looking for something to give me that happy, fulfilled feeling. I was a dedicated wanderer, traveling all over the world, dabbling in different religions, and willing to try anything once…or twice. In short, I was a well-intentioned mess.

And, there was ample support for all of my crazy choices, choices which were mostly thought of as "free-spirited," even though they actually caused incredible pain for myself and others. Even my grandma encouraged me to seize my freedom, to go and do and see. Wait to settle down, wait to have children—keep snatching up experiences and bucket-list moments. And so I did. In a way, relationships were just another adventure for me.

After all, each new relationship was full of possibilities: Who would I be now that I was with this person? Would we live forever in Africa, and take safari vacations? With another person, would I start going to church again and do a complete 180? (And wouldn't that be funny?) I thought nothing of the challenges of marriage. Notably absent from the daydreams about the future were discussions about, well, *being married*. Who would work? Doing what? And who would raise the children? Would there be children? Getting married was thought of as a culmination of the good times we were having, and after the ceremony and honeymoon there would be many more good times.

Predictably enough, my second marriage didn't work out. Marrying because my work visa was expiring, we had to live apart for a year, during which I committed adultery. That time left me broken and divorced...again. And, predictably enough, everyone saw it coming and no one was surprised. Or perhaps they were surprised that I thought there might be a different ending.

So there was a healthy dose of skepticism on my part and probably everyone else's as I became engaged for the third time—*here she goes again*. But this time, faith played a role. I'd started going to a Lutheran church again, and my fiancé was baptized and confirmed a few months before the wedding. He had been raised by his secular Muslim mother and spent his youth with her New Age husband. He believed in God but had never been religious or had clearly defined beliefs, aside from "there is a God" and a supernatural bent with a large dose of superstition thrown in.

So now with a faith in God, and doing our best, and committed to each other, we married and moved across the country so that my husband could attend law school. Those were a difficult couple of years. In some ways, I expected our marriage to fail, wanted it to fail, and was absolutely certain that he would let me down. And in some ways, this has proved true. Turns out, marriage is actually hard. Even a "good one." That's something that never really occurred to me. To my way of thinking back then, either marriage was hard and that meant it was bad, or you hadn't found "the one," or you shouldn't have married at all, *or* you should keep looking—until you found that magical unicorn of marriages, which was basically an endless date with your best friend.

But marriage isn't like that.

In addition to all the normal challenges of marriage, we were both very wounded by past relationships—and the example of our parents' divorces and remarriages and re-divorces. Added to that was a long period of infertility and a blistering curve ball that I never expected: My husband decided he wanted to become Catholic.

We fought a lot. I defended Martin Luther. I was Lutheran. I would die a Lutheran. I wanted to celebrate Reformation Sunday in peace. Lutheranism was the only religion I wanted to be part of, and it was the only shred of tradition I had inherited from my family: We were

Lutheran. Several generations had been raised in the same area, baptized in the same church, and had grown up singing the same hymns. I clung tenaciously to that. I remember telling my husband, "I would never, ever have married a Catholic."

But then, just two weeks before our long-awaited daughter was born, I saw a podcast on his laptop about Mary and asked him if he was going to be okay with raising our daughter Lutheran, because I wasn't about to convert and I was tired of the tension. He promised that he would be okay with that, but only if I agreed to read a handful of books he recommended. If, after reading them, I still didn't want to be Catholic, he would let it go. So I started reading. Within days I was open to the idea of becoming Catholic.

Funny enough, his desire to convert came about because of the Church's stance on divorce. He couldn't understand, reading the notes in our Lutheran study bible, how divorce and remarriage was not regarded as an ongoing sin. It was unfortunate, but not wrong. One simply moved on. And, being children of divorce, we both knew it wasn't that simple. Being twice divorced myself, I saw how much harder it became for me to trust a husband, to commit to marriage, and to accept that marriage meant a lot of sacrifice, work, and dedication—even when it didn't feel good, even when it wasn't easy or fun.

We now have three small children, and we are raising them with the understanding that marriage is forever. Even when we disagree, even when things are hard, we are always a family, we will always be a family.

But the past still hurts. Despite all the graces, and sacraments, and my lifetime confession—all of which have helped immeasurably—I still often wish things were different. That our parents had made different choices. That I had made different choices. That we could turn back time and get another chance, another bite at the apple—or the chance not to bite it. But sin has consequences, and they remain.

The thought that gives me hope, when marriage feels hard, when the past feels oppressive, is knowing what a difference my husband and I can make in the lives of our children and grandchildren. In just a couple generations, the history of heartache can change. Our children will not face the fractured family dynamic we have struggled with in our own families—a dynamic that has only become more difficult as we've gotten older and started our own family.

Our children will be able to look to us as an example, and their children will be blessed to have parents and grandparents (that will be us!) as ongoing examples of holy matrimony. What an inspiration this is on the hard days, to think of how our grandchildren might experience marriage and family life, and the effects of our efforts on future generations! God is truly merciful, and it is such a blessing to have been given another chance to choose to do right and choose to love.

Marriage is not about our feelings or about being happy all the time; rather, it's an opportunity to sacrifice for another, to give of ourselves, to take up the cross with Christ. Marriage is often more sanctifying than exciting, but on the other side of sacrifice, there is always true joy. I realize more every day that 50th wedding anniversaries are made up not of large moments but of a million small sacrifices, and that those choices are made, those vows are renewed, each day, in each moment, until death do us part. [21]

Not sure how well I can get across my message, but I want to try. I'm the daughter of parents who had a very difficult marriage. My dad has depression, anxiety, PTSD, and bipolar disorder, and growing up I saw and heard a lot of things that a child should never see or hear. Many people might say that my mom should have left him, that we would have been better off if she did. I can say that I am so glad she didn't.

My dad was ill. Mom wanted to leave many times. She got out the door with us. But she came back. She persevered. We did learn by example—by *her* example: Sometimes you love people who are acting unlovable. Who don't deserve it. You don't allow yourself to be walked all over, but you stay. You fight. You have healthy boundaries. You help the sick to be treated. You don't use sickness as an excuse to break the marriage vow.

My dad got treatment eventually. I suspect his motivation was Mom's unfailing love. He is madly in love with her, always has been, and is never afraid to say it. He is a hopeless romantic. My dad has no religion, and he feels utterly beyond forgiveness for things he did in Vietnam. Mom said he hit a family of ducks the other day while driving and wailed like he'd hit a child. He is a very sweet, sensitive soul. He went on medication for bipolar disorder. It's tough to keep people on bipolar meds, because they go off the meds when they feel good—a big mistake. But Mom drew a hard line of motivation: "Trust me," "You need it," "We aren't staying here to be in harm's way if you can't manage to stay on it," "We will help you, but you have to help yourself by doing this part,"—that sort of thing. She's learned how to navigate his illness and to mitigate the damage it could cause people and finances. She loves him through it.

We lived through some traumatic times, including walls punched, broken plates, and even a threatened suicide attempt. We learned that loving someone isn't all roses and greeting cards. It's often hard times and heavy crosses. But my mom did have boundaries, and we learned that, too.

My sisters and I are all functioning adults who learned from all these experiences. We are empathetic, strong daughters, and we have our own boundaries. We have solid marriages. We were always loved beyond measure by both parents, and we had happy family memories, too. A camping trip here or there and trips to my grandma's. We never had any money, but it was a good childhood in so many ways.

My dad isn't perfect, but I am able to see his amazing qualities clearly now. He is able to be the best person he can be in this life, and I am proud of that person and proud to be named after him (mine is the feminine version of his name). He is a great dad to me now, and I am so glad he is in my life. I just love him so much. My mother didn't hurt her four daughters by staying. She was a wonderful example, which is all she could control. I am so grateful to both of them—and, they just celebrated 50 years.

I want to say this for mothers who have husbands who aren't the fathers they want them to be....All is not lost. Continue to be the example to your children. You never know what the future will bring, and hopefully you will see fruit in this life. But if not, that's not what it's about. Sending love and prayers to each of you. [22]

My husband and I met in college when I was on the rebound, and we were married less than four months later. Tom was kind, caring and moral. He did not try to take sexual advantage of my vulnerability, as did the previous boyfriend. I had doubts about the wedding, but as a child of divorce, I thought: "I'll just get divorced if it doesn't work out, but at least I'll have children."

I asked my dad what he thought about Tom. He answered, "It's your choice; I don't have to live with him." Secretly, I'd hoped he'd tell me to really consider my decision to get married.

Tom and I knew so little about each other, including what we believed about God; neither of us attended any church. I was away from my Catholic faith, and I agreed to allow a Protestant minister to marry us.

In Catholic school in the 1960s, I was taught that marriage was permanent and that use of contraception was a grave sin. These teachings were deeply ingrained in me, although, when I married, I was ignoring them.

Tom expected me to use contraception for a few years. Later, he said he didn't want a child because he was afraid of losing me, in the sense that pregnancy could jeopardize my health or life. Analyzing this now, I think he really was afraid of losing me emotionally; he sensed that all I ever wanted was children.

Tom and I shared very few of the same interests or goals. We each had unrealistic expectations of one another, and he was critical of me and my family. I considered divorcing him, but because I could not figure out a way to do it without hurting him, I never pursued divorce.

In the fifth year of our marriage, Tom desired to go to church. Personally, I was becoming even more hostile to God, but I went with him to visit churches anyway. If he was serious, then I at least wanted to be somewhat comfortable with it (I had no intention of going back to the Catholic Church).

At one church, the minister gave a sermon that made me realize that God really did love me. A few months later, I met a woman who shared her conversion story with me. These two things brought me to surrendering my life to Christ, but not to the Catholic Church.

I finally had peace with God for having returned to Christ; however, there was still an emptiness. I found a church I liked, and Tom and I began going there, but we changed churches many times through the years—and I still had no child.

I was never able to conceive. Contraception was detrimental to our marriage, and I have had to forgive my husband for asking me to use contraception, something I never wanted. My deep desire was to get pregnant as soon as we were married. However, I must take responsibility for choosing an IUD, a type of contraception that completely destroyed my fertility.

After many years of marriage, we finally adopted a newborn baby. The moment Christopher was placed in my arms was the happiest moment of my life. Unfortunately, motherhood did not make me as happy as I had hoped it would, and my husband and I were not in agreement on many parenting issues. Tom was often critical of me in front of our son, which in turn caused my son to disrespect me. I became very sad.

If I hadn't been a stay-at-home mom and attending a strong evangelical church that frowned on divorce, I may well have divorced my husband then. But my desire to stay home with our son was greater than my desire to leave my marriage and have to take an outside job. Tom was willing to provide.

I visited a Catholic Mass with a friend several years later, and when I saw the Eucharist consecrated, I began to desire to return to the Catholic Church. Deep inside, I always believed in the Real Presence of Christ in the Eucharist, but, having been away, I hadn't realized its true significance, and that only an ordained priest, consecrated by a bishop who had true apostolic succession, could transform the bread and wine into the Body and Blood of Jesus Christ. In the weeks following, as I continued to attend Mass, I came to the realization that communion in a Protestant church is merely a symbol, as they claim it to be.

I finally went to confession, and the spiritual and emotional healing began. Healing continued through frequent, honest confessions, receiving Communion, and praying at Adoration.

Since I was baptized Catholic and we were married outside the Church (something known as "lack of form"), we did not have a valid marriage. Before the paperwork for our marriage was sent to the archdiocese, the priest advised me that once we received the sacrament of matrimony, there was no turning back. I thought to myself, *I have been in this for 35 years; I guess can endure it to the end of my days.* We received a "radical sanation" (*sanatio in radice*), which means "healing at the root." Unlike a convalidation, which validates a marriage from that moment onward, a radical sanation is when the bishop *retroactively* dispenses an impediment to marriage, in our case due to my husband's sincere belief in the validity of our marriage from the start.

Many times, people suggested that I could benefit from counseling. I was resistant because of previous destructive experiences from counseling when I was a teenager dealing with childhood traumas. My husband also felt negatively about counseling, but suggested I talk to the priest first.

Fr. Steve began with prayer, listened to me, and asked some questions. He gently helped me see that some of my responses to my husband were not normal, and he suggested I learn to offer up my sufferings to God. He also explained that it would be very hard for a man to have worked hard to provide for his family, as my husband had done, and then have his wife leave him. This comment gave me the strength to determine that I could not morally, nor will I *ever*, leave my husband.

After my encounter with a priest empathetic to my pain, the Holy Spirit helped me to see my own part in causing my unhappy marriage. I realized that I had actually hurt my husband, too. I think I went to confession three times that week. This helped me more easily accept the difficulties in my marriage, because not only could I see how flawed I am, but I could also see great redemptive value in offering my sufferings to God.

When I originally came back to the Church, divorce seemed preferable to living with my husband's jealous resistance to my renewed Catholic faith. I resented that he was—or so I thought —"holding me back spiritually." Then I realized that by willingly carrying my crosses and by becoming a better person through the sacraments, which are channels of sanctifying grace, my husband would see that I love him more, not less. Tom is now respectful of my Catholic faith.

Here are some important truths I'd like to impress upon anyone struggling in a marriage as I have:

- Just because a marriage *can* be declared null does not mean it *should* or *must* be, or that it will make life better. There is a more excellent and better way. Fix yourselves, love better (1 Cor. 13) and validate the marriage. There is no need to break the family.
- The day I accepted that my husband might not ever change was the day things changed for the better. The day I took the burden off of my husband and my child to make me happy was the day I found peace. Once I realized and accepted that God alone is the source of my happiness, I was free to love even difficult people.
- Accepting everything from God as gift—even the losses, hurts, and disappointments—is a source of great joy, and it was in this understanding that I finally lost my desire to divorce. Because Jesus suffered so much for love of us, accepting my share of sufferings is a great gift I can give back to God; offered suffering is *redemptive* and has real meaning (Col. 1:24).

I still have many struggles in my marriage, but I recognize that I would have similar struggles no matter to whom I was married. We have been married close to 50 years now, and I am at peace. My love of God gives me strength—and a greater ability to love my husband. [23]

As I begin writing this account, I am on a clipper ship somewhere in the Strait of Juan de Fuca in the Pacific Northwest, on a trip celebrating our quarter-century of marriage. This beautiful adventure is a well-earned exhale after 25 years of many worrisome moments that often inched sadly close to the dreaded "D-word"—divorce.

Nothing but grace can explain how it is that we're not only still together, but truly enjoying each other. Indeed, it is a miracle that brings us to this point. While I suspect more suffering ahead, we seem to have endured and overcome the worst, and I hold much hope for what is to come.

We met young, both 18, both on the rebound from previous relationships, both wounded children of alcoholics, both angry inside. Finding each other was like a toxic lure. We were, in large parts, drawn to the interior mess of the other because it was familiar. Our relationship quickly turned co-dependent.

We were on-again, off-again, not understanding what comprised a healthy relationship. After many break-ups, we decided to marry after college graduation, with reservations. I remember being obsessed during our engagement about whether we could manage to avoid divorce. One positive was that both sets of our parents, despite tumultuous years themselves, remained intact. This, and the few divorces in our extended families, gave us some confidence that maybe we stood a chance, too.

And yet, there was a pervasively nagging doubt, and it wasn't long before things began to get very rocky. A lack of trust on both ends made our marriage especially vulnerable, and while the birth of our five children (in 10 years) gave us something important to focus on, it also brought a great deal of stress. Financial woes and uneven faith journeys only added to the pressure. The threat of alcohol abuse and the fear that our kids would endure the same misery and worry I had as a child gripped me. Despite some high points, I wondered if we'd made the wrong decision, and I'm sure my husband felt the same. We knew we were damaged, and facing the root cause seemed like the scariest thing in the world, but we knew we had to try.

Many therapists later (at least a few made matters worse), and after rivers of tears and truly feeling that our situation was hopeless, grace began to take hold. This long, painful process included several years of Al-Anon, in which I learned how to respond better to situations that seemed so wrong and out of control. As I began to change my responses, little by little, my husband seemed to respond differently, too. Looking back, I see how I had focused on *him* changing—and how much of my misery was because of that. It wasn't until I realized I could change *myself* that our marriage began turning around.

During those times when we were tempted to part ways rather than face the demons within our relationship, another force—something invisible—seemed to keep us together and trying. Our competitive natures began to soften as we worked together to help our children in their difficulties; with common goals, selfishness faded. Rather than blaming one another, we found ourselves looking to one another, and to God, with open arms to seek help. Moment by moment, slowly but surely, grace began to find more openings.

The combination of therapy, Al-Anon, Marriage Encounter, supportive family and friends, the grace of the sacraments, and a common focus on our children's wellbeing worked to bring us closer together. But one thought stands out: Had we sought divorce, *we would have been seeking a permanent solution to a temporary problem*. It's the same with issues such as abortion, sterilization, surgically "changing" one's sex, and suicide. So often we make decisions based on what we are experiencing at that moment or during that season, forgetting that that moment or season will pass—and with its passing comes the possibility of brighter days ahead. We don't give grace a chance. We don't give life a chance. We don't give God His time to work.

God gave me the saving grace to think about the future—graduation parties, weddings, and family reunions—and to realize how painful those events would be if we broke the family. At one point, I even glimpsed further out, to my deathbed, thinking about whom I'd want by my side at the very end. Peering through the painful haze of the abandonment and disillusionment I often felt, I was surprised to see that our history mattered, that each of our children was a visible sign of our union, and that, yes, I would want my husband to be there with the rest of my family in the last days of my life. In fact, I would want my husband there most of all! We'd been through so much, and only he had known me this long. I realized that I really do love my husband. And the more I've seen him as a child of God who needs

God's healing, too, the more hope I've seen in us.

The experience of being at my own father's deathbed six years ago, with my small, intact family of origin by his side, only firmed up this idea that life is best, and most pure, when we stay the course despite difficulty. My own parents' example of this had led to a most beautiful, holy death for my father, after many years of tumult. He'd come back to the Church after a 35-year absence, and, as he passed away, the tear in his eye said everything to me. It was a gift and a reminder that to be faithful to God and to one another is worth everything.

Addendum:

It's been two years since I wrote the above, and as I read over the account, I freeze right here: "While I suspect more suffering ahead...."

So much suffering has happened in these last couple years that I can't help but look at those words now and see them as innocently prophetic. Just a few months after we returned home from the Pacific Northwest, my husband learned that his heart was in a critical state. During treatment for an unrelated issue, we were stunned to learn that cords in his mitral valve had prolapsed, and the only fix included open-heart surgery. My husband, who had never stayed overnight in a hospital before and had been the picture of health for 49 years, went into survival mode—and the specter of death surrounded us.

I'd like to say it the surgery went smoothly, but in truth the three-hour surgery turned into six. We'd later learn the reason: His heart had flat-lined upon his chest being opened. The surgeon had to think fast and work quickly, massaging his heart back to life. Essentially, he had died on the table.

Through the last three hours of surgery, I began desperately pleading with God to spare my husband's life. God granted that gift, but the recovery would prove brutal, especially emotionally, for it seemed like something within my husband had been damaged when his heart stopped. As in those earlier years of marriage, I began to feel alone again, unable to reach him. It felt like 200 steps back.

Within a year, my husband came back to his more gracious self and hope returned—just in time to learn that the valve was leaking once again, and my husband was facing a second open-heart surgery. Upon hearing about my husband's return to ill health, a friend who suffers greatly with her own devastating diagnosis said to me, "This will be a chance to love with a purer love." Immediately, I understood the otherworldly wisdom in her words.

As we prayed the Surrender Novena at my husband's request, he became determined that the words of the novena, "O Jesus, I surrender myself to you; take care of everything," would be the last he would utter before going under anesthesia. Should something go wrong again, he said, he wanted these to be his final words.

To our great relief, the surgery went well, though we will not claim that he is out of the woods completely. We've realized that his life, and mine—and all of ours—are truly in God's hands at every moment. The Lord is always with us, and, through our sufferings, we are continually being readied for heaven.

And so I return again to my earlier words: "While I suspect more suffering ahead...." But this time, I read through to the end of that prophetic line: "...I hold much hope for what is to come."

This is marriage. Amen. [24]

I'm reluctantly telling the story of my deeply painful struggles in my 31-year marriage. My husband had an affair after we had been married for 14 years. It had been going on for four years, with a coworker whom he had introduced to me as a friend. She was struggling in her marriage and he was "helping her." I confronted him after discovering certain things that didn't seem right....

I think the most painful part of it all was that I had no idea he was so unhappy in our marriage. The betrayal was gut-wrenching, and I don't know if I am completely over it. Maybe there will always be scars that I will live with, my cross to carry. We tried to talk to our priest about it, but he didn't seem interested in helping us. He did give us the name of a counselor, and she was okay. I was in such deep pain that we tried a handful of counselors. I don't think anyone really helped that much....

What helped me to stay in our marriage?

First, prayer. My husband and I had a reversion to our Catholic faith, realizing we had been cafeteria Catholics. This actually happened after I discovered the mess our marriage was in....Funny how you turn to God when the bottom drops out of life. We had been getting more help from evangelical sources than Catholic ones, but the prayers of many led us to a deeper understanding of the Catholic Church. (I'm not going to lie—because of the mess our Church is in, I've wondered if we were led to the Truth. But then...the Eucharist; how can you leave the Eucharist?)

Second, I was determined to protect my three kids from the pain I had experienced due to my own parents' divorce.

On to the crazy part. My husband had gotten a vasectomy after my last high-risk pregnancy when we were both 28 and had only been married for six years. No one discouraged us from sterilizing our marriage, and we came to understand that this decision hurt our marriage profoundly. In fact, a catalyst for our reversion was seeing this sin for what it was.

Believing that we had to right a wrong (though we know it is not strictly required), my husband had a vasectomy reversal ten years after the initial procedure and about two years into the discovery of the affair. I had three pregnancies after that, each one ending in miscarriage. That was devastating, and was I angry at God, but he healed my broken heart through our adopted children. I look back at all the intense pain I had experienced, and I see that being able to raise more children with my husband helped our marriage tremendously.

How do we keep our marriage strong? I think the biggest thing is acceptance. We are two imperfect people coming together to do our best. We really have to work at taking time for each other. I also have to catch myself when I default to the "if he would only do this" mindset. And as an adult child of divorce, I keep everything inside, which is something I have to work on—he's not a mindreader.

This is more recent, but I'm just now seeing the destruction that feminism has caused in our marriage. My mother and mother-in-law both worked outside the home (giving us the example that "this is what you do"), and I mostly worked outside our home. The juggling of it all was really stressful, and I'm sure that led to "how could we possibly have more kids?" which led to the vasectomy, which led to the downfall of our marriage....Such a red-pill moment that I'm slowly digesting....

After all these years and through so much pain, our marriage, while far from perfect, is so much better than I ever could have imagined! We are God's work in progress. [25]

I was enamored with Daniel from the start. His confidence was so attractive, he treated me unbelievably well, and I felt like a precious jewel in his care. He was thoughtful, fun, and on a track to success. He accepted me totally, and he made me feel safe and beautiful. We talked for hours, about everything and nothing. I often thought in those early years of marriage, "Life is too perfect! How did we get so lucky?" I was just waiting for something that would crash the party.

We eventually became parents and didn't handle the change well. Our marriage was a slow fade and falling apart in the small ways: neglecting to go on dates, doing activities separately, ignoring each other. We had moved away from home for my husband's job, and I stopped working to stay at home with our two-year-old daughter. Multiple stressors came upon us all at once, with the added loneliness of living 700 miles away from home for the first time. It was the perfect storm.

I watched my husband become lured away, escaping to do anything outside of our home. I remember saying to a friend, "I'm so disappointed in the man Daniel is becoming, and I don't know what to do about it." He was distant, cold, uncaring towards me, and becoming more and more uninvolved as a father. For four years, he was in a constant sprint away from us, which I chalked up to a crisis of faith and negative peer influence. For four years, I spent hours in Adoration and praying rosaries for his conversion and the resurrection of our marriage. I would drop our children off at school, then head straight to the Adoration chapel multiple times per week.

On a random weekday, my world came crashing down. Just after we tucked our children into bed, my husband sat me down and told me that he couldn't love me any longer, was moving out, and had consulted a lawyer about a divorce. I was devastated and caught completely off-guard. Like Jesus being scourged at the pillar, I couldn't believe this man was so brutally hurting my heart and causing me such pain. The image I had that night was of our family being in a boat with a storm raging all around us. It felt as if Daniel had thrown me into the water without a life preserver and set the children on a raft next to me while he took off to get out of the storm.

I didn't have a job, all of our family lived hundreds of miles away, and I felt abandoned, alone, and overwhelmed. I knew we had been unhappy for four or five years by now, but, as a devout Catholic, divorce was never an option for me—and nothing we appeared to be dealing with seemed to call for such drastic measures.

For the next 40 days, I walked around like a zombie; I barely ate or slept, and I prayed for Jesus to intervene. During that time, I discovered that not only was he leaving me, he was leaving me for another woman. A woman that he'd been having an affair with for nearly four years. Everyone surrounding me told me to burn his things in the yard, run away, and move on. But one person, a priest, challenged me to honor my vows. And through quiet miracles of grace, God granted me the strength to show my husband love in each small moment. For example, I went so far as to ask if I could wash his clothes, even if it meant knowing he would then pack them in a bag to leave.

In my time spent in Adoration, through the tears, I kept hearing Mary saying, "Bring him to me...." I completed the novena to Our Lady of Fatima for the 100th anniversary of her apparition, and, in God's divine grace, my husband joined us for Mass on Mother's Day. With our son clinging from his neck during the consecration, my husband looked up at the statue of the Virgin Mary within arms reach of him and said, "I'm so sorry, Mother...." His heart had finally broken, he set down his foolish pride, and he came home that day.

Much like the slow fade of our marriage into destruction, the rebuild was just as slow and painful. Daniel's addiction to his affair did not magically disappear, and by the time we later attended a Retrouvaille retreat five hours away, Daniel had lost his will to restore our marriage. In another small moment of grace, though, he took the advice of one of the attendees, and prayed, at least, for the will to *want* to try.

We returned home and began the painful journey of healing. People often comment, "How do you go back to a marriage that is so broken?" My answer is, "You don't." That old marriage must die and a new one must begin. Daniel ended things with his affair partner, and for the next six weekends, we traveled four hours one-way to attend follow-up sessions with other couples to start our renewal.

It was not an easy path. Holding my husband while he mourned the loss of his girlfriend was something I didn't see coming. Reflecting on the call to imitate Christ's love for us and all He endured for our sake was the only way I was able to make it. During our recovery, I constantly reflected on the fundamental nature of *what marriage is and what our wedding vows really mean*. I knew that the vows were not for the easy times in a marriage but for times such as these. For better or worse. In sickness and in health. Until death do us part.

There are no exceptions listed when you state your vows before God and witnesses.

Our vows are not "for better or worse (unless you cheat on me)." Our vows are "for better or worse." Period. And this was the "worse" part that I had promised to love Daniel through. In spite of what our culture tells us, love is not a feeling, and it's not about being happy. Love in marriage is not about liking a person (it had been a very long time since I'd liked Daniel). *Love is a choice.*

We had several couples in our lives who encouraged us and walked beside us. It was not an easy path, and both of us had to look in the mirror and decide every day to love each other a little more. It required a cooperation with God's grace, and specifically understanding the grace available in the sacrament of matrimony given to us on our wedding day. In time, wounds began to heal, forgiveness became possible, and we fell in love all over again.

Today, I can say we've never been happier in our marriage, and I feel like the 22-year-old who first met Daniel and fell in love. My dad recently referred to us as newlyweds! To understand all that is possible through Jesus Christ, we need only to pass through the fire while trusting in God's promises that He will never fail or forsake us. His ocean of mercy and grace are endless.

The conversion I have witnessed in my husband has been breathtaking and an answer to so many hours of prayer. I'm so grateful that I chose to stay and fight for my marriage, as it is often the case that the better comes *after* the worse. I lived through a dead marriage renewed, and I would relive it all over again if it gets us to where we are now.

By the grace of God, and through Our Lady's intersession, one year to the day of Daniel's return home, we were blessed with evidence of that renewal—and her name is Mary Grace. [26]

My oldest memories are not the sort that any child should have. My childhood was filled with uncertainty, tears, and a feeling that I was the fruit of a very unhappy marriage where unkindness, pride, and selfishness were dominant. Strong words, broken plates, slammed doors, and car engines driving away were the only constants.

The first seven years of my life were tainted with sadness, but (thankfully) never with despair—even though things never seemed to get any better. It was ugly and it was painful. It really looked like our little broken family had reached its lowest, deepest point of suffering and would have to endure the final blow of separation. My parents' relationship had very little chance of survival; it was a relationship that had lost its dignity and seemed very soon doomed to die.

I don't particularly remember what led to the events of that night or maybe that day, but what I do remember is that things had gotten so bad that my mother drove my sister and me to my grandparents house and left us there. We were going to be sleeping there for a while. I am not quite sure for how long—days, maybe only a few weeks—but it certainly felt like months.

Suddenly my dad was out of the picture, and I would only see him on the weekends. I would peer from the balcony, all dressed up and waiting for that moment that I'd looked forward to all week. With a mixed feeling of fear and excitement, I would patiently wait for his car to arrive. The fear was that our "date" would fly by way too quickly, and the excitement was anticipating a day full of surprises that would probably leave me with a new toy or extra pocket money.

But parents cannot buy their children's affection forever, and as the excitement wore off, I was left only with the realization that weekends like this would become part of my routine. And, I knew there was no toy in the world nor any amount of money that would fill the hole that this separation was causing.

There was sadness all around. Yes, I loved staying at my grandparents' house, but, more than that, I wanted my parents to love one another. I enjoyed the attention we received from my aunt who was trying with her whole self to compensate for the unfortunate situation in which we found ourselves, but, more than that, I wanted my parents' attention.

It looked like we were a broken family, with no direction or future. The world around us seemed to say that my parents should stop trying to save what seemed un-saveable. That they should run— far away from a suffering that was too hard to bear, suffering that was not helpful to anybody, suffering that would have crushed us all.

And yet that was the moment when God intervened. I suddenly saw a man and a woman surrender to God, recognizing that what they had to offer to one another (and ultimately to us) was very limited and wasn't always what was needed. I saw them stripping themselves of any ideals they once had of one another and accepting that they needed something else, some real help that came from outside of them.

So they gathered their courage and went to speak to the parish priest who was also a very good family friend.

I can only imagine the pain that comes from admitting to oneself that one's marriage is an utter failure, but I saw that when they did just that, it looked like a burden had been lifted off their shoulders. The blame game was finally over.

My parents, together, started attending some Catholic formation sessions that were being held in the parish, and there they received an ever deeper understanding of the moral sense of the Word of God— they were put before the immense love of Christ! They experienced Love in their brokenness, Love that is merciful and unconditional, and they accepted this Love, Love that was revealed little by little in this new journey of faith that they had firmly decided to take together.

It was precisely when they had lost everything that they found the whole world! We slowly became a family that enjoyed each other's company, a family that went to church together, a family that prayed together. And in the midst of this suffering, our family met Jesus Christ and, without my parents even realizing, some solid foundations were being built beneath us.

My parents are no saints, but in witnessing their humanity and their fragility, we children could clearly see the marvelous things that happen when you invite God into your life! They say that what you see, you cannot unsee—and that goes both for good and bad things. I believe it is possible to have a successful marriage, because I have seen it. And when I am tempted to doubt my faith, the actions of God in my past are always before me and the memories still vivid. I witnessed a miracle! I have seen Jesus Christ bringing life to a place that had no life left. I saw Our Lady present and I tasted that supernatural wine of Cana which only comes once the natural wine has run out.

I was not afraid to get married, nor were my sister and brother. We had seen the formula for a successful marriage and we were going to treasure it!

This year, to thank Our Lady for having watched over our marriages and protecting us during the most difficult times of our lives, we all traveled to Lourdes for a thanksgiving pilgrimage. There, we were fortunate enough to have a special Mass celebrated for us at the Conventual Friars' Convent. The Word of God (Acts 16:22-34)—which we did not choose, but which were the readings of that day!—spoke of us, spoke of my dad and his family: "Believe in the Lord Jesus, and you will be saved, you and your household."

Dinner in Lourdes that night was particularly beautiful. Surrounding my mother and father were their three children and 14 grandchildren *like olive shoots around their table* (cf. Psalm 128:3). I had yet another confirmation of the greatness of the Lord as I saw His promise to my father fulfilled. Laughter filled the table and gratitude filled our hearts—gratitude towards our parents who stuck together and who recognized that they couldn't do it alone.

Forty years later, here I am, the fruit of what started off as a very unhappy marriage. I am married to a wonderful man, and we have seven children (and counting...). The graces keep overflowing as we receive what was promised to my dad.

Our past, our present, and our future belong to Him before Whom we have exchanged our wedding vows. With our "yes," we invested everything in Christ. We know that the source of every grace we need in marriage is Christ Himself, He Who is the fountain to Whom we must return over and over again, to quench our thirst for love and forgiveness, to find renewal and inspiration.

In the Eucharist, we are loved and fed by Christ Himself, and having received that love and communion, our marriage can be healed and restored. Around the dining table we are at the service of one another as a couple, and of our families. We speak of what matters to us—our work, our life, and our faith—and every meal can become a source of nourishment, not just for our bodies, but for our minds, souls, and relationships, too.

We have learned that when an argument has gone too far, so much so that we can't even remember what caused it in the first place, and when there are no more words to say and the struggle seems too entangled to untie, it is then that giving ourselves as a gift to our spouse, and holding nothing back, has an incredible effect. There is no storm that this gift can't help to calm. In the sacredness of our marital bed, the sacrament of marriage is renewed and the bond between husband and wife is strengthened—year by year, day by day—so that the sun may never go down on our anger (cf. Eph. 4:26), and that in becoming one flesh, we may more and more enter into deep communion with the One who is True Love. [27]

My father was an alcoholic. I'm the youngest of eleven children, and when I was about five years old, a couple of my older sisters pressured my mother leave our dad. One of the sisters ultimately told him to get out, with a call to police to back it up. He left. Years later, my mom received divorce papers, which broke her heart, but which she ignored.

Mom was a devout Catholic, and I could feel her intense pain in this situation. Every evening at 6:00, we would all gather to pray the rosary, and Mom's prayer was always, "Lord, please don't let Ray die alone in the streets! Let him come home and allow me to care for him." *Every night!* It seemed a reasonable request to me, but I can remember hearing a few groans from my older siblings.

Fast forward about 20 years. My brother is on vacation in California and decides to see Dad. He finds him extremely ill, loads him in his car, and brings him back to Idaho.

There's a knock on my door, and it's my brother telling me he's got Dad in the car and can he bring him inside while he goes to talk to Mom, who lives a few blocks away. It's an awkward moment, but I say yes. I hadn't seen this man in years. My two children are there, and I introduce them to their grandfather. Ten minutes go by—it feels like forever—and my brother returns and announces, "Mom says it's okay to take him home."

We took Dad to the hospital where they drained six gallons of fluid from his belly. His last two years were spent reconnecting with his wife and children, and getting to know his grandchildren.

Shortly before he died, I was in the hospital room with both Mom and Dad. They started talking about personal things, and I said, "I'll wait outside." They both looked at me and told me to stay. Besides the gift of life, this was the second best gift my parents gave me. They went back to talking as if I weren't there: He told her, "I never stopped loving you," and she answered, "I never stopped loving you, either."

In my father's final days, all of his children got the healing and happy ending with our dad. Imagine him surrounded by all eleven of us, our spouses, his grandchildren and great-grandchildren—about sixty of us at the time! Dad died a beautiful, peaceful death as two of his daughters held his hands, prayed, and sang hymns. His last word was "ama"—which means "mom." He was 73. Mom lived to be 90, and she was the best mom ever! A witness to unconditional love. [28]

My parents contributed to 200 years of marriage.

In the 1960s and '70s there was so much turmoil, uncertainty, arguing, screaming, throwing, pounding on tables, crying, accusing, and threats of divorce in our home of nine. The marriage began in 1952, with the first son born exactly nine months later, the next son in 1954, the third son in 1955, then I was the first daughter born in 1958, the fourth son in 1959, the fifth son in 1963, and the sixth son in 1967. There were seven of us, 15 years apart. We were the largest family on our post-WWII bungalow-lined street.

My parents moved from the city of Cleveland to the suburbs, where they literally helped build one of five Catholic churches in Parma, Ohio in 1958. On a construction foreman's wages supplemented by a part-time nurse working nightshift, they sent seven children through Catholic elementary school, with five attending Catholic high schools. We learned the *Baltimore Catechism*, attended daily Mass until Vatican II, and fasted on Fridays. My brothers were altar servers, and I worked at the parish rectory all four years of high school with the Franciscan Friars.

There never was any money. Just enough to pay the mortgage, buy food, and pay for Catholic school tuition—barely. Dad was often laid-off in the winter months. Mom worked 11 p.m. to 7 a.m. a couple of days a week. I rarely saw her sleep. All of my brothers worked a large paper route, handed down from one brother to the next. Many times, my mother had to use the paper route money to buy food.

Dad worked hard, played hard, drank hard, and apparently gambled away his paycheck at times. Oh, the arguing. Mom would scream, "Where is your paycheck? How will we pay the mortgage? Who will feed the kids?" I can't count the times that Mom threatened to leave my dad. We "ran away" several times. Mom's version of leaving was packing up the station wagon with all the kids, stopping at the local Lawson's for milk and cookies, and spending the evening at a drive-in movie. She said we were never going back home. Every single time, we went home. When my parents were screaming at each other, I heard the words, "I am divorcing you." The morning after the fights, I would ask my older brothers, "Did they get divorced last night?"

We looked sort of normal. Our house was full of super-high-achieving athletes and motivated children. Dad coached every sport, started the Holy Name Society, worked the local political campaigns, was a Grand Knight in the Knights of Columbus, and ran the big church fundraisers. Mom worked nights, the only working mom in our tight-knit neighborhood which included hundreds of children. She also took care of her mentally ill father, belonged to the church's Lady Guild, and was an all-around amazing woman and mother. Besides the paper route, all seven children worked by age 13.

While we looked good on the outside, the storms were constant in the house. The houses on our street were so close together you could hear the neighbor's toilet flush. We were a bit hard to contain as a family of nine in a tiny house. During the hot summer months with the doors open, my dad's loud voice could be heard. But it was all "kind of normal." Everyone loved my dad. They would say, "He is gruff on the outside and a teddy bear on the inside." True. So true. So difficult. So lovable. Mom was considered a saint for putting up with him. There was so much tumult, but my parents stayed married. I don't know if they said, "We are Catholic; we can't get divorced." But they lived that out in unspoken ways. It just was. You just stayed together no matter how many times you talked about leaving.

When I was in high school in the 1970s, I realized that my parents did not get divorced. They kind of stopped talking about it. They did not stop yelling at each other, though. Until one day, I just noticed how much they liked being together. They did everything *together*. After college, I remember being bold enough to ask my mom why she stayed with my father. She said something like, "You just do." All I ever wanted was for my parents to stay together. I had a lot of fear over many years about what life would be like if they did divorce. Through thick and thin, through medical crises, financial ruin, infidelity, drug use by a child, death of a child to AIDS, and other scandals, my parents managed to stay married.

When my dad died at age 72 in 1997, after 45 of marriage, the family and community was crushed. This bigger-than-life man was gone. My mother's spouse, lover, best friend, teammate, was dead. Yes, despite the troubles, the marriage vows won!

By today's standards and sensibilities, they should not have still been married. How did they make it? Why did they stay together? Yes, they loved each other. It was way more than that, though. Way more. There was something in their soul, their being, that they "had" to stay together. It was a commitment that today seems "old-fashioned," that defies logic.

That sense of, "You must make it. You do not stop trying even when it all seems hopeless"…stuck in the hearts and souls of their six children who married. As of today's writing, their children have 200 combined years of marriage among them. *200 years.* Had my parents divorced, it would have made it so much easier for us to do the same. Of six marriages, I know for certain that five of us very seriously considered leaving our spouses at one time or another. At some point, every single issue that my parents faced became issues in our own marriages. By all modern accounts, my brothers and I should have left our spouses, should have divorced.

After this many years of marriage amongst my siblings and myself —43, 40, 33, 31, 28, 25 years—we are all glad we stayed. The turmoil has melted into the fabric of our marriages. We are best friends, world travelers, soulmates, caretakers of our spouses. We talk at intimate family gatherings, wondering aloud how different everything would be if mom and dad had divorced, or if we had divorced. Those pieces could not be put back together. Divorce—literally "to turn aside"— severs and ends. But the tumult in our marriages, because of the example of loving for better or worse, could be tilled into rich soil by staying together.

In the end, the staying together was better, best, and gratifying— and smart. It is not about happiness. There is a lot of comfort, love, and satisfaction, though, and yes there *is* happiness, but that is not the end all, be all. Whatever hell we thought we were going through was worth it. We can breathe, we are still together, we feel like warriors, we wear badges. With honor. We are married.

Two hundred years. [29]

When my parents celebrated 50 years of marriage last summer, I hadn't anticipated just how much it would mean to me. I look back through their lives, and my life with them, and see what a miracle it is that they stayed together—and that they have grown in grace to become the affectionate, sweet couple they are, when it was not that way during the majority of their years together as man and wife.

When my folks were first married, they were like most newlyweds, full of hope for the future, though they carried some heavy baggage from their pasts. Both had come from single-parent, fatherless households, and both had survived a kind of Great Depression poverty that many (including me) will never understand.

The problems began early on. My dad drank, was indifferent to his Catholic faith, had a terrible temper, and there were hints of infidelity. My mom's successes at work and her ability to provide for her family before she married sort of made her the "man of the house." This uncommon situation, in addition to the way she was treated by men, enabled her to accept some of the ideals of feminism that were being heralded at the time. In fact, much of her advice to us girls about marriage and men was negative.

My parents likely even had grounds for annulment, which was harder to come by in those days. My dad's mother had a legal contract with all of her sons, stipulating that half of their pay would be sent home to her. My father did not disclose this to my mom before marrying, and she found out only after she had my sister, when things were already going very badly. My father hadn't wanted children, and he didn't have much to do with his first daughter. My mom had had enough and wanted to leave him, but she didn't give up entirely. They remained living together, but in a semi-separated state, until they eventually worked out the financial situation with his mom.

Still, things were hard. During her pregnancy with me (I was their "accident"), she had undiagnosed preeclampsia. The on-call doctor who delivered me allowed my mom to hemorrhage and broke my nose during the botched delivery. At one point, she was even declared dead, but the Lord gave her more time. The night she brought me home from the hospital, my father broke a chair on her. She called the cops, had him arrested at work the next day, but didn't press charges. She did tell him that if he ever laid a hand on her again, she would press charges. For the most part, he did as she said. And for the most part she protected us from him—though he did not protect us from her violence against us—she was the more violent of the two and was also psychologically abusive.

My brother was conceived two years later, next to a tumor—and my mother was again warned (as she was with all three of us) to abort the child or die. Even her priests told her it would be okay, because her life was in danger. In spite of the lack of support, she chose life every single time. For this, I will always be grateful.

During this time when we three siblings were little, both the economy and their situation were poor. My dad had a degree in engineering, but struggled to find and keep work in difficult economic times that were rife with racism (my folks are both Hispanic). He worked in refineries and saw dreadfully dangerous conditions, which co-workers of color were made to endure. He witnessed injuries and even the death of one person.

Eventually, we moved to Illinois, and both were stretched more than they could have imagined. My father traveled weeks at a time, so my mom was mostly on her own, including for two of the worst blizzards in history. At one point, she was forced to fight against the state, when a corrupt state agency tried to take my baby brother under the pretense of a failed hearing test. (In David vs. Goliath fashion, she won—all on her own, with her own research, her own testimony, and probably many desperate prayers.)

The neighborhood situation wasn't much better. It was a nice area and my folks' first house, and they thought things were looking up. But when my mom went to a welcoming "party" by the neighborhood wives, she was shocked with the veiled threat: They had worked hard to get here and didn't want "her kind" ruining things. The following year, a cross was burned in the front yard of the only other minority family here.

Mom was relieved when it was time to move back to Texas. Things began to normalize, and my dad was able to spend a few more days at home, traveling only 3-4 days a week. My mom's spirits lifted. And when I was an early teen, my father began to delve deeply into his Catholic faith, learning more and more as his heart caught on fire. Despite these positive changes and a turn toward God, he was still an angry man, still disconnected from all of us (though more affectionate with us children than Mom). They still fought, each wanting the last word or the upper hand. Mom's cancer diagnosis added another stressor to their very difficult lives.

Through the years, we often thought they'd divorce, and we wondered if it would be a relief. But they stuck it out. When I was 14, they switched parishes. They had petitioned Pope St. John Paul II for a Latin Tridentine Mass—and were granted an indult. It was life-changing for all of us. I was a lukewarm Catholic, and I began to fall in love with my faith. My father's authoritarian style of parenting wasn't ideal, but the Lord used it for him to lead us in saying the daily rosary, going to First Fridays and Saturdays, and going to Adoration weekly. Little did we know how much we children would need these graces in our own lives. Fast forward to today, and all three of us siblings are still active Catholics, carrying on this most important aspect of life that my parents gave to us, in this most crucial time for the Church.

So as they celebrated their 50th, we children found healing with them and with each other, and we witnessed their healing among their own siblings. My folks are sweet to each other now, and you'd never know they had such a terrible marriage. Through good times and bad, through sickness and health (to the extreme!), they have not just survived, but have grown in grace, in spite of not having a firm foundation.

Today they are in their late 70s, are growing more feeble with health issues, and lean on the Lord and each other. They take a drive almost every day by the coast, and pray the rosary as my mom looks out at the water, contemplating the eternity for which she longs. My dad goes to Adoration nearly daily, attends daily Mass, and still sneaks in fasting (against the doctor's wishes). Since she was a child, my mother has always leaned on Our Lady, the perfect Mother, even in the bad days when she herself was not a good mom. Perseverance, patience, and time brought us all forward in God's plan. I am convinced that all of the good fruits we see in our family today stem from my parents' commitment to their sacramental marriage, a fount from which graces continue to pour out on all of us, 50 years later. And I am grateful. Thank you, Jesus. [30]

My parents have very different personalities, and they are almost complete opposites. They come from two totally different cultures, backgrounds, and continents, and I find it hard to believe that they got together in the first place. Oddly enough, when they announced to their families that they were getting married after dating for only two months, the only thing my maternal grandfather wanted to know was if my father was Catholic.

I grew up in a very tense household. My parents fought all the time, sometimes even physically. I absolutely hated being home. They fought about everything, and I mean everything. If a paper was misplaced, it was an argument. If something broke, it was an argument. When my father traveled for work, things were much more peaceful, and I started to wish they would just divorce to make the fighting stop. We would even tell my mom to just get divorced like all her friends so that we could have peace.

My parents were Catholic in name only, not really practicing the Faith. There was no regular Mass-going, no confession, no family prayer, etc. During my teens, my mom dabbled in the New Age, playing around with crystals and tarot cards.

My childhood had some good moments, but the day I left home for college at age 18 was one of the happiest days of my life. In the years that followed, I kept waiting for the call saying that they were getting divorced. It never came.

Years later, by the grace of God, my parents returned to their Catholic faith. For my mom, her return to the Church was gradual, and it started with a prayer to God that she not fear Him irrationally (the fear of getting "zapped" if she did something wrong). And, it was tied to an understanding of the permanence of marriage. When I asked her, my mother told me, "Deep down, I knew marriage was for life. I knew I had made a contract with God that I couldn't break."

But there was something else. My own marriage had started out disastrously. I almost called off the wedding, and I was filled with ill-will toward my husband even on our wedding day. The anxiety of the whole situation had made my parents feel desperate, and they began to pray in earnest, reaching out to God like never before. Instead of taking on her future son-in-law and risking a strained relationship, Mom decided to stay silent and pray, resulting in the change and softening of her own heart.

Most surprising was my dad, who was never a very religious person. I remember specifically giving him St. Faustina's *Diary: Divine Mercy in my Soul* after I read it. This was right about the time that my husband and I (who had eventually become estranged) started getting back together. He said to me, "This book is changing my life." He now wears a miraculous medal, prays the rosary and never misses Mass. My mother also prays the rosary every day and frequents daily Mass.

God used a horrible start to my own marriage to bring not only me back to the Faith, but my parents—and eventually my husband—as well!

After 51 years, my parents have learned to accept each other's differences. It may have taken them longer than most, but I believe they are truly happy now. Family gatherings are fun and joyful, and they do everything with us. The tension I experienced as a child is not an issue anymore.

It is only now, after starting my own family—and after learning and reading what children of divorce endure, even decades later—that I am so grateful that my mother didn't listen to us or to her friends who were encouraging her to divorce. The temptation must have been very strong. I am so grateful that my parents remained faithful to their vows. Thank you, Mom and Dad, from the bottom of my heart. [31]

Our story isn't ended yet. I have no idea how it ends, but, for my part, I made a commitment before God, so I'm still here.

My experience with advice from priests has always been very solid, but once our pastor sent us to counseling at Catholic Charities. When we told our *Catholic* Charities counselor how important *Catholic* guidance was to us, she responded, "I use to be Catholic, and I even still sometimes go to Mass." It got worse from there. While discussing our very wounded history—things like both of our childhood sexual abuse, becoming parents as teenagers, his porn addiction, struggles with his sexual identity, and his cheating—we also mentioned that, for several months, we had sex for several hours every day. Of all the things we told her, that last bit was what she focused on; she was fascinated by his "sexual stamina," which in fact wasn't stamina but an inability to climax due to over-exposure to porn! She was also shamelessly flirting with him right in front of me. Our one "Catholic" counseling session was not over soon enough!

One thing I now clearly understand is that marriage here on earth is "until death do us part." My real and true Bridegroom, my eternal Bridegroom from Whom I'll never be parted, is Christ. He has a purpose for me to be here.

It's weird how many lessons I've learned through this marriage. For example, I truly believe it's better to be dysfunctional together as a family than dysfunctional apart. And, having a spouse who sins against you in these ways doesn't necessarily mean he doesn't love you...anymore than my sins against him mean I don't love him. For example does yelling at a spouse (which in most cases is a sin) mean you don't love him or her? No, it means you are choosing a non-loving act. We are all sinners. We all married sinners. God knew we would, and He still said "no divorce." I've also learned that feelings shouldn't always be trusted when trying to discern God's will. The devil can twist emotions in us so easily.

It is very important to be diligent in seeking help that aligns with our Catholic faith. So, we have to know our faith! And if a person can't find help aligned with the truths of our faith, it may be better to struggle alone with Christ. [32]

I met my husband in college. We were a little older than most college students and a bit cynical about the opposite sex. Both of us came from broken homes and had to fight to trust people. We had an almost instant connection and were brutally honest with each other. We met in August and were married by a justice of the peace in April—he was about to be commissioned in the Army in May, so no time for Pre-Cana.[6]

Less than a year later, we had an infant and were living overseas, and I was expecting again. He was gone 24 out of the 30 months that we were stationed there—ten months of which he was deployed to a combat zone. Alone with two babies in a foreign country, I was so tempted to pack up and go back to the States, but my grandmother talked me out of it. My grandfather had served in WWII and she encouraged me to stick it out through the rough parts, saying that my husband was worth it. So I stayed.

Reintegration did not go well. He didn't know where he fit in the family when he came home, so he didn't help. I had a routine and, after all, he was just going to leave again. The kids were scared of him, because they didn't even know who he was. It was incredibly difficult. We moved twice the year we returned from overseas, and my husband was gone to schools for half that time.

When we finally settled into a duty station, 9/11 happened. The fort closed ranks. Armed soldiers patrolled the housing areas, tanks were on the gates. The world was falling apart, and we weren't even married properly. All those people who died never had a chance to set things straight. I went to the Catholic chaplain. Fr. Jack counseled me and my husband, together, then apart, then together again. Fr. Jack insisted we go to a class given by another military chaplain to help us learn to communicate with each other; he said if we didn't learn to communicate, we would be divorced inside ten years. It's true that we'd had very few examples of good communication, but we thought we were muddling along okay; his assessment was a shock to both of us. We went, and it was eye-opening.

So...Pre-Cana was next. Both of us laughed when it was suggested —*not* the reaction Fr. Jack was expecting. We had always wanted to be married in the Church, and both boys had been baptized, but because my husband was gone so much (understatement), we couldn't make it happen. Fr. Jack set up an intensive Pre-Cana weekend workshop with onsite childcare and had food brought in. Seventeen couples were in the same boat. Friday came, and my husband was called out for training in the back reaches of the installation. Convinced that Pre-Cana wasn't ever going to happen, I went to Fr. Jack with my two toddlers about an hour before the workshop was to start. I was in tears. After determining that the training was not mission-essential and that the unit could do without my husband until Monday, Fr. Jack pulled rank and sent the assistant chaplain out to get him. Fr. Jack convalidated our marriage and blessed our rings that fall. He cemented our relationship with each other and with God. That was a turning point for us.

Fr. Jack helped me fit my husband into the family with excellent advice. He helped both of us unload some of our childhood insecurities and baggage. We're still brutally honest with each other, but in a kind way—which was not the case early on. Twenty-two years, nine duty stations, and five children later, we're still going strong. Against all odds, we've made it. God bless that priest. [33]

About eight years ago—after two-and-a-half years of marriage and with an 18-month-old son—I accidentally discovered that my husband was a sex addict and had been since before we were married. He'd become addicted to porn as a teenager, and things had spiraled out of control from there.

His addiction had gotten so bad that he was becoming careless in covering his tracks, and I stumbled upon his latest affair when he left evidence on our kitchen counter. To say I was shocked would be an understatement. I thought that, of all the men in the world, my husband was the least likely to be unfaithful. But he was not just unfaithful, he was repeatedly unfaithful in all of the ways one can be unfaithful in a marriage.

Now, of course, looking back, all of the warning signs were there. He had become increasingly depressed and was drinking too much; he had lost a job and was unwilling to find a new job; he was short-tempered with me and would stay up all night, never coming to bed. But we had a young child, I was the sole income provider, and we didn't live near family. So, I essentially ignored him as he got worse, because I was so stressed with trying to keep us afloat that I felt like I couldn't deal with his issues as well.

My first move after finding out about my husband's addiction was to go see a divorce lawyer. I was in so much pain that I could only see one way to move forward: Get rid of the cause of the pain. However, my lawyer informed me that because my husband was not working, he could potentially be designated the primary caregiver for our child should he choose to fight for that. I knew that my husband was in no position to be caring for our toddler, but because he was in such a wrecked emotional state, I thought he might fight for primary custody as a way of trying to regain control over his life. He had refused to move out of our house (and I couldn't force him to leave), so I knew that he was grasping for some sense of control. I decided to drop the divorce filing and, instead, get all of my ducks in a row. I wanted to make sure it was clear that I was the primary caregiver before trying to file for divorce again.

This is when my story began to change. I started attending S-Anon, a 12-step group for those affected by someone else's sex addiction. There, I met amazing women and men who had been through many of the same trials as I had. There's something really sacred about those basement meeting-rooms in churches. While I struggled to find my place upstairs at Mass, I found comfort in the basement. I started learning about addiction, and that I couldn't control or cure it despite all of the ways I had tried to force my husband to be faithful. I had tried being more sexy, withholding sex, doing everything around the house so that he didn't have any responsibilities, doing all of the childcare so that he didn't have any reasons to be stressed. I even tried begging and pleading with him to just. stop. being. an. addict.

Obviously, none of that had worked. Instead, I started seeing a Catholic counselor and working on my own stuff. I discovered that I avoided intimate relationships, I had trust and abandonment issues, and that I was super-controlling. All of this was my attempt to cope with a childhood that had been filled with uncertainty and chaos. This did not excuse my husband's behavior, of course, but it made me understand why I was attracted to him in the first place, and also how I could be difficult to live with at times. I started to heal parts of myself that I hadn't realized were broken.

I learned about the concept of boundaries, and, after a year of knowingly living with active sex addiction, I decided that I was ready to set boundaries to protect my health. I sat down with my husband and told him that I could no longer live with active addiction. I wanted him to move out and get help. We were already in serious debt as a result of his addiction, and he had risked my health through unsafe sexual practices with others. I was so worried that I would not stick to my requirements that I went ahead and filed for divorce, knowing that I had a 90-day waiting period to change my mind.

My husband reluctantly agreed to move out. I felt a freedom from the burden of addiction for the first time. I continued to work on my own issues, focusing on being the best possible parent I could be to our son. My husband, through God's grace, began to get help as well. He took it seriously and showed me over the course of a year-long separation that he could handle his own finances, therapy, and employment—he even got a full-time job. It was nothing short of miraculous. I had dropped the divorce proceedings, and we moved back into the same house.

But it wasn't easy. At first, I regretted moving back into the same house with him. I was "free" of the addiction and all of its consequences for a year, and having him back in the house meant that addiction, even though it was addiction in recovery, was right back in my face. However, my son was ecstatic to have Dad back, and eventually the regret stopped. We now have a second child, and my husband sponsors addicts in 12-step while continuing his own program of recovery. I continue my own program as well, because, to stay healthy in our marriage, I need it just as much as he does.

It's not all sunshine and roses in our marriage. I still struggle with anxiety about his sobriety and wonder about the "what ifs" of tomorrow. My husband struggles to stay sober, and often his addictive nature comes out in other ways. But I do firmly believe that we are doing the right thing for our family in staying married. Our kids deserve this effort from us, and, luckily, though my husband and I do not see eye-to-eye on much, we are united in placing our children's needs above our own.

I've realized in the years since we've been living in the same house again that life is full of more nuances, crosses, and uncertainty than I once thought. My original understanding of marriage was completely distorted. I thought that my spouse's role was to make me happy and to meet all of my needs. I have since learned that marriage isn't about me, and even less about me when children are involved. Marriage is about a child's natural right to a family (with both Mom and Dad present), and it's about helping your spouse get to heaven. For me, that has meant sticking firmly to healthy boundaries, giving up control over life's outcomes, and putting my faith in God rather than my husband.

I am forever grateful that I did not listen to my well-meaning Catholic friends and family who told me to cut ties and run from my husband. I am so thankful to my friends in 12-step who showed me examples of how I could live within my marriage and actually be happy, regardless of whether or not my husband chose recovery—and I wish that more Catholics studied 12-step and saw how closely it is integrated with Catholic teaching.

I'll end with my favorite quote, from Archbishop Fulton Sheen:

"In family life, two hearts do not move on a roadway to a happier love; rather, every now and then, they seem on the brink of losing their love, only to find it on a higher level." [34]

My husband and I had been married for almost 15 years and had six children when he became an alcoholic. For another 16 years, I lived a kind of nightmare, trying everything to get him to stop. I suffered anxiety, depression, and just feeling generally helpless and devastated, hopelessly wondering when and how it would all end. I was afraid he would end up dead or in jail, and then what would become of us?

There were periodic reconciliations and short bouts of sobriety, and three more children came along. Anyway, long story short, he has now been sober for almost a year and seems to be utterly determined to remain so. He is peaceful and happy, as I have not seen him in many years, and our marriage is healing.

This is, to me, a miracle—and rock-solid proof of God's faithfulness to those who are faithful to Him. I can't tell you how many times it was helpfully suggested to me, including by priests, that I should throw the bum out. And, believe me, I was tempted! I was so angry with him and couldn't understand how he could do this to his family. But I knew that my children would suffer irreparably by being separated from their father, and I knew I had made a vow—before God's altar!—to be faithful to him "in good times and in bad" until death. So I held on. I clung by my fingernails. I threw myself on the mercy of God, begging Him and His Mother to help us, and to help me know and do His will in all things.

I would have voted to get this miracle a whole lot earlier, but of course it had to come in God's time—not mine. I consoled myself that St. Monica had to wait 15 years for hers, and I knew that these refining fires were burning away much in me that was not pleasing to Him, much as I would have liked to escape them. I now feel like I've been freed from prison, like a great weight has been lifted from my shoulders. I praise God all day long for His great love and mercy.

It just makes me weep when I hear or read stories of people who've given up on their marriages because they're unhappy. It really stinks to be unhappy, but if they only knew what God can do when we turn it all over to Him and just hang on for the ride, even when it seems utterly impossible to endure it for one more second.

I could go on and on, but I'm sure this message is already too long. Ultimately, we are bound together by the vows we made, by the decree of Christ that "the two shall become one," and by the children that we share. Besides the mutual help that we owe to one another, our kids need us to remain a family until death. That's it. That's what I live by. God has a plan, He knows what He's doing, and He wants the very best for us. My job is to simply cooperate with Him to the best of my ability. With grace. Always grace. [35]

Coming home from work in 1993, I experienced an inaudible warning to be "cautious at the light"—just before my car was hit by a red-light-runner. Thanks to my guardian angel, I walked away from a crash that could have killed me. I will be forever grateful for the accident, as my soul-saving walk with God began that day.

I was 18 when I moved to the West Coast in the 1970s. I had a great job; life was good. A year and a half later, I met a nice guy at work, and eventually we started dating. Two months later, we became intimate, and three months later, he was ready to get engaged. I was thrilled.

Even though my fiancé grew up without any faith, he appreciated mine and agreed to a wedding at my parents' Catholic parish. We wanted to save money to cover honeymoon expenses, so we decided to live together during our six-month engagement. We told my parents about our plan; however, as I was the oldest of eight, it was to be kept a secret from the rest of the family so as not to cause a scandal.

Looking back, the '70s were wild. In fact, I thought I was pretty wholesome by comparison, even though we were "living in sin." I had no idea that this grave sin would be the beginning of a slippery, downward slope toward misery. Those times were all about "love, love, love." Pre-Cana classes were fluffy, and the exhortation to "be nice" and "love each other" wasn't really going to prepare us for married life. There was no one-on-one couple's time with a priest, nor confession before the wedding.

My parents made a huge mistake by not telling me that we were offending God by living together, but they themselves may not have been well-formed in the Faith, or perhaps their pride would not allow them to be "hypocrites" by telling us we were sinning.

We had a delightful wedding, but we kept God at arm's length, due to the effects of our sins. The ceremony was an external formality that ended our secret of living together.

Part of our first year of marriage was in a foreign country. We were open to life, but we could not conceive. Near the end of the assignment, I was finally pregnant, and happy to be heading home. A month after our return to the States, I had a miscarriage. The medical term for miscarriage is "spontaneous abortion," and I did not like the way that sounded. Even though I was not well catechized, I knew I didn't want anything to do with abortion.

Eventually, we had the blessing of children, born and baptized; however, we weren't attending Mass weekly, and I slid further away from my faith. I was content caring for our children at home, but soon realized that the world did not value motherhood and keeping the home. I also realized that my husband's Saturdays would nearly always center around golf. I felt alone most of the time, except for two dear stay-at-home mom friends whom I was devastated to leave behind when we moved again. I hadn't planned on reentering the workforce, but when a job dropped into my lap after the relocation, I found good daycare and started working.

Nearly all the people my age at work were single. They periodically went out for drinks together after work, but I rarely joined them as I had my children to consider. My husband was on another field assignment (which left me feeling like all I did was work), and when he was home, I was competing with golf. He was still a nice guy who took care of us and made great sacrifices, but life together was far from my vision of "true love."

Growing up conditioned to believe that love is a romantic feeling, I began an affair of the heart with an attractive guy at the office. It was never physical, but I was desperate to feel deeply loved. At this point, only God could save me from myself.

Within a year, we moved back to the Coast to find employment after both companies shut down. We were financially devastated and filed for bankruptcy, and I went back to work at the company where we'd met. By this time, my heart wasn't in our marriage, and I gradually withdrew my affection from my husband; my indifference led to our separation. One night I went out with friends—and stayed out. I had never done that to him before, and it scared the hell out of him. Instead of fighting for our marriage, he chose flight. After yelling at me in great anger, he decided to get an apartment and go. I had broken his heart by not loving him the way he knew that I could.

During one of his early visits with the children, I sat upstairs alone, weeping on the bedroom floor, wondering what was wrong with me. I thought that someday in future decades someone would do a study to discover why so many couples weren't happily married.

After a year, I switched jobs and was pursued by a couple of married men (whom I rejected, thank God, but temptations in the workforce are real). I loved my children, and hated the weekends when they weren't with me. I appeared happy, but my soul was dying as I naïvely went on offending God. I was on a slippery slope moving ever downward.

Sin begets other people's sin, often in the worst ways possible. One spring day, my mother called, asking for help with something that turned out to be the greatest regret of my life. My sister was to have an abortion, and it needed to be done before the eighth week when the baby "begins to develop"—a deadly lie peddled by the enemies of life! My mother told me that all I had to do was drive my sister to the office. I loved my mother dearly, and I did what she asked. My own sins had dulled my conscience and darkened my intellect. I was no longer horrified by abortion, and I had no thoughts of God during any of my participation in it. I know that I am forgiven through sacramental confession, but I will never forget my part in killing another human being. I believe that, had our marriage been healthy and holy, we would have encouraged adoption, or raising the child ourselves.

Throughout our separation, my husband never abandoned us; he was a decent man and offered what he could for the children. He secured their religious education at our local Catholic parish, and he became interested in the Faith. Then, one Easter, he was baptized and entered the Church! I had nothing to do with his conversion. He owned it. It was his journey. Prior to that glorious day, I was his guest for dinner at a parishioner's home. An older woman quietly asked if we were back together, and I gently shook my head while looking at my husband, and she kindly replied, "Well, maybe someday." Across from me, I could see a man who didn't want to give up hope that we would be together again. However, at that moment, I just felt rotten and wondered, "Why can't I just be happy?"

It wasn't until many years later that I was hit with the reality that I had been sexually assaulted, just a couple of months after I'd left the safety of my marriage and the protection of my husband. I had met a man for dinner at a resort hotel, and subsequent manipulations and veiled threats to my life led to an attack that was just short of rape. It was only in revealing this to my therapist (much later), and seeing her reaction, that I came to understand how broken I had become during those years of separation. The results of sin, and now sexual abuse, had taken their toll.

So, how did I get to a point where I could begin healing, choose to love my husband, and end our separation? Two summers before the car accident, my husband offered me the use of his full-size car for a two-week trip. I accepted on the condition that he stay at my place during the trip, and he agreed. After returning from vacation, I asked him if he would like to stay, to see how we might put our family back together. That had to be the grace of God, because I was only thinking about our children; I was pleased for them that he could be a full-time father again.

A few months before the accident, even as we continued living as "brother and sister," my husband suggested that a house, and not my condo, would be better for all of us. We eventually found a ranch-style within walking distance of the children's school, and a few days before the move, the car accident happened.

By moving day, I was experiencing pain and limited in what I could do. Nearly six weeks after the accident, the pain increased to the point that I didn't want to live; I didn't want to kill myself, but I wanted the pain to stop. The clinic doctors told me I would have to learn to live with the unbearable pain, and I knew then that no one but God could help me. I prayed, cried, and prayed some more. Through a remarkable string of events, I was referred to an orthopedic surgeon, who, after months of trying every other avenue, performed major back surgery.

In my convalescence, I had to depend on everyone for everything. I surrendered all to God. Recovery took several months, and during that time, I prayed and I fell in love with Jesus. I came to realize that no mere human being could ever make me truly happy, and that I could only be happy with what Jesus had to give me. From *that* love, I could love—and learn how to be loved by others. I recalled how during the previous years, the words, "What God has joined together..." had come to mind many times. Those powerful words of Jesus, once a warning, had now become an invitation to repair our marriage.

If ever a man was in the position to hold his family together and keep us afloat during a long battle with the demons from below, it was my husband. I am certain that his baptism sanctified our marriage and helped drive the demons away. Confession and therapy brought me to a healthier place, spiritually and emotionally, allowing me to heal childhood wounds—wounds caused by others, and wounds that I caused.

The six months of living in sin before marriage and the six years of separation during our marriage were related. If I could take back the pre-marital sex and living together before our wedding, I would do it in a split-second. For whatever we thought we gained, we lost so much more. Sexual sin, even when it is called love, has consequences. Satan hates marriage. Run away from sin before marriage, and run to confession during marriage; I am convinced that the grace of Christian marriage will help others to avoid sin, saving them, body and soul.

The debilitating pain and suffering that almost destroyed me after my accident became a truly *redemptive* suffering, for which I am eternally grateful. My suffering brought me to fully love Jesus Christ, my Healer and our family's Savior. My husband and I have been married 42 years, and we are very blessed! [36]

From my earliest memories, my parents fought a lot. My dad traveled for his job and was usually only home on the weekends. My mom would let me sleep with her during the week (I think she mostly did this because she was so lonely), but because I slept in her room, often my last waking memory would be of her crying or yelling into the phone at my dad. I missed my dad very much, because, of the two of them, he was the nurturing one.

I think that the fighting started sometime after my baby sister's death. She lived only four days, and I know my parents were devastated. Her death was followed by a late miscarriage of another sister, and then by the birth of a healthy baby brother. So, it was my older brother, myself, and our baby brother—with two very broken parents.

My dad began to drink heavily. He was a functioning drunk for a good deal of my childhood, and, thankfully, he was a happy drinker and never missed work or treated us badly because of it. He also never missed Mass, and while he wasn't very vocal about his faith at the time, his faithful Mass attendance made a huge impact on me. I remember my mom also making sure we got to Mass when my dad was away, but my mom checked out in her own way; she was very depressed and slept a lot.

I looked after my baby brother and felt a lot of responsibility at an early age. Because my dad was gone during the week, and because they fought so much when he was home, I often felt lonely and anxious. My parents also struggled financially, which fueled the fighting and increased the anxiety. I remember coming home from school and frequently finding the power, water, or phone shut off or disconnected. And, there were times when the cupboards were bare. I tried to take care of my baby brother, and I mothered him as best a little girl could who was only five years older. My older brother stayed in trouble. In hindsight, I think he was just seeking any attention he could get—good or bad.

When I was about ten, my parents separated. Although what I really wanted was stability and an end to the fighting, I had begun to pray that they would get a divorce, and it seemed my prayers were being answered. Our family was so broken, and I longed for peace! The separation didn't bring peace, though, only more heartache. My older brother chose to go with my dad, and I really wanted to go as well; however, I didn't want to leave my baby brother all alone, and I knew it would shatter my mom if I chose my dad over her. Making a child choose which parent to live with is a terrible burden to place on small shoulders.

My mom's depression got much worse after the separation. We had to move to a smaller house—it was dark, and it remained dirty and undecorated. It was just a place to stay, not a home.

One Friday, my dad came to get us for the weekend. My mom seemed so sad that I hesitated to leave her, but I was also longing to spend time with my dad and get a break from the heaviness. (I couldn't have worded it that way back then, but that's how it felt with my mom—dark and heavy.) We left the house, and Dad suggested that we go by the store to get Mom a gift to try to cheer her up. When we got back with the gift, I took it in and found my mom passed out on her bed with an empty bottle of pills beside her. We didn't have phone service at the time, so I ran back out to alert my dad and then ran next door to call 9-1-1. The ambulance came, and her suicide attempt—another really unfair thing to do to a child—failed. I know it was God's grace that brought us back to the house that night.

After this, I think my dad realized that divorce was not the answer. A few days later, I came home from school to find my mom and dad sitting on the front steps together. When they told me that they had decided to get back together, I was happier than I'd been in so very long. Dad was going to stop traveling, we were going to move away from the dark, heavy house, and things were going to get better. Dad also stopped drinking, and just having him home every night made a huge difference for me and my brothers. My parents still fought, but less frequently, and although things weren't perfect, it was definitely better for all of us. We had more stability in our family than we'd ever had before.

As an adult now, with a husband and children of my own, I can look back on things through a different lens. My mom struggles with mental illness, and, because she refuses to admit it, she has never gotten treatment. She continues to be very up and down. It is hard to have a "normal" relationship with her, especially for my dad, who has chosen to stay faithful to his vows, despite my mom's erratic and often irrational behavior.

My dad was ordained to the diaconate ten years ago, and he now ministers to everyone who comes into his path. But most especially, he ministers to my mom by continuing to love and care for her. In my own experience, I have found that not a very easy thing to do. One Sunday not too long ago, he gave a homily about taking up our crosses and loving people, especially the ones we find most difficult to love. His main point was, "love anyway." He never alluded to my mom, but sitting in my pew with tears running down my face, I knew.

Looking back, I am so thankful that my parents decided to fight for their marriage and family. They are still together, 40+ years later. That witness to us kids (now all adults) of sticking it out despite the great temptation to walk away is, I think, the greatest gift they ever gave us. In so many ways, it is a heroic witness with far-reaching and ongoing benefits for us, our children, and all the family and loved ones who know their story. Giving up might have been easier in some ways, but persevering spoke volumes about self-denial, determination, and sacrificial love. I continue to see the beauty of my dad's love for my mom—a love that isn't just "talk," but the real "take up your cross and follow me" kind of love. [37]

My father and mother married in 1945, when Mom was 18 and Daddy was 19. His parents did want them to get married, as my mother was

Catholic and my dad was not. Dad was drafted within two weeks of the wedding and was gone for two years. My mother wrote him on a regular basis, and, when he returned, he told her he wanted a divorce. He told her they had married too young, and he felt like he did not know her anymore.

He didn't go through with it, and within a year of his return, their first born child was born. My mom would say that every time they almost got a divorce, there would be another child. They had eight kids in 14 years, and I was the youngest, born in 1962.

At certain points, it was my mom who wanted out of the marriage. One time she was thinking of divorce when a traveling priest came through town and saved her marriage then. Later, after decades of struggling through child rearing, debt, and my dad's infidelities (coming home with lipstick on his collar that was not her color), my mother thought she'd finally had enough.

They were approaching forty years of marriage when my mom contacted a lawyer to file for divorce. That call was on a Friday, and meanwhile, we, her children, had been planning their surprise 40th anniversary party for the following weekend. My 7-year-old niece was riding with my mom (her grandma) that Friday to spend the night with my parents, when she let it slip about the party—an innocent, childlike mistake that we are so grateful she made.

With the knowledge of the upcoming party, Mom spent that weekend thinking, "What am I doing? How can I do this to my children?"

Mom called Monday and cancelled the appointment with the lawyer.

She would later say that the next decades were the best years.

They were married 67 years when my dad died in 2013. Their love had become so deep after wading through all the shallow years of ups and downs.

How did they push through to the other side after so many decades of marital strife? My mom was a strong woman. When she was nine, her own father died tragically when a bridge collapsed in a flood as he was on his way home. Her mother (unknowingly pregnant with Mom's youngest sibling) never remarried. These tough early years built up my mom's fortitude, and she was a strong-headed firstborn to begin with.

Mom was also a strong Catholic who believed in the sacraments. Throughout her life, she went to confession regularly, and she took all of us to Mass, no matter what, no excuses.

She drew on that childhood strength and her Catholic faith to carry her through all the hard times in her marriage, even when she was wondering, "Why did I ever get married?"

Ultimately, faith and family meant so much to my parents, and, even despite the hard times, there were many wonderful family times, too. We eight children cherish those good memories, and we have always thought the world of our parents.

There was a great humility that my mom learned in those later years of marriage, and when I would talk to her about my own occasional struggles with my husband, she would smile and say, "You will come to see one day that a lot of it was your fault." All of the sufferings in her marriage had helped (forced!) her to let go of her own stubbornness and pride, allowing her to see her own sins more clearly.

Their love grew through the years, and when my daddy was dying —when I saw her over him, holding him and crying—I saw how deeply she loved him and forgave him. I thank God every day that my parents stuck it out till death parted them. [38]

I have never once seen my parents organically, lovingly embrace. They are not shy; growing up, my parents simply always despised each other. Rarely a day passed without incident—not even birthdays or Christmases were agreeable. My mom was especially open about her distaste and routinely demanded, "If I leave your father, who would you rather live with?" She knew the answer was her. Divorce was always on her mind and is sometimes still threatened. Ultimately, she has refused because of her Catholic faith.

As a now-married adult looking back, I realize that both my parents, individually, suffer from their own deep emotional and mental wounds that became complicated by their mistreatment of each other. Most, if not all, of the child-rearing responsibility was shoved onto my mother, who was already severely depressed and lethargic. My father was emotionally empty (with the exception of anger), absent but physically there. To this day, he rarely leaves the house and can be found in his natural habitat of recliner + television. Since I was very young, he has slept there and not with my mother. Meanwhile, other than to argue with my father, my mom wouldn't get out of bed for weeks, except maybe for a necessary errand or Mass; I dreaded childhood summers, because they were spent doing absolutely nothing.

To complicate things, my parents were physical and emotional aggressors in the household and terrorized each other. Occasionally, we kids were caught up in it, too. I still suffer from nightmares, and I end up screaming or muttering in my sleep, according to my husband. My parents constantly argued at the top of their lungs. Every. Single. Day. (By high school, I actually entertained the idea that they enjoyed arguing and mistreating each other, but in greater wisdom I no longer believe this to be true.) My mother routinely stood in front of the TV and provoked and belittled my father until he had an explosive response. Both parents have physically mishandled or abused me (my father, being a man, was by far the greater physical threat, and my mom dominated in the emotional abuse and betrayals).

I know readers might be thinking that my life or my parents' lives could have improved if these behaviors had been reported. That is plausible. Would my life have improved had they suddenly divorced, or if people had told my mother to leave? The answer is certainly no. There are a total of three options to my scenario: 1) my parents stay together miserably, 2) they divorce, or 3) they work on themselves and improve for the sake of the kids and each other.

Let's dissect the divorce option.

My explanation of how my suffering would have increased by divorce is three-fold: 1) my mother did leave on occasion, without plans of return, 2) I can compare my own feelings to those reported in *Primal Loss: The Now-Adult Children of Divorce Speak* and draw stark differences in our sufferings, and 3) I have witnessed both parents improve later in life.

First—When my mother left on occasion without a plan to return, she tore the family apart. She chose certain of my siblings to go with her and abandoned me and another sibling to our father, who basically ignored us except when he was angry. It was a new wound on top of all the other wounds, and much deeper this time. I have been asked in my adulthood of my worst memory ever, and the memory of my mother leaving me and separating the family is the absolute worst of all—it cuts deeper than the physical battles. I wanted my parents to resolve their issues, not separate.

Second—I can clearly compare and contrast my trauma to those of the children of divorce. Wounds we have in common are that I have a deep fear of rejection: Some days I have to wake up and convince myself that I matter to anyone, including to my sweet husband and God. I regularly suffer from a complete lack of managing my emotions appropriately and expressing my feelings in an effective way. Other related issues are that I struggle with self-acceptance and self-criticisms; I have to be careful, because I accept blame very quickly in order to make problems go away. I have also been in a string of bad relationships, including one that ended in filing an injunction against a college boyfriend. I married a wonderful man, but his normalcy and upbringing with happily married parents highlight my learned responses. Thanks be to God, I am not my parents, and I humbly utilize counseling regularly. I accept my cross and set out to do much better than they did. My children will not know my past. In *Primal Loss*, some of the children of divorce reported feeling the same way I just listed, but their struggles seemed more prolonged and impossible to control.

Here are some of the problems I *could* have had if my parents had divorced on top of the pre-existing trauma, *but which I don't have*: fear of commitments; fear of marriage dissolving unexpectedly; insecurity about potential infidelity; doom regarding the effects on future generations (over which I have much more control than a child of divorce); lack of a home to go home to; need to constantly please my parents (I am free to displease them, ha, ha); loss of income during childhood; lack of trust; skeptical of promises; lack of faith in God (all of my siblings and I are still practicing, faithful Catholics). I could go on. I am thankful for the accounts of the children of divorce, because I can now be grateful my parents stayed married. I suffered heavily, but all my sufferings would have been multiplied under the realm of divorce, not solved.

Third—Improvements!!! Both of my parents are actually more patient with one another now! I'm not talking a night-and-day change; a more accurate comparison would be the difference between 7:00 a.m. and noon, but improvement nonetheless! This growth is unexpected in light of their past, and I guarantee it would not have happened under the pall of divorce.

I left my childhood feeling deep resentment and hatred towards them, and I'm sure divorce would have complicated these feelings. Now that I have never had to "choose" a parent, I have been able to forgive them and move past resentment towards actually kind of liking them now. In a weird twist of events, I have observed moments where they seem to like one another! My father has notably taken great steps to correct himself. He no longer lashes out physically (my mother followed suit), and he mostly ignores my mother's attempts to antagonize. He also has apologized to me for his actions, which has helped me heal so much.

Recently—in a total miracle—my dad became Catholic after his 50+ years of non-practicing Christianity. My mom delightfully calls Sundays their "Mass dates," and I have seen glimmers of girlish happiness in her that I never saw growing up.

I recently remarked to someone that reading *Primal Loss* made me feel more profoundly loved than ever before in my life. It makes me feel loved that my parents were more willing to suffer literally every day than to destabilize or traumatize all of us kids more than we already were. They did not like each other, and they suffered a lot for our sake, and I am grateful for that. I admire their flawed but steadfast commitment to marriage.

I am realizing every day that there is great hope in the suffering and sacrifice, and while the cross doesn't dissolve itself, God sends moments of grace and joy when I realize just how fortunate I am to have my whole family intact forever. [39]

I begin my story by giving all the glory to my Lord and Savior, Jesus Christ. Without Him, this story would have a completely different ending. It would have ended in divorce, as so many marriages with infidelity do.

My husband and I were happily married in 1991. We both wanted children but initially struggled to get pregnant. After a few years, God gave us the beautiful gift of a daughter.

On the surface, everything appeared to be going well. We both worked full time jobs and were raising our child. However, we were so busy working and taking care of our daughter that we forgot to pay attention to each other, and we both withdrew into our own selfish worlds. We stopped having intimate relations, but we never fought. There was no physical abuse or name-calling. We went to church every Sunday and sent our daughter to Catholic schools. We were a family and were looking good!

Then one day in the fall of 2006, my life fell apart. I learned through my two siblings (who worked with my husband at the same family company) that my husband was having an affair with a woman in their office. I was completely devastated and filled with anger.

I cried, screamed, yelled! I tried to gather myself to think of what to do next. Not only had my husband betrayed me, but my own family had also betrayed me by not coming to me or my husband when they first suspected the affair (many months prior).

During our crisis, my family and even some close friends distanced themselves from us. They completely abandoned us and did not speak to us, and one family member handed me information to see a divorce attorney. It blew my mind.

My family may have abandoned us, but God showed up in a big way! He sent His angels to support us through our tough trial. My husband's family was also very supportive. They wrapped their arms around us tightly, walked with us, and encouraged us to fight for our marriage. I also had a dear friend who stepped in and worked every day with both my husband and me. God truly anointed her to nurture us back, to be able to see His love and grace. She spent many long hours listening to us and reminding us of God's love for us and our marriage.

I needed to separate from my husband in order to begin healing. My husband moved in with a relative so that our daughter and I could stay in our home and keep our routines of school and work. Through this separation, we stayed connected and maintained a relationship through our shared commitment to our daughter, who was our first priority.

We placed our faith in God and asked for His help and guidance. My husband had reached out immediately to our pastor at our church. Knowing God was with us and having immediate access to confession and the Eucharist was such a comfort, and the sacraments began our healing process from the inside.

We both started going to a Christian counseling center, seeing different therapists. We did this for a few months, and we slowly started to talk and recognize where we had neglected one another for so many years. As our eyes opened, we began to address how each of us had failed to care for the other and our marriage. After a while, we began seeing my husband's therapist together.

I struggled with forgiveness in a big way—it was the hardest thing I have ever had to do. It took a good year to truly forgive my husband, and I had to check myself on that at times. My faith is what enabled me to forgive; I would contemplate what Jesus endured through His passion and crucifixion, and it helped me through my struggles. The healing process took time, but we eventually grew in our relationship. I must say, I never felt like giving up, only because I saw the work my husband was doing and the change that took place in his heart. God, in His mercy, allowed me to see that firsthand. Our faith in God did not allow us to end what God put together.

Today, we are not a surviving married couple, we are a *thriving* married couple! We make the time to pay attention and really talk to each other every day. God gave me back a new husband, and I became a new wife for him. We are better connected today than when we dated!

There is always hope. Hope in Jesus Christ. He died for our sins—all of them—and has redeemed the world. He saved our marriage when there were many people telling me it would fail. The naysayers now stand back, years later, only to see that we have defeated the threat to our family and restored a marriage that secular society believed should have ended in divorce. Every day, I thank God for where He has brought us and for where I know He is taking us. Praise the Lord for He is merciful! To Him be all the glory! [40]

I was raised Greek Orthodox. My dad is Greek and immigrated to America when he was 19. My mom (an American and cradle Catholic) became pregnant with me, and so they got married. I don't think it was ever a happy marriage. They had a messy divorce, which started when I was 16—that's when Dad began sleeping on the couch, then later moved to my brother's room until I was 18. Although we went to church, the faith was never lived. We celebrated all things Greek, and I had loads of cousins all around me, but I never witnessed faith lived deeply or a loving marriage, just lots of fighting and unhappiness.

I met my husband in college. He was raised Methodist but did not practice, and I did not practice my own faith and was far from God. When we were 25 years old, we married in the Methodist church. My husband is a native Bermudian, and we moved to Bermuda two months after the wedding, which was not an easy move for me. I had a large extended family, and my husband did not. After living with his parents for the first year, we got our own place and had our first baby, followed by a second baby 17 months later. Three years after that, we had our last child, and, at this point, my husband was immersed in his career, and our relationship began to spiral down. I felt very alone; it seemed he never truly listened to me when I expressed my needs. I started going to therapy (he refused).

To back up a bit....When I was pregnant with my third child, I had a St. Paul-style conversion! I went to a Magnificat breakfast event with my mom in the States (the first trip I took back home without my husband or kids). I only went to this event to make my mom happy—it was not my idea! At the end of the event, there were prayer partners waiting to lay hands and pray for anyone who wanted to be prayed over. My mom wanted prayer, and I was in line with her. (The Holy Spirit was already busy at work. During all the praise and worship, all I wanted to do was cry, and I couldn't understand why.)

I decided to have prayer for my marriage. Two beautiful woman prayed for me. One knelt in front of me and placed her hand on my pregnant tummy and the other stood behind me and placed her hands on my shoulders. They started praying in tongues, and I had no idea what they were doing, but the tears started to flow like never before. I can recall that as they were about finished, my tears and runny nose were clean and dry. The woman standing behind me was sobbing, and they both hugged me and told me they would continue to pray for me. When I stood up, I felt like I was floating. As I walked down the aisle to meet up with my mom, all I could say was that I felt really strange. I realized that the stone wall around my soul had broken away. (Before this time, everything religious repulsed me.) When we arrived home, I wanted my mom to read her spiritual book aloud. I was changed.

I was afraid to say much to my husband, who was and is anti-Catholic (he'd had a bad experience in the Catholic school he'd attended). A few months later, I decided to go to RCIA and become Catholic. This did not go over well. My husband persecuted me terribly, and he started fights with me every time I was headed to class. I had to hide all things religious, and I went to church alone, because he would not let me take the kids to Mass. I continued with therapy, but I was still deeply unhappy in my marriage and frightened to take any action with three young children and no career of my own.

However, when our youngest was about a year old, it finally got so bad that I gave my husband an ultimatum. I told him that if he didn't pick up the phone and make an appointment with the therapist, we were through. He didn't want me to leave, so he called, and we started therapy together.

At this point, my love for my Catholic faith was unshakable, and I began to recognize that my therapist (a former Catholic) was deep in the New Age. I felt very strongly that she was siding with my husband and not remaining neutral. My being Catholic was a huge problem for my husband, the therapy was not helping, and at the last appointment I attended, I felt like I was being assaulted by the evil one. The therapist and my husband were slinging one question after another about the Church at me, and, being such a new Catholic, I was unable to adequately answer them. I finally stood up and walked out.

I met my husband in the parking lot and told him I would never go back to her again. I drove straight to church and knelt before the Tabernacle. I poured my heart out to Our Lord and surrendered my life and marriage to Him. Although I felt not one drop of affection for my husband (and hadn't for a long time), I begged Jesus to help me find love for my husband again.

God truly answered my prayers.

It didn't happen overnight, but He put it in my heart to be a loving wife. I decided that love was going to be an act, not a feeling. I stopped nagging him for the things I needed and wanted him to be for me, and I did the things that I thought he needed instead. I brought him his breakfast in bed every morning, and I served him lovingly even though I felt no love for a long while.

Eventually, my husband started to listen to what was important to me, and he did the things I needed. He started to see Christ in me and started to appreciate and love me for the woman I had become. We were both able to let go of the poison of resentment and unforgiveness in our marriage.

That was 21 years ago, and we just celebrated our 30th anniversary. We have been through so much, especially in the last seven years. Our oldest son had a near-fatal motorcycle accident, and his life and ours have drastically changed. Without my Catholic faith and a strong marriage, I don't know where we would be. I am so grateful for the grace I was given to recognize and face my own sins and weaknesses so many years ago, which changed the course of our family, forever. [41]

When I saw that you were asking for marriage success stories, it occurred to me, to my surprise, that I am one.

My husband and I were both raised Catholic, so we shared a belief in the Church's teaching on divorce. However, 16 years and three kids into our marriage, we were barely limping along, and he had an affair. I was devastated. I did not know how I could ever forgive him or trust him again, but I did not want to break up the family, which I felt would make our kids pay for his sinful acts. I resolved at that time to stay with him until our youngest child was out of the house, at which point I would leave him.

For ten years, I kept putting one foot in front of the other, and during that time we settled into a pretty comfortable life with each other. After our youngest left for college, we hit another rough patch, and I learned that he was in the process of becoming involved with a woman at work. I moved out of the house. I contacted a marriage counselor to help me figure out what to do. To my surprise, my husband decided to come with me. We went to counseling about once a week for probably nine months or so. It was hard and sometimes painful work, but it was effective. We stayed together, and we were happier with each other than we had been for many years.

Four years later, I was diagnosed with breast cancer. Biopsy, followed by lumpectomy, followed by 12 weeks of chemo, followed by bilateral mastectomy and reconstruction—the process took most of the year. And through it all, my husband was a rock, a prince. I can't imagine how I would have gotten through all of that without him. Now, as empty-nesters, our marriage is the happy, supportive partnership I always hoped it would be.

All those years I thought I was sacrificing my happiness for the sake of my kids. Turns out, I was just as much a beneficiary of my decision to stay with my husband as anyone. God works in mysterious ways. [42]

According to my sister, I once said that I thought I was supposed to marry him but didn't want to. Apparently, I said this long before there was ever a reason to anxiously await double-pink lines creeping into a tiny test window. And frankly, I don't remember saying it. Nevertheless, eventually I did marry him, and not just because of the baby we created. It seemed like the Lord was calling us together.

I am so thankful that we got married in the Church, because we would desperately need the saving graces that come with a sacramental marriage, especially in the first seven or so years. The same sister I mentioned above made a speech at our wedding reception about the changing nature of our relationship, which touched on the promise that God makes all things new. Looking back now, it seems prophetic for what was to come.

Those first years were so far beyond difficult, and not just because of the normal marital woes. We both had a lot of baggage, and my dear husband was never taught how to love unconditionally, nor how to properly treat a woman. A victim of his own parents' divorce and of an abusive father, he was angry and abusive himself.

The harsh reality of my existence was that I was the recipient of verbal, emotional, and even physical abuse at times. It wasn't daily, mind you, but it was happening. To be clear, I was not the perfect wife, a spotless victim in all that happened. No one should be mistreated, and my actions weren't the cause of that mistreatment. But if he was guilty of abuse, I was too, in smaller but real ways. This is something I don't think a lot of people will admit to. They will try to justify their own bad behavior because of the treatment to which they were subjected. This is not a judgment; it is a statement of the fact that I, like so many other women I know, have been influenced by this line of thinking that is so prevalent in society. It seems to me that its roots are found in the feministic ideology that says men are just tyrannical beasts and women are victims of their "toxic masculinity." With this image of men, these women will always view themselves (and the world) through the lens of a victim, making it easier to leave—and to not only avoid the crosses of marriage but also to avoid taking upon themselves any responsibility for its survival.

In all honesty, if my husband and I had to do things differently (in order to endure less of each other's awfulness), we might have chosen temporary separation with on-going therapy, with the expressed goal of going back to living in the same household when things improved. However, we can't rewind our life to that time. I have no idea what would've happened had we chosen that path. Perhaps we would have loved our freedom a little too much to want to save our marriage. Who knows? All I can really say is that I am truly thankful for God's grace in all of what happened, no matter the cost.

I'd like to validate the fact that not everyone in an abusive situation should continue living in such a circumstance. The discernment process on that is difficult, and I don't make light of it at all. But, the truth is, not all abusive people are monsters who love to hurt their family members, something that would require perhaps even a permanent separation.[7] Mine is not a popular opinion in this day and age when the main focus is self (*self*-care, *self*-love, *my* happiness), and where modern psychology basically teaches that if someone is rude to you, insults you, or upsets you in any way, you need to leave the situation—even the permanent and sacred commitment of marriage. The truth is that *any* act against another human being by which that person's dignity and worth are disrespected—i.e., any sin against another—is a general abuse of humanity. But there is a vast spectrum of such sins, and oftentimes we make no distinctions within that spectrum when we cite "abuse" as a reason to leave the marriage. And we also forget that marriage is a covenantal, binding partnership that, even if we get a "divorce," is still actually indissoluble.

Despite the reality of what my husband and I went through, I still believe that sometimes the cross of enduring unloving behavior by someone you have given your life to in marriage far outweighs—in value and glory given to God—the freedom and "happiness" one seeks when they walk away from their marriage covenant because of that cross. If viewed in the proper perspective, one can easily see that a cross is meant for salvation.

What made the change for us, from misery to happiness? I really believe that it was not only our prayers, but those of family and some friends, that solicited the grace we needed to stick it out, to begin to see our own worth and that of each other with the merciful and loving eyes of God. If we had listened to so many others, or to the world, we wouldn't have made it to where we are now, and most of our children wouldn't exist.

I'd love to say that our willingness to persevere was a conscious, concerted effort to work toward the common goal of saving our marriage, no matter what. But in reality, neither of us had any grandiose ideas of what we were doing, at least not at first. In the beginning, neither of us had any thoughts of *"I need to endure this to show my spouse God's love, to save our marriage, to do the right thing."* The realization of our goal, and the means to reach it, came after a few years of enduring—and more so in the recent years, when we have looked back on what has taken place and recognized exactly what He, the One Who makes all things new, did with our willingness to stay.

A lot of people would say that the bad examples that were set are damaging to the children, something that should be considered, and they'd be right. But I believe—and have experienced—that any damage that may have occurred is just as prone to divine healing as the tumultuous events that brought that damage forth. The Lord can do anything with the most decaying pile of junk that we—*with innocent faith, true contrition, and trembling hands*—place at His precious, wounded feet. Despite how we felt at times, and by God's merciful grace, we could never have chosen to "save" our children from our bad examples (especially when they would still see a thousand more throughout their lives from their all-too-human parents), only to pile on the desperation, anxiety, depression, guilt, and utter, ongoing loss they would've experienced if their family had been dismantled through divorce.

I once read this quote by Robert Anderson: "In every marriage more than a week old, there are grounds for divorce. The trick is to find, and continue to find, grounds for marriage." The *"...continue to find..."* is foundational here. If I could say that there are any grounds for saving a marriage, it would be those precious children in our keep, no matter their age. And, it would be the fact that we should not presume God's mercy in our sin, but should pray for it in our pain. He truly does make all things new, and a marriage, even in its darkest moments, cannot be hidden from His light.

Our relationship now is just so incredibly beautiful. My husband and I make a dynamic team, and we both have servant hearts focused on sacrificing for the good of the other, and for our family. We get so many compliments from people who truly know us, who know we are not just putting on false pretenses, especially those who have known us from the beginning. I am so blessed to say that our marriage not only survived, but is thriving! We are not perfect, and there will always be mountains to overcome; such is the way of a fallen world. But as we continue to draw closer to the Lord and each other, we are given the strength and the grace needed to keep fighting the *good* fight. [43]

My parents married in 1960 and had their first child (my sister) in 1962. I came along almost two years later, followed by three more siblings.

When I was a little girl, I didn't know that my dad was an alcoholic. All I knew was that we had to be very quiet in the morning because Dad didn't feel good a lot, and he would be mad if we woke him up. I didn't become aware that there were problems in my family until my mom left for a week when I was eight. Prior to that, I had heard her talking to a neighbor on the phone, saying, "I just can't take it anymore. I have to get away from here." I remember being scared and thinking it was because we kids were too noisy all the time and were "driving her crazy," since she would tell us that a lot. I didn't connect any of it to issues with my father.

My grandmother came and took care of us while my mother was gone. We missed my mom so much, and I overheard my dad and grandmother say that Mom "may have had a nervous breakdown." She did come home, though, and I was thrilled. I tried to be very, very good so that she wouldn't leave again. I loved my mom.

When my dad was feeling good, he would play with us for hours and hours, horsing around in that way that kids love so much (but that moms hate because they worry that someone will get hurt). He had a great sense of humor and was always teasing us and kidding around. When he was happy, we were all happy. I loved my dad.

We moved across town when I was nine, and it was at our new house that I began to suspect that my parents were struggling in their marriage. One night, after my siblings and I went to bed, we heard terrible screaming coming from downstairs. We all crept out of our rooms and were huddled at the top of the stairs listening to my parents fight. Suddenly, our mom yelled, "That's it! Go pack your things and get out of this house! Right now!" On the stairs, my brothers and sisters and I were all hugging each other and crying. We didn't want our dad to leave.

When my parents saw how upset we all were, they told us not to worry, and things calmed down for awhile. My dad started going to Alcoholics Anonymous, and my mom to Al-Anon.

When I was 14, my dad got a butcher's knife from the kitchen drawer and tried to slice open his wrists over the kitchen sink. (I am sorry to recount that so starkly. Even now, it is hard to write about.)

My dad was hospitalized three times over the next four years before he was finally diagnosed with bipolar disorder. My parents' marriage almost fell apart during these years. The doctors were trying all kinds of medications to treat my dad's mental illness, and it was a rollercoaster of ups and downs, manic phases followed by deep depressive episodes. Up, down, up, down. I never knew what I would walk into when I came home from school. Friends of Mom were suggesting my mother "dump him" and were recommending divorce (which I really resented). It was a very painful time for all of us, and I was aware that my mom was thinking about walking away and "getting us away from our father." We pleaded with her not to do it. We loved our dad.

My siblings and I were a wreck. I was constantly anxious and afraid, and my grades in school plummeted. I went from being a straight-A student to barely scraping by. I remember in 7th or 8th grade, I had to stay after school to make up some work (I was missing a lot of school), and no one came to pick me up. I waited and waited, and no one came. I remember how nervous and upset I was, walking home five miles in the dark and cold, with cars whizzing by me on the overpass. My parents were so wrapped up in their problems that they forgot about me—more than once. I felt "erased" (for lack of a better word), and I started acting out.

My best friend's parents were going through a divorce at the time, and she and I would go sit by the brook through the woods in my backyard, and we'd talk about these things. One day she said, "At least you still have both your parents." She had a point there. What I was going through was nothing compared to what she was going through—it completely destroyed her family. At least I had mine, as messy as it was, and I was grateful for that.

My friend loved coming to my house, but we avoided hers like the plague; chaotic as my house was, hers was worse. Think of a mom with five kids, ranging from 16 to seven, suddenly having to survive without a husband/father. He left her for another woman and moved across the country, so my friend barely saw him after the divorce. I'm sure you've seen what happens when girls are abandoned by their fathers, and that story sure played out in my friend's household. Teen pregnancy, abusive relationships, alcohol and drugs. Teens find numerous ways to fill that hole in their hearts caused by a missing father.

When I was 14 or 15, I came home drunk. My mom was so angry that she threatened to kick me out of the home. I was devastated and begged her to let me stay. She took me to a counselor instead, where I sobbed openly during the session; however, because the counselor suggested that the problem might be my home life, we never went back. When we left the office, my mom was livid, saying, "She doesn't know what she's talking about!" and adding, "You are just like your father!"

Her words crushed me, because I knew what she thought about my father at the time. I became very introverted and struggled with feelings of hopelessness. I considered suicide more than once. (One day I was in the bathroom with a bottle of pills in my hand, in despair, wondering if there was any reason to stay alive. But then I remembered that it was a mortal sin, and I didn't want to go to hell. So, I changed my mind. Ha! The "Catholic" in me never really left!)

I share this because I want to point out that my mom's anger toward my father—and, by extension, toward me—caused me far more pain and grief than my father's mental illness ever did. It felt like her rejection of my dad was a rejection of me. Every time she mentioned divorcing my father, parts of me would shrivel up and die. After all, I was "just like him."

Looking back, I believe I acted out because anything was better than the feeling of being like a ghost in my own home, feeling "erased." I saw myself as a girl who had to look behind her as she walked, to see if her feet still made imprints in the sand. Acting out made the footprints deeper, and I suspect that's why I did it.

But here is the redemption: With time, awareness, and forgiveness, things began to get better in their marriage. I believe the change came when my parents really took notice of the deep impact that their dysfunction was having on all of us. My mom had a strong Catholic friend, and I think she played a big part in bringing my mom back to the Lord. She gave Mom Catholic books, talked to her about God, and went on pilgrimage with her. Mom began receiving the sacraments regularly, and this changed her heart. Mom's friend reached out to me as well, bringing me books, rosary beads, and prayer cards. Looking back, I can see that the seeds of my own conversion/reversion were being planted by her, though it would take years for them to sprout.

For my dad, I think the catalyst for his return to the Faith was his suicide attempt, the hospitalizations, and the desperate understanding of how much he needed God. When you are brought down low, you see your helplessness and your total dependence on God. He became a very prayerful and humble man. Doctors found a medication that helped my dad's bipolar disorder. He was able to quit drinking after that, and he has been sober ever since.

For years, my mom had forgotten the "in sickness and in health" part of her vow, but once she started praying more (and focused only on her own sins), all thoughts of divorcing my father left her. God showed Mom the inner workings of her own heart, and she began to see the part she had played in the (almost) destruction of her marriage and family. Once my mom got past her anger and resentment towards Dad, she was able to see how her responses to family trials had *added* to the burden everyone was carrying. Let's face it, resentment and despair are the heaviest things in the universe. No one can carry that kind of load—not parents, and definitely not kids.

My mother's transformation was more stunning than my father's. She became kind, compassionate, forgiving, and completely trustworthy, and she became solid as a rock, because she finally had a Rock to stand on. When your heart changes so deeply, the world around you changes as well. My mom was able to forgive my father, and their relationship, over time, grew strong again.

Because there was no divorce, and only forgiveness, I was able to watch my family become whole again—this, in turn, led to the healing of my own heart. One of the great things about my parents' example is that it taught us to stick with things, even if the road gets rocky. My sisters and I have all been married to our respective spouses for decades (25, 28, and 34 years), and there hasn't been a single divorce in the family.

Today, my mom has Alzheimer's. I went over there this morning, and my dad was shuffling along behind his walker, bringing Mom's morning coffee to her, with one sugar and lots of cream, just the way she likes it. He wakes her up in the morning, makes her breakfast, and then helps her get dressed if one of us isn't over there yet. Sometimes she forgets he is her husband and calls him "Dad," but she never forgets to thank him sweetly for his help. He plays music for her "because she likes it," or sits on the porch with her, reminiscing about the old days. She can remember things from the past pretty well, but very little about the present. He treats her like a queen. They love each other very much.

Leila, watching them interact is the cutest thing ever! He is so gentle with her, and she loves him so much! It always makes my family smile! She goes and looks for him if he is gone for more than a few minutes at a time. My father never wanted a divorce; my mom was the apple of his eye. They kept their promises through it all, and God was faithful, too. We are all so grateful that they never got a divorce, but saw their marriage—and our family—through to the end. [44]

I grew up in a Catholic family, with a great devotion to the Blessed Mother, and that set the course of my life. I entertained the thought of becoming a missionary nun...but then came out of high school having completely lost my faith.

I went to college for ballet, got a job at the Pittsburgh Ballet Theatre, and later went to New York to audition, trying to support myself. Winter came and I got the flu. All alone in my little room in Hell's Kitchen, I was thinking, "I don't want to spend another winter in New York!"

And then...the circus audition! They were promising we'd go to Florida! Steve had joined the same circus: Ringling Bros. and Barnum & Bailey. He was hired as a clown, and I was hired as a showgirl. I introduced Steve to my parents while we were leading a very hedonistic lifestyle:

"Daddy, I'm moving to Florida with this clown!"

My parents were flabbergasted: "Our daughter, who wanted to be a nun—now she's marrying a clown?"

One day, I lost my grip on the net and smacked down to the ground. I couldn't stand up straight. I was crippled and had no health insurance....My mother said, "Come home; we'll have you go to the hospital here, and you'll have the surgery."

And it was during this time that the Blessed Mother called me back.

When I was in rehab and when it was time to go back to Florida, I said to Steve, "I want to come back as your wife. I'm not living with you in sin."

Wha—? How could this be? Suddenly, I was changing his plans! He hung up the phone sad, and I just said, "Oh, Lord, what did I do? I've lost him!"

Steve was angry. He came from a broken family, and he'd say, "My dad's not married, so I don't want to get married." And yet, at the time I suggested marriage, he was living in this trailer, sleeping on the floor with the dog—and a lightbulb went off: "I'm saying *no* to this woman I love, for *this*?"

So he called me and said, "Yes, let's get married!"

In the meantime, I was struggling to find my way. I said to the Blessed Mother, "Give me my faith that I had as a child!" I started praying the rosary, and when I made my wedding gown, I sewed appliqué roses onto it; I offered each rose to the Blessed Mother.

Trying to live Catholic with an unbeliever is very hard. So I would just give Steve ultimatums. One day I came home, and I told him: "No birth control!" And he just couldn't *fathom* that! (At the time, I was already pregnant but didn't realize it, so it ended up being a moot point!)

What really brought me back to the Church was the pro-life issue. I decided I would go to the annual March for Life, and I came back transformed. I started giving talks at church, going to pro-life meetings —and then I got involved with Operation Rescue.

Because of those rescues, I was getting my photo on the front page of the paper, and I was a total embarrassment to Steve! That's when my marriage started deteriorating. Now Steve was thinking, "We're going in two different directions, and never the twain shall meet." He was Indiana Jones, the big shot at Disney-MGM—and he had an affair with a young woman. This was the most devastating thing that ever happened to me.

During that time, I got pregnant! Our first child was four years old, and I had not been able to get pregnant in all those years.

Steve was angry with me: "How could you let this happen? The irresponsibility!"

But you know, Steve was raised with some moral responsibility. The girl he was having an affair with kept asking him: "When are you going to divorce your wife?" and he'd say, "She's pregnant! I can't leave right now." A whole year went by....

But oh, the pressure from well-meaning friends! "What are you doing, Anna? How are you still holding onto this guy? He's just taking advantage of you!"

I kept saying, "Lord, what do I do?" And in all of my anguish, I never heard Him say, "You need to leave him." I'm waiting to hear that! And that whole time, with all those stabs to the heart, I would say, "Lord, You laid down Your life. I'm laying down my life for my husband's conversion....I just give it to You."

Now, when you pray the rosary, you will often receive "signal graces." One of my best friends was an elderly lady; when she died, she gave me her statue of the Infant of Prague, and I developed a devotion to Him: "The more you honor Me, the more I will bless you." One day, our son was playing, the statue got knocked over, and the Infant was decapitated.

What kind of a sign was this?

Now, you know how the Baby Jesus has His two fingers raised? I decided I'd fix it. So I formed two fingers out of putty, and I put them on. I glued His head back on; I painted everything. I admired it, with the two little fingers together, and I heard:

"The two shall be made one."

In the midst of this awful, awful time! What was broken off (those fingers—one shorter, one taller—were broken) would be made new, made whole. With those words, I had something to hold onto.

Another amazing thing: When we used to do the trapeze in the backyard, Steve would take his wedding ring off, and one day it was lost in the backyard. Now, three years later, my neighbor said to me, "My little boy found this! Here it is!"

It was Steve's wedding ring! It looked like it'd never been off! A sign! A year had passed; we had had the baby, and the girl was starting to get really angry that he hadn't left me.

Even at my worst, I never cursed him or yelled at him. I was trying to let God do the work. And that fed into his procrastination... pressure, pressure....

Things started to change. He was more open to me....Remember, I had given our marriage to the Blessed Mother, and she was not about to let it fail. She gave the grace for him to procrastinate and for me to hang on!

On our anniversary, I gave him the ring and told him it was a sign. And he just broke down. He put that ring on his finger and went, as Indiana Jones, to work. His girlfriend saw the ring, and my friend told me later that Steve and the girlfriend sat in his truck for a very long time that night. I was absolutely ripped apart, crying, "I thought it was over!" But I heard the Blessed Mother say to me: "I thought it was over, too, when He bowed His head and died; but then they pierced His heart with a sword."

She was there with me, feeling that pain. Then she told me that, after this, it would indeed be over. And that was true—the conversation in the truck was about how he was going to come back to me.

He did, but in a shaky kind of way. He would say, "I love you, but I'm not *in* love with you"—you know that tired little phrase? *Ten years* of that. It was not good, but it wasn't awful.

Now, his physicality was what Steve was about—and then he had his career-ending knee injury. He was trying to support us in other ways, we had the electricity shut off, and then, suddenly, he was going to California. He'd hatched a plan that didn't include us.

He told me: "I want a divorce." And I responded: "Well, can't we stay together for the kids?" We couldn't, he said. I kept trying to get him to come home, and he wasn't falling for it.

I said, "Lord, I have done everything I could possibly think of to save our marriage. I have prayed, I have sacrificed, I have put up with everything; everything I know how to do, I have done. Lord, I give him to you. Not my will but yours be done." And I had to trust that God was going to do—something! But, I was absolutely devastated and having a hard time functioning. I called him on Father's Day.

"Happy Father's Day. You want a divorce? Go. Get your divorce. I won't stop you."

And he was so happy, he started weeping! I said to my Blessed Mother, "How could you let Satan do this to my marriage?" And I heard these words:

"Only for a short time; but I will make of you a beautiful city with a beautiful garden."

I said to her: "How do I know this is true? What if it's just me wanting it so bad?" And she told me:

"You will know it because it will happen."

I told Steve, "If we're getting divorced, I'm going with the kids to live with my mom."

"What? You're not going to live in Florida?"

"No, why would I live in Florida? I was living in Florida because you were there! I have no support system, no job, I have to go to school, learn a trade. I can't do that if I'm by myself with two kids."

And he said, "But—but—I don't think I'll ever come to Pennsylvania. I'd be in Florida, 'cause I'd have jobs in Florida."

Again, we'd be messing up his plans!

I continued crying out to the Blessed Mother, doing novenas. I talked about coming back to see him, that we'd figure things out. His tone was more conciliatory.

Through all of the years, he'd rejected my suggestion for marriage counseling, but now he said to me, "I'm thinking about the kids....I'll never see them....Maybe we could try this marriage counseling thing...."

Oh! Oh, boy. "Okay...."

So we went to this wonderful marriage counselor at the church. He said to Steve, "You have a remarkable wife. She's stayed with you through all this...." And the counselor said to me, "Ten years of putting up with all this; you must have a lot of anger and bitterness toward Steve."

And I thought about that. I went home, and I realized, "No anger. No bitterness. All I have is love for him." I told the counselor: "I never held onto it. I always said, 'Lord, it's yours. Use it for his conversion.'"

The counselor went back to Steve and said, "You'll never believe this!"

And when Steve knew that I held nothing—*nothing!*—against him, that gave him the freedom to say, "Yes, I want our marriage to work."

And from that moment on, our marriage was transformed. It was like we were newlyweds again. Steve became the husband and father that I had prayed for, that I had dreamed about. That's the power of forgiveness right there. If people could understand that! It transforms what was so awful to the most beautiful thing! [45]

My daughter Audrey and her husband James were 19 and 22 when they met. After 10 months of dating, she became pregnant. Her immediate thought was marry quickly—and *never* to have an abortion. She knew her dad and I would be disappointed, but she also knew that we would be grateful that she believed in the value of human life, no matter how that new person is created.

They were both happy at the thought of becoming parents. Our parish priest advised our daughter to wait until after the baby was born to marry so that they could go through Pre-Cana counseling, and also because James had been out of the Church for several years. About a year and a half after our precious grandson was born, the wedding was scheduled to go forward. However, my husband and I had noticed problems in the kids' relationship, including some things that James had done that put up red flags. We both told Audrey that this may not be the right time for a marriage, but she insisted that she wanted to do what God wanted—and that was to make her relationship honorable in the eyes of God by marrying and giving her son a proper family.

The wedding proceeded.

The Mass was beautiful, but many of the immoral goings-on at the "after party" were a sign of things to come. James' family were not church-going people (although they said they were "believers"), and although James had been baptized in the Church as an infant, he had never again been taken to Mass.

When the kids were married, they attended Mass weekly and James had "intentions" of being fully initiated into the Church, but they wound up civilly divorcing just five months later. He said he wasn't ready for marriage, and he felt Audrey wasn't either, so he had packed her things, along with the baby's, and sent her back home to us. Lawyers were sought and fees were paid. Fighting later ensued over custody of their son. We geared up for the custody battle and an attorney was again put on retainer. Ugly words were spoken, and lines were drawn. Ultimately, the judge ordered that Audrey be given permanent custody of the baby, with his father allowed weekends, and child support given to Audrey. This lasted for six long years, with both good and bad times throughout. James was an excellent father, but not a very good friend to Audrey—although they never let their son see anything but good.

When her son was eight years old, Audrey took him on a weekend road trip to see an MLB double-header. They attended the Saturday game and went shopping afterward. On the way back to the hotel, they were in an accident involving a deer, and Audrey's car was totaled. Instead of calling her father and me, her thought went to calling James —who was actually on a date at the time! When James heard that his "family" was hurt, he apologized to his date, paid the bill, and said he was leaving. She told him that she couldn't believe he was leaving her for his ex-wife. He responded that he was leaving her for his son and for the mother of his son, and he was sorry if she didn't understand that.

My husband and James met up and drove to bring them back home. The first thing Audrey said to James when she saw him was, "I love you. Thank you for coming." James later told me that she was the love of his life. Audrey said that the accident had to be a *Godly* thing, because so many people had been praying for the restoration of this family, and it took *this* to make her accept what she was fighting. They were remarried civilly (their marriage was never annulled) and now have a happy home together. One night after their reunion, their son sat between them on the couch and said, with childlike joy, "Now, *this* is a family!" To add to the joy, he has been blessed with a new baby sister! So many prayers answered. God is good all of the time. [46]

"I, William, take you, Theresa...I, Theresa, take you, William...to have and to hold from this day forward. For better or worse. In sickness and in health. For richer or poorer. I will love you and honor you all the days of my life."

And with those simple but ratifying words, my parents "tied the knot" in 1958 at St. John the Evangelist Catholic Church in Los Angeles.

Neither may have deeply pondered the profound meaning of what those words implied, but when it came to living them out, they radically practiced the vows they had made. Their new life had begun, and in short order the children came, ready or not.

My mom came from a quiet, affectionate family, having never heard her parents argue. My father's family was stricter and more inflexible; his parents simply argued in German so the kids couldn't understand. Verbal or physical affection was not shown in his family—"you just knew" that your parents loved you. His mother passed away after childbirth when he was only fourteen years old, leaving his father to provide and care for four young children.

While with friends, my parents met on a beach in California in 1956, when she was still in high school and he in the Marines. In a matter of three months, he deployed for a remote assignment, and she graduated. They married five months later, upon his return. Their temperaments, dispositions, and styles of addressing everyday life were very different and often at odds, but both were practicing Catholics and continued to live their faith and attend Mass.

Dad had a challenge adjusting from the single military life with his buddies to family life. Where he came from, it was duty first, then drinking with the boys after work. His personality was such that he could be very controlling. He did not allow Mom to socialize with neighbors or friends. It was his way, always—and it felt like a dictatorship to her. So, she learned to lie about and hide projects that she wanted to do that he wouldn't like. Their communication as a couple was confrontational or sketchy at best. Mom was too ashamed to talk about his drinking even to her own parents, and so she had no support system in these particularly challenging times.

This is where they were in their marriage when, one winter day in March of 1967, Dad awoke to find that his legs were paralyzed. They were living in Colorado by this time, had five children ages eight and under, and he carried mail for the Post Office. He was 31 years old.

I was their oldest child, and, although only eight years old at the time, I can remember this day profoundly. I had been snuggled deep beneath the covers in the room I shared with one of my sisters, when a commotion in the hallway woke me up. Curious, I got out of bed and peeked out the door. My parents' door was open, lights on, and in the hallway was a wheeled stretcher. My father was being lifted onto this stretcher by medics as my mother stood by watching. I walked over to my mother's side, and she leaned over and told me, "He will never walk again."

Dad was out of our home for a couple of months in rehab, learning the skills required for his new normal. The doctors were unsure of a diagnosis and experimented with various drug combinations to deal not only with the paralysis, but also the pain. Unfortunately, the prescribed medications caused him to be more agitated than usual, and Mom bore the brunt of that.

We soon found out how inaccessible our home was. Ramps were built, and hand-controls were put in the vehicle so Dad could drive. Helpful strangers came and went, often bringing food and necessary items. Thanksgiving and Christmas that year were provided through their generosity. My parents took what we needed and passed on the extra to others.

We learned very quickly to be quiet as mice when Dad was sleeping, so as not to disturb what minuscule respite from the pain he might have. Someone from the parish had recommended that he begin to read Scripture; we also had the Pilgrim Virgin statue in our home and began to say the rosary regularly. I can often remember seeing him lying in his bed, tears running down his cheeks and a rosary in his hands, as he tried to cope with it all.

As the months turned into years and he was no closer to recovery, his frustration grew and the marriage was stretched to its limits. Mom was now the main breadwinner and was coming home exhausted. Dad wanted her for himself, so there was little left for the children and nothing for herself. He was able to attend to most of his own personal care and cooked for the family intermittently. His ability to drive the modified car allowed him to experience some freedom from the home, weather permitting. We took some family vacations to our parents' hometowns occasionally, and, before departing, we would all pray before the Shrine of the Sacred Heart of Jesus in our home.

Needing to escape the snow and ice, our parents decided to move us to Arizona several years later. Mom was able to transfer with Mountain Bell; however, the move itself was not paid for, which further strained their very limited budget. Sadly, the move did not improve their ability to communicate as they pushed through the everyday challenges of life. Dad's irritation and orneriness intensified as the years went on, and Mom returned little affection. Hiking clubs and work trainings took her away from Dad and the kids on occasion.

Dad took advantage of an opportunity to go to accounting school, which heightened his self-esteem, and he then worked part-time for a neighbor who was a CPA. At this time in their marriage, my parents were still praying the rosary and were becoming involved in the charismatic movement.

Communication was still strained between them, and, as Mom

relates to me now, she "didn't like him very much during this time." She loved him and was committed to the marriage, but they just began to "do their own things." Dad's inability or unwillingness to communicate without directing anger toward her had the effect of pushing her further away.

They were stuck in a cycle of miscommunication and nursing old wounds that blocked their way forward. These bad habits continued for years. Eventually, Mom was able to retire early, and they began to say the rosary together daily.

A watershed change came forty years into the marriage, when Mom was journaling. She was going to write about the harsh words that Dad had spoken, when instead she was interiorly moved to pray the Our Father, a prayer she had said her whole life. For the first time, she really pondered the line that instructs us to "forgive those who trespass against us." She began to ask herself if she was really forgiving him. It was a grace-filled turning point for her, and she realized that she, too, would be judged—just as she had judged her husband.

She began intentionally to make small attempts to be present to him, to listen better when he was speaking, and to make eye contact with him. She gently, affectionately, began to touch him again. These small changes on her part effectively began to improve communication and their attitude toward one another, almost immediately. Her heart had been profoundly healed, and they fell so deeply in love again.

Both would agree that they were "jerks" during a long period of their marriage, and that it wasn't "any one person's fault." They had withdrawn from and reacted poorly to each other in their hurt, rather than remain receptive and compassionate. The apologies began to flow more freely and frequently, as well as the willingness to forgive. A new tenderness emerged between them.

On February 1, 2019, Mom and Dad celebrated 61 years of marriage in a very different place from where they had started so many years before. Love truly conquered all. Prayer, faithfulness, and a determination to live out their vows won out. They honored their vow of commitment in this "culture of quit."

On July 13, 2019, my father passed away in his sleep. The witness of their marriage continues to impact all of their family and friends.

My mother recently wrote this to me, "Until I died to self, I did not know how to love. God loved me so much he gave me Bill." [47]

The last three redemption stories are provided by public figures.

Christine Bacon, Ph.D., hosts the radio show Breakfast with Bacon: The Relationship Doctor *and is the author of* The Super Couple: A Formula for Extreme Happiness in Marriage.

A few months ago, my husband and I celebrated our 36th wedding anniversary. That's quite an accomplishment in this day when marriage is no longer valued and more babies are born outside of wedlock than within. It's a double accomplishment for me because our marriage—by all worldly standards—should never have survived.

My husband and I had sex very soon after we met, and I got pregnant the very first day we had sex. I can't even express just how traumatizing that was to me. I even considered abortion, though I am staunchly pro-life. *That's* how terrifying it was to me. The term "baby-momma" hadn't yet become *en vogue,* and there was still great shame associated with teen pregnancy. I didn't want to be pregnant. I had my whole life ahead of me. Yet I found myself in that same gut-wrenching position as so many other girls.

My then-boyfriend was much less traumatized. He was madly in love with me and told me immediately he wanted to marry me and raise our child together. While that did not remove the trauma, it certainly brought me a modicum of peace, knowing I had a man at my side whom I'd eventually come to know as a man of great integrity. So many others are much less blessed.

So, after knowing my husband for an extremely short two-and-a-half months, we ran to the Justice of the Peace and married. We were 18 and 20. Our precious daughter was born a little over six months later. We were happy.

As a military family, we moved from Wisconsin to New Hampshire ready to begin "the rest of our lives." We were so happy, in fact, that we decided to grow our family, and I got pregnant within a month. I can't stress enough that WE. WERE. HAPPY.

Two months after getting pregnant, I began an extramarital affair.

That revelation likely shocks you, because it shocked me, too. I couldn't believe what I was doing. What happened?! I was happy! I was pregnant!

I felt filthy. I remember the day when I physically entered that dirty, dark, and sinful relationship. I actually thought to myself *on that day* that I could never again call myself a faithful wife. Funny, isn't it? I willfully walk into a sinful relationship, and my thoughts are immediately of my broken vows.

As I sit here typing that putrid part of my story, I desperately want to hit the delete button on my computer. My mind is racing to the judgment you and others will place on me in knowing a part of my story that I have spent thirty years trying to forget. But God. He gives me the strength and the courage to speak the truth, because He alone can convict me, and He has already forgiven me. So has my husband.

I didn't understand infidelity back then, because society had already taught that infidelity can only be borne out of an unhappy marriage.

Society was wrong.

I figured that, because of these powerful feelings I was experiencing for the other man, I must have never truly loved my husband. So, I decided that our marriage was over. I'll never forget the day he moved out. He was being transferred to South Carolina, and he stood outside of our door with his seabag on his shoulder and tears in his eyes and pled, "please come with me." I was unmoved, and I remained where I was with our two daughters, ages five months and three years. I'm crying again at my computer, recalling that day. The pain on his face is seared into my memory *still*—and I hope never again to cause him such excruciating pain. Thank you, Jesus, for forgiving me.

We were separated for four years.

In the time we were separated, my husband changed his posture from one of sadness to one of meanness. He said and did hurtful things—things that "proved" to me that I'd made the right decision in leaving him. I know now that his cruelty came from a hardened heart due to the hurt I had caused, and—possibly more so—due to the voices of all his "friends," who were constantly telling him to "move on" and that "he deserved better than an unfaithful wife." Our society is filled to the brim with well-meaning friends who are, in part, responsible for the breakdown of their friends' and family members' marriages. Either the true causes and outcomes of divorce are unknown to them, or they have experienced divorce themselves and fall into encouraging others to divorce as well. You know, so that their friends can also be "happy."

It took me two years to realize what a bad man the "other" was, and I finally left him. I was now a single mother raising two little girls, and I figured it was time to file for divorce. I didn't necessarily *want* to file. I just figured that was the next logical step. My husband was in South Carolina. I was in New Hampshire. We'd been apart two years. We were *supposed* to get divorced then, right? No one told me otherwise. No one told me I was making a mistake. No one told me to stand for my marriage. No one told me divorce would devastate my children.

Ironically, it was the divorce filing that seemed to awaken something in my husband that caused him to stand up and fight for our marriage. He quietly refused to sign the papers. He'd make changes to the documents and then deploy. There's a silly little (awesome) law that says you can't divorce a military man while he is deployed and unable to defend himself. My husband's maneuvering would delay the proceedings for several months. I'd make changes and return them, and he'd again hold on to them, make more changes, and then deploy. I now know this was God's way of delaying a proceeding He didn't ordain, while simultaneously softening both of our hearts.

Over the year while this was taking place, my husband and I, unbeknownst to the other, began to attend church again. I became actively involved in my Catholic parish, joined the choir, and had our daughters baptized. My husband began to talk to a preacher who encouraged him to reach out to me and reconcile. He started to pursue me again. He flew to New Hampshire and visited the girls and me more often. He sent Christmas gifts and Easter baskets. All the while, I resisted. But most importantly, he'd call and ask, "Can we please try again?" I want to stress that it was his persistence and humility that won me back. He did then what Jesus had done and teaches us to do: The *offended* humbled himself before the *offender*. How beautiful is that?

In time, we moved back in together. His persistence had paid off. I'd like to say things were great at that point, but they weren't. We just jumped right back into marriage with no guidance, formation, or training whatsoever. It took time before we figured out how to make a marriage work—and we did, eventually, figure it out.

In the thirty years that have passed since those dark days, I have come to understand that we were held together by two things: 1) the God we both loved madly—a love we showed by our deep prayer lives and our unwavering Mass attendance, and 2) the silent vow I made to myself the day I agreed to reconcile. That long ago day, as I stood in the living room of my apartment with the voice of my discarded-yet-faithful husband coming from the phone at my ear, I vowed to myself that, if we got back together, this time it was for life. I never realized until decades later, and becoming a marriage researcher myself, just how important that vow was in the long-term maintenance of our now-thriving marriage. There *cannot* be an escape clause. We must absolutely burn our parachutes and know that our only option during difficult times is to stand and to fight.

These days, I save marriages for a living. I hope somehow my marriage story helps to save yours. No marriage is perfect—neither ours nor yours. But extreme happiness after infidelity *is* possible. Do it for your kids. They're worth fighting for. Too often, the same parents who would take a bullet for their kids are willing to duck and let the kids take the divorce bullet. Don't be that parent! Re-learn how *to love* their other parent. It *can* be done. It *must* be done! Then one day when your fourteen-year-old looks you in the eye and says, "Thank you, Mom, for not divorcing Dad," you'll know it was worth the fight. *You're welcome, Jessica. You were worth it.* [48]

The following essay by Catholic journalist Doug Mainwaring originally appeared at Public Discourse: The Journal of the Witherspoon Institute.[8] *Reprinted with permission.*

The most riveting, wise, and helpful statement I have heard in recent years was shared by Ifeyinwa Awagu of Lagos, Nigeria, in a short video prepared for the 2014 Vatican *Humanum Colloquium* on the Complementarity of Man and Woman:

> The couple is the locus, it's a starting point, but it's a ripple....Whatever I do in my marriage, the circle keeps increasing, keeps widening, until it covers the whole world. Marriage is beyond us. It's about the society. It is your own project for the world.

Ify's statement is pure gold, displaying immense truth and gravitas. To illustrate why, I begin with this example from my own life.

While my wife and I were still divorced, our younger son, Chris, would occasionally spend the weekend at the home of his middle school friend, Ray. When he arrived back home, he wouldn't say anything in particular, but I could read his body language and perceive what was left unsaid. I didn't need to be a rocket scientist to understand that Chris really liked spending time at Ray's house, and the reason was clear: He loved their family life.

All I had to do was look into Chris's eyes to see that he wished he had a family like theirs—a family with a gregarious, big-hearted, and affectionate Mom and Dad who clearly loved each other. I knew that this was precisely what I had deprived Chris and his brother of.

It was this very loving marriage that first caused me to wonder if I had made a huge mistake in divorcing my wife and breaking our family apart. And after each of Chris's subsequent visits with Ray's family, I became more convinced of my grave error. I knew that I needed to repair what I had broken. Yet Chris never made a single direct statement about this. He never said why he enjoyed spending time with their family or explicitly compared it with ours. Although I don't know if he could have articulated it if he had tried, I received the message loud and clear. Eventually, I realized that I had no choice but to find a way to bring our family back together.

Meanwhile, Ray's family simply carried on life as usual. They had never made an attempt to address our family situation; they just simply lived their lives as faithful Catholics and as faithful loving spouses to each other. They had never spoken a word of judgment, encouragement, or advice to me, and I had never once said a word to them about my broken marriage. In fact, at that stage we barely knew each other except to say "Hi" at our sons' football games. Our lives touched only through our sons, yet that was enough.

This family had no idea how much good they were doing for me and my broken family just by the way they were living their lives. Somehow, their Catholic faith, their joy, their love, and their faithfulness overflowed and cascaded into my life via my son.

Were it not for this family, I'm not sure I would ever have had that first thought implanted in my mind about bringing our family back together. Although I was completely irreligious at the time, it seems to me that this was God's gentle way of getting me to see that I had erred and needed to do something about it. God didn't send somebody to club me over the head or rebuke me. Instead, He brought me into indirect contact—into the distant outer orbit—of a couple whose lives deeply, quietly touched mine. I am one of the beneficiaries of the ripples emanating out from their loving marriage.

When I finally had lunch with Ray's parents a few years later and thanked them for what they had done, they were completely taken by surprise. They had no inkling of the important role they had played in our lives.

Yet the ripples of their faithful marriage continue to expand. Not only have my wife and I been back together for nearly six years, I also returned to full communion with the Catholic Church after a nearly twenty-year absence.

None of us can truly gauge the impact of our lives on others. Yet, even without your knowing it, the witness displayed by your faithful marriage might be the lighthouse that guides and helps others to hold their marriage and family together. You could be saving a family from the destructive influence of the world. You could be leading someone to the threshold of faith, and you may never even hear about it.

You probably have no clue of the enormous good you do by cherishing your marriage, your spouse, and your family, and by simply living your life as a faithful Christian. Your personal relationship and commitment to Christ reverberates all around you, sending out ripples that affect the lives of others in unseen and unexpected ways.

This kind of impact is extremely personal and therefore difficult to quantify or measure. Yet legitimate social science seems to bear out the point I am making. As Kay Hymowitz has observed, children "have a better chance at thriving when their own father lives with them and their mother throughout their childhood—and for boys, this is especially the case." She continues:

> A highly publicized recent study by the Equality of Opportunity Project comparing social mobility by region found that areas with high proportions of single-parent families have less mobility—including for kids whose parents are married. The reverse also held: Areas with a high proportion of married-couple families improve the lot of all children. In fact, *a community's dominant family structure was the strongest predictor of mobility*—bigger than race or education levels. This research suggests that *having plenty of married fathers around creates cultural capital that helps every member of the Little League team.* [emphasis mine]

* * *

In miraculous manner, the blessings and benefit of intact families spills out of their homes and into surrounding households. I'm not a social scientist, but history, observation, and common sense all support Ify Awagu's statement: "Whatever I do in my marriage, the circle keeps increasing, keeps widening, until it covers the whole world."

Marriage is bigger and more important than either husband or wife alone. Perhaps that more easily resonates as true for couples with kids, but it is just as true whether children are present or not. While marriage has been under attack throughout human history, beginning in the Garden of Eden, in recent decades it has suffered catastrophic blows thanks to the ongoing sexual revolution, a revolution that has produced countless casualties.

Through my own marriage—with all the mistakes and detours—my wife and I have created something that is irrevocable and unmovable. What we began at the altar in 1985 in front of our families, guests, and God can't be undone. Two became one, and an entirely new entity came to being in the universe. Not a metaphoric creation, but a reality. A wonderful, utterly unique new alloy was forged. It can be ignored or abused, but those choices don't undo the mandate that fell into our laps that hot July afternoon nearly thirty-two years ago. When my time on this planet has reached its end, my marriage will have been the single most important contribution I will have made.

There is never a good reason not to uphold your spouse's dignity— in front of the kids, in front of friends and family, in private conversations with your spouse, and even in your own mind where nobody else can see or hear. Belittling, cold-shouldering, name-calling, and tearing down or undermining your spouse's dignity in any way is always destructive and never helpful, demonstrating an absence of unconditional love. Even negative humor is far from harmless. It's not funny; it's a visceral personal attack on your spouse's dignity.

In my marriage, we've had to deal with my same-sex attraction, family histories of addictive behavior, financial difficulties, major health issues, and much more. Sadly, a combination of those things once led to our separation and divorce, for which I take full responsibility. But, in the end, good has outweighed bad, and human dignity and love have slowly and steadily triumphed over animosity and isolation.

How do you heal a relationship that self-destructed, which had lost its moorings for more than a decade? I have no easy answer, but I do know that the first step is this: You must choose to recognize the importance and irrevocability of your covenanted relationship and to uphold the dignity of your spouse and your relationship every day, no matter what, repenting when necessary.

Since reconciling (and that's too weak a term—it has really been a complete change of heart and a hard-fought renewal of our minds), we have continued to face both big and small challenges, one after another. Rather than allowing them to tear us apart or let our relationship fray at the edges, to give up or to say "this is too hard for me," my wife has upheld my dignity as husband and father, and I have upheld hers as wife and mother.

My wife's love for me, especially during the darkest times when I've been at my most weak and vulnerable, has been a direct conduit of God's love to me. In fact, the greater the personal challenges I have faced, the more she has honored me with dignity and respect. There is a miraculous, inverse relationship between the weight of difficulties and weaknesses present and the degree of dignity accorded. It's counterintuitive. It's the opposite of the way things work in the world, but it's a reflection of God's unconditional love. Upholding each other's dignity allows grace to flow into and lift our marriage day after challenging day.

For every objection or fear, worry, regret, or apprehension I can come up with, I've taught myself this two-word response: "So what?" Our marriage is more important than any reservation I encounter.

– I'm unhappy. So what?
– I'm same-sex attracted. So what?
– I'm disappointed. So what?
– We're having financial difficulties. So what?
– We've become incompatible. So what?
– We've gotten older and gained weight. So what?
– My spouse has developed bad habits. So what?
– I didn't bargain for these medical or psychological problems. So what?
– I've met someone I like better. So what?

Here's what I say: "I can handle that, and I do so with pleasure. We can address and overcome these problems. We'll navigate difficult waters together, even if it falls upon me to do all the paddling and steering while plugging all the newly sprung holes in the hull."

Instead of fretting or wistfully daydreaming about something that might have been better, realize this: There is no better option, because you have no greater, more important mission.

If it weren't for the presence of dark times, I don't think godly, unconditional love and dignity would have ever had a chance to take root and grow between my wife and me. Personal experience has taught me that the Church truly is a field hospital within our own home. That makes sense, because the domestic church is right up on the front lines where battles can be treacherous, and where wounds, both old and newly inflicted, can often present themselves. If willing, spouses can serve as medics. The very best medics.

Don't be caught by surprise, don't despair, don't give up, and don't be afraid. Instead, resolve with all your might to hang on to your life's greatest mission and treasure. Even if it feels like a daily burden, it remains a pearl of great price. Ify is right: "Marriage is beyond us. It's about the society. It is your own project for the world."

Ify first spoke these words in Lagos, Nigeria: "Whatever I do in my marriage, the circle keeps increasing, keeps widening, until it covers the whole world." I first heard her words in Rome, Italy, and they have continued to have enormous influence on me and my family here in the United States. I owe a debt of gratitude not only to Ray's parents, whom I now count as friends, but to Ify and her husband, Chidi. We have never met, but their marriage has touched my life in a profound way.

Marriage is the big project that I have chosen for myself and it's the big mission that I've been charged with. We have solemnly created our marriage, God has solemnly blessed it, and now we must solemnly live it. It is our project for the world. [49]

I'm ending this section with one of the most poignant stories I've ever read, from one of my favorite Catholic luminaries, Professor Anthony Esolen, who writes about his wife's parents. This piece, "Culture of Divorce, Culture of Death" from InsideCatholic.com, *is reprinted with permission.*[9]

"Come sit over here," my wife whispered to me. "Let's give Dad a chance to be alone with her."

It was a quiet room in a hospice, the only sounds the muffled pumping of oxygen, and the softer and slower breathing of my mother-in-law, Esther, as she lay a few hours before her death. Her husband, Herb, stood by the bedside, stroking the gray curls on her forehead, a slight gesture. It seemed to wave away 50 years of sorrow and disappointment and strife, leaving only the love he felt for her in the beginning, like a seedling under the ruins of a city.

He could have abandoned her years before—not for another woman, but for what the world calls peace. Dad is not a Catholic, so he had no Church precept to warn him against divorce. He didn't need any. "You never know what you'll get in life," he put it to me once. "You have to do the right thing, because if you don't, you'll probably make things worse." So he never left, and at the last moment of Esther's life he was there, fulfilling a patient vigil, his eyes red with weariness and loss.

"Moses allowed our forefathers to present their wives with a bill of divorce," said the Pharisees to Jesus. "For what cause do you think a man may put away his woman?"

Consider them the pundits of that time, eager to learn whether on this matter of public policy the preacher from Galilee would position Himself on the left or the right. Would He agree that you could divorce your wife for burning the soup, or would He hold out for a far narrower range of grounds—adultery, for instance?

But Jesus rejected the terms of the question. "Moses permitted you to divorce," He said, "because of the hardness of your hearts; but it was not so from the beginning. Therefore you have heard it said that a man should leave his mother and father and cleave to his wife, and the two shall become one flesh. So I say to you that any man who puts away his woman—I am not talking about fornication here—and marries another, commits adultery." He concludes with a stern admonition: "What God has joined together, let no mere man put asunder."

We may be too familiar with these words. They should strike us with the same shock that once silenced the Pharisees, or enraged them, when the Lord reached back behind all the history of the Israelites, behind the Temple and the kings and the judges and the tribes, behind even creation itself, as He said, "Before Abraham was, *I AM*." Here alone, in this discussion of marriage, does Jesus answer a question about good and evil and human life by appealing to the time before the Fall. "It was not so," He says, "from the beginning." It was no part of God's plan for innocent mankind. It can be no part of God's plan for man regenerate in Christ.

Jesus has presented to us two potent truths, each unbearably alive and full of import for fallen man, yet leaving it to us to connect them.

The first has been celebrated joyfully by Pope John Paul II: Man and woman are made for one another. Our bodies, our very souls are stamped with a nuptial meaning, and in the embrace of man and woman, an embrace that in God's providence can bring into being a living soul, we recall our innocence in the Garden, and we share in and anticipate the wedding feast of the Lord. The second? We were not made for sin and death, for alienation from one another and from God, our life. That too was not so from the beginning.

Make the connection. Culture of divorce, culture of death.

If any man had cause for procuring a divorce, short of adultery and mayhem, my father-in-law had it. Esther was a difficult woman to live with. Over a trifle, as when we should leave for the diner, she could go into a towering rage, then storm off to her bedroom, her face set like flint, certain that she was right, that she was ill-used by everyone, and woe to my wife if she tried to reason with her. "Gram's on the warpath," she'd say. She could jest about it then, nervously, but when she was a girl she didn't dare bring any of her friends to the house, for fear that her mother would cause a scene. Hers was a lonely childhood.

What caused this habitual anger, I can't say. Perhaps a deep insecurity, a hunger to be loved; her own mother was by all accounts a tyrant in the household. When Esther returned home with Herb from their elopement, her father said to him, "If you can live with her, more power to you." And she was her father's favorite.

For a few years they lived together happily, in unlikely conditions: quarters for married midshipmen at a naval base in the Bahamas. They always spoke about that time with wistful humor. The poverty was something they shared and couldn't help, so they took it in stride, and made jokes about how much they grew to hate bananas. Esther was also one of those women who genuinely enjoys the company of men, and whom men will treat with a big-brother jocularity and kindness. Those years were good for them.

Then they settled down in New Jersey, where they would live most of their lives. Dad is a sharp man and a hard worker, holding down two and three jobs all his life before he retired. But for a while money was tight, and though Esther grew up with eleven other children in a rented house with an earthen floor, or maybe because she grew up in such straits, she never learned any measure in her spending. She was one of the most generous people I've known, lavishing my children with Christmas presents, but she spent on herself, too. She wanted nice things they could not afford. So she upbraided her husband about his pay, and went to work herself.

My wife was born then, and maybe all would have been well had Esther been able to trust her husband's industry and thrift, and had she not been afflicted by a painful condition that compelled her to have a hysterectomy. It was a severe loss. In her frustration she took a job at a monstrous candy mill, working at rotating shifts, two weeks in the day, two weeks in the evening, two weeks in the dead of night. The body never accustoms itself to that; it is always sleep-deprived. So she took to having a nightcap before bed. Then she fell in with some cynical companions at work who also liked to drink. Soon she was an alcoholic.

Many readers will be able to fill in the details. She was impossible to predict; sometimes ingratiating, sometimes as unappeasable as rock. She would throw cups and dishes about the kitchen. Her fists were not idle. She'd shut herself in her room for days of terrible silence. She insisted on separate bank accounts, throwing it in Dad's teeth that it was her money, that she made more than he did (for a year or so this was true), and that she could spend it as she pleased. My wife cannot remember when they shared the same bed.

But to her credit, Esther recognized that Dad was a terrific father, and in her own way she was true to him. Nobody else dared criticize him—but she would humiliate him publicly. He didn't care, or didn't let on. They could unite only in their love for their daughter, whom they showered with gifts, partly to compensate for their inability to give her what she wanted more than anything, namely love for one another. Finally, when she was 15 and presumably capable of surviving the blow, her mother approached her with bad news.

"I can't take it anymore! Your father and I are getting a divorce."

But divorce was still rare in those days, and my wife hadn't entertained the possibility. It was as if someone had told her that her little world, so fraught with suffering, so fragile, yet so beloved, would be smashed to bits. She broke down in bitter tears. Her mother backed away, and God would bless her for it. The word "divorce" was never uttered again.

Divorce destroys a world; it smothers an echo of Eden. What was the Fall, if not man's first attempt to divorce? "Where are you, Adam?" calls God in the cool of the evening. "You haven't come out to meet me as you used to do." Adam is steeped in shame. He doesn't want to be seen. Consider the unselfconsciousness of little children who parade naked in front of their parents, because they sense no separation; they feel themselves to be at one with mother and father. Only later, with a growing sense of separate identity, and a growing loneliness, does the child wish to hide. Adam is hiding not because he is naked, but because he is alienated from God, and it is that separation that causes him to look upon his nakedness, an emblem of his own being, with shame.

But the severance could not end there. When Adam and Eve admit their guilt—a graceless and skulking admission—they chisel the fissure more deeply, divorcing themselves from one another and from creation. "It was this woman you gave to be my help," says Adam. "She gave me the fruit, and I ate it." Eve passes the blame in turn. "It was this serpent you created! He tricked me, and I ate the fruit."

There you have the motto for a culture of divorce. Cain's words assume that the brother, the parent, the spouse, the neighbor is not worth keeping. What to do with one who obstructs my will, or casts a pall over my daydreams? If I can get away with it, and if I am angry enough, I put him away. No matter. Around any house or barn there's plenty of noisome matter to be buried, shoveled over, cast into a pit, or burnt. We rid ourselves of the sights and smells.

Cain begins in Genesis a saga of family strife, occasioned by lust or greed or envy. Lamech is a multiple murderer, and proud of it. Men begin to take several wives. Lot listens to his grumbling men and separates from Abram, taking that fateful left turn toward Sodom. After Sarah finally conceives a child, she cannot bear the sight of the woman she had encouraged to become Abraham's concubine, so she forces her husband to send Hagar and Ishmael away into the desert. Though God would bring forth good from her guile, Rebecca causes deadly enmity between her sons when she tricks Isaac into giving his blessing to Jacob and not Esau. Jacob's uncle Laban tricks him into marrying Leah, whom he does not love, and then extorts seven additional years of work from him in exchange for Rachel, whom he does love. The intense rivalry between the two sister-wives causes a rift in the family between the sons of Leah and the sons of Rachel, whom old Jacob favors. One of those sons, Joseph, is hurled down a well by his brothers, then sold into slavery.

If heaven is filled with life and light, a wedding feast to celebrate the marriage of the Lamb to His bride the Church, then hell, as C. S. Lewis imagined it, may be the Great Divorce, a realm of alienation, whose "citizens" detest even the thought of a city, and who wish, in an endlessly fissiparous parody of the Heavenly Jerusalem, to move further and further away into the outskirts, to put as much distance between themselves and God (and their neighbors in damnation) as possible. Dante saw it too: One of the traitors in his *Inferno*, fixed in ice up to his head along with all the others of his ilk, defines his neighbor simply as that one "with his head in my way to block my sight"—a head that will annoy him for all eternity, and that he would gladly lop off if he could, with no more compunction than if he should swat a fly.

But Herb and Esther never departed for that gray city that promises much and delivers nothing. They stayed with one another; they endured. They kept their vows. "Son of Man," said the Lord God to Ezekiel as he stood before a valley of dry bones bleaching in the desert sun, "tell these bones to rise." And from those vast dead sands they did arise.

Not immediately. They sent their daughter to college, and after years of wandering in the academic wasteland, joining a tent revival, falling away, brought closer to the Lord by a rabbi, a musician or two out at heels, a good old girl from Tennessee, a motorcycling professor of Milton, and a lover of Crashaw, she ended up in North Carolina, where we met; and I had left my own footprints over many a desert mile. Each of us became the instrument by which the Lord brought the other one home. We fell in love; we worshiped together at Mass. At our wedding, our priest delivered a sermon on the Song of Songs, and on the righteous souls in Revelation, the communion of saints whose robes have been washed white in the blood of the Lamb.

I have a picture of Herb walking down the aisle with my wife. He looks embarrassed, as if he couldn't tell how he had come to be there. He had been raised in an evangelical church. His father, a sternly righteous man, took the Faith seriously, but imparted little of the joy of it to his children. Herb's churchgoing did not survive the Navy. Esther, meanwhile, had been raised with hardly any religion at all. She may have attended a Dutch Reformed church for a few years as a child, but her parents paid so little attention to it that they failed to have her baptized. By the time we were married she had given up drink for good, and the AA meetings she attended may have turned her toward the Bible; or maybe she had turned on her own. In any case, though she was ashamed to be found in a church on Sunday, she read a little of the Bible every night, in secret.

I don't know if, except for marriages and funerals and an occasional Easter long ago, Herb and Esther had ever been in a church together. I do know that *our* marriage, and *our* increasing steadfastness in the

Faith, made them happy. They suddenly had something new to unite them. If they could not love one another, or at least not admit to it, they could together love my wife and me, and then the little girl and the little boy we brought them—the only grandchildren they would ever have. Esther was a hard woman, but she had also the corresponding virtue of loyalty. If you hurt someone she loved, she might never forgive you, but if you loved the one she loved, her heart would swell in gratitude. Now she and Herb had unexpected reasons to be grateful to one another. They could tattoo their house with pictures of the toddlers, who adored them in their turn, as was just.

"God is not the God of the dead," said Jesus to the Sadducees, whose hearts were too cramped to believe in any resurrection, "but of the living." To accept divorce as a way of death—no way of *life*—is to deny the very being of God as revealed by Jesus. It is to say that love can, or should sometimes be permitted to, die utterly. But had God so acted toward us, all this universe would have winked out of existence at the first sin of Adam. With every sin we commit, we pretend to sever ourselves from the fount of our being, as if we were lords of life and death; yet should God respond to us in kind, we would find the divorce complete, and would fall into the nothingness of everlasting loss. But He does not do so, and at the last moment, like the thief on the cross who joined the others in their jeering, but who then thought better of it—and maybe it took the torment of crucifixion to wake him —we may turn to Christ and hear Him say, "This day you shall be with me in Paradise." Christ did not put away that dying criminal. So much the better for us, who are all criminals, dying.

Esther too was dying, though nobody but my wife noticed it. "Something's wrong with Gram. She remembers things that never happened." Old age, I supposed. Esther did not look like she was about to depart. She still fought mercilessly with her husband. She still squandered her money, though it had been many years since illness had forced her to retire from the factory. She still raged against how badly everyone treated her. She still slammed the door to her room, to hide, to be miserable; and, at night, to open her Bible, though she never talked about it.

But she was suffering a series of small strokes, as we learned much later. These strokes compromised her memory and her ability to get things done around the house. Herb never complained. He'd always been handy, and now he began, unobtrusively, to take on chores she could no longer perform, sweeping and vacuuming, loading the washer, tending the garden, along with all his old chores and his hard work, post-retirement, at his auto junkyard. The strange thing was that as Esther's memory faded, so did her rumination upon all the wrongs she thought people had done to her. Weakness wore away the edges of her anger.

All this took more than ten years. It was punctuated by times of madness, when she would storm out in the dead of night and pound on a neighbor's door, because a "strange man" was in her house—her husband; or when on a snowy Christmas night she forgot that she was visiting us 250 miles away, and insisted that she was going to walk home. I had to sleep in front of the door to bar her way. But in general she was softening, mellowing. When, after his open-heart surgery, Herb could no longer take care of her and she had to move to the county home, she was pleasant to the nurses and the beauticians, and would brighten up whenever anybody came to see her. Herb visited her three or four times every week, which was as often as her condition could bear, wheeling her down to the solarium where they would talk with other patients and visitors for the whole afternoon.

Esther could be most kind when she wanted to be, and could accept kindness too, but for much of her married life she would not accept it from her husband. Now, as she grew more helpless, she was glad to accept it from him, and he gave it without stint. She called him, in a moment of tenderness and lucidity, her "savior." She was not far wrong. His most important act of kindness he performed just before his operation and her entering the nursing home. He'd become friends with a local Presbyterian minister, a genuine believer in Christ. Now he knew that Esther was too ashamed to admit that she hadn't been baptized. He also knew that if he were to suggest a baptism, she would reject it in anger and hurt, and that would be the end of that. So he told everything to Pastor Forbes, and invited him to visit now and then, so that Esther would get to know him. Then the subject might come up unbidden, or certain suggestions might be made. So he did; and, not long before the time would pass when she could reasonably make any decisions she would remember, without any prompting she asked to be baptized. A few days later, Pastor Forbes baptized my mother-in-law, a frail old woman but at last a daughter of God, in her own kitchen, christening her in the name of the Father, and of the Son, and of the Holy Spirit.

We in a culture of death hunger after life, but on our own terms, and at the expense of others, even at the expense of their lives. But some of us will only begin really to live when we have lost all capacity to pretend that we are our own. That is one of the meanings of Jesus' mysterious saying, that unless we become like little children, we shall not enter the kingdom of God. Esther now entered that childhood, and Herb was there, to feed her, to wheel her about when she could no longer walk, to talk to her even toward the end, when a massive stroke had left her still wishing to speak, but unable to form more than one or two intelligible words.

And he was beside her those last few days, making sure, if by some miracle she regained the ability to swallow, that the hospital staff would not abandon her to starvation. He would not allow them to hasten her death with morphine, prescribed less often to alleviate pain than to soothe the onlookers and free the doctors and nurses from the ennui of a natural death. We watched by turns at the bed of the dying woman, not because we believed there was something magical about squeezing out each breath from the clamp of death, but because it was the right thing to do. She was going to die, but we didn't want her to die alone. The dying life was a mystery. It was not our place to abandon it, to cast it away as inconvenient, as trash, as we are urged to do to so much else in our barren lives.

How can we know what fleeting notes of grace came to her in those last hours? If God wills, who can obstruct Him? After nearly 53 years of struggle and disappointment, yet 53 years of faithfulness and duty, Herb stood by, never divorced. The Lord God, against whom she had sinned the more mightily, never turned from calling her back to Him, and as a child of over 70 years she finally answered that call.

What keeps people from believing that a good God loves them and desires never to be parted from them, unless they themselves should flee that love? Look in the mirror, and see the cause of despair in others. Do not repeat the words of the great divorcer at the bottom of hell, who says in his loneliness and misery, "I am my own, I am my own." Say rather, "I am a wayward child, and the one I am called to stand beside is a wayward child." Do not dare mull over your "quality of life" and your "fulfillment"—wrapped in a shroud of deadly self-regard, while the Lord of life, who dies to bring you to life, gasps for His last breath on the cross above. If anyone had grounds for divorce, He had; no one ever loved as deeply as He, and no one was ever betrayed as He. You, reader, have betrayed Him shamelessly, as have I. Yet He remains faithful, and waits for us, to bring us life:

And I John saw the holy city, new Jerusalem, coming down from

God out of heaven, prepared as a bride adorned for her husband. And I heard a great voice out of heaven saying, Behold, the tabernacle of God is with men, and He will dwell with them, and they shall be His people, and God Himself shall be with them, and be their God.

And God shall wipe away all tears from their eyes; and there shall be no more death, neither sorrow, nor crying, neither shall there be any more pain: for the former things are passed away.

And He that sat upon the throne said, Behold, I make all things new. [50]

THE STANDERS

My mother encouraged me in praying for my future spouse when I was barely 12 years old. Taking her advice to heart, I made a sincere effort to draw this mystery man into prayer. I asked God to prepare his heart for mine and to protect him on his journey. Some 17 years later, my mother's affirmation echoed my own discernment. I had found "the one" for whom I had been praying. Our year-long engagement and preparation for marriage was built upon the foundation of a shared faith, a love for family, and our parents' examples of faithfulness in marriage.

As a young married couple, we immediately received instruction in Natural Family Planning, which we practiced the entirety of our marriage. We prayed together and attended weekday and Sunday Mass. Our pastor asked us to become sponsors in the RCIA program, which led to our involvement in several other ministries. The mutual sharing of our spiritual and intellectual gifts came together most notably when we were asked to head up a marriage apostolate. We recognized the honor and privilege of walking alongside other couples as we presented topics on St. John Paul II's *Love and Responsibility*, communication, conflict resolution, suffering together, and family of origin issues. For our ongoing dedication and commitment to marriage ministry over many years, our archbishop bestowed upon us a prestigious honor at a diocesan event.

Our family life also flourished during this time. We welcomed four beautiful children into our arms and three into our prayers after miscarriage. Every pregnancy required medical intervention almost as soon as a positive test was confirmed. Complete bedrest for months and constant hospitalizations were the norm. My husband was a champion in caring for the needs of our home and graciously joined me in sacrificing for the sake of a safe delivery. As a homeschooling family, we used these sacrifices as teaching moments on a day-to-day basis. We befriended many other young couples and regularly opened our home for family gatherings and social events. We became godparents for many children during this time, and we celebrated three marriage vow renewals over a span of 18 years.

I believe these details about our faith, family, and community life testify to graces attributable to the marital bond.

There were many joys in our marriage, but sufferings as well. In addition to the miscarriages and months of complete bedrest I mentioned earlier, there were premature births, severe hurricane damage to our home, the burden of two mortgages, my mother's unexpected death, and a family member's crippling disease. Suffice it to say, these and other crosses reminded us of our dependency and reliance on God. This dependency consoled us in the knowledge that we would never suffer alone. Our perseverance always brought a blessing in due time.

Given the stability of our marriage and family life, the time was right for my husband to pursue his doctorate. This was my opportunity to support him as he had supported me during my pregnancies. His published dissertation included a tribute thanking me for countless hours of reading and editing his work.

Upon completion of his doctorate, however, there was a noticeable shift in his views on faith and morals. He claimed his doctoral studies in the social sciences had enlightened him. As a result, he rejected the existence of absolute truths in exchange for relativistic views. As he focused more and more on his secular experiences, he began to doubt his faith. He expressed confusion about a God who "lets" bad things happen and loathed the idea of the cross.

I tried every way to comfort him and to offer clarity amid his confusion. The more I tried, the more he resisted. Even the compassionate accompaniment offered by many family members and friends could not console my beloved spouse. He fell into grave darkness, and my heart shattered into a million pieces.

During this painfully bewildering period, I turned to Scripture and sought the wise counsel of trusted spiritual advisors. When I think back, the sufficiency of grace amazes me still. I found a strength and clarity to proceed patiently and mercifully. I offered forgiveness and an ongoing commitment to healing. The pastoral interventions were endless. I even sought the help of my bishop to declare a separation with the bond remaining (per canon law, 1152) for the purpose of encouraging my spouse to retreat and receive pastoral care. Unfortunately, I have since learned that no U.S. bishop follows or implements the canon on separation, even when petitioned, as required, by the faithful.

It became clear that without my husband's active will to remain faithful to our marriage, there was little I could do. After a series of complicated and traumatic details, he departed our home. I continued to care for our children, all the while assuring both my husband and our children that healing and marital reconciliation were a priority. I reiterated that I would never ask the court to rule for divorce because I believed our marriage to be valid and indissoluble. In forming my conscience over the years, I had developed integrity of self; I found discernment of truth and goodness and right action intimately related to achieving interior peace. Through this process, I was able to integrate grief and loss with hope and purpose. It is also how I dealt with my children's pain and anger in discovering that their father had begun to date another woman.

Many months later, my spouse initiated and obtained a judgment for divorce. He married civilly outside of the Church because he had not obtained a declaration of nullity. He eventually petitioned for nullity and was denied after a protracted period of scrutiny. He appealed that decision, and, when it looked like the process would not overturn validity, he renounced the appeal altogether. The favor of the bond was upheld. My children embraced in a group hug upon hearing the news. Some teared up, and some offered words of affirmation and gratitude. The overall tone was of celebration and joy!

"We knew it! We knew that what we believed to be true based on our own experience of your marriage and our family life was in fact real and true!"

"It feels like we just finished a marathon and we won the whole thing!"

"Mom, thank you for standing up for the truth and for defending our sacramental heritage!"

Our children's response was so powerful that I realized my offering of fidelity, in conjunction with their faith, was the greatest gift I could give them.

A few weeks later, I got out our family films at the children's request. It was the first time I had watched them since my husband left our marriage. The children and I marveled as scene after scene reflected the richness and beauty of our domestic church. Our wedding anniversary is referred to as the birthday of our family, and that is how my children and I now celebrate it. I am grateful they recognize this goodness and that it remains at the core of their identity. This blessing guides us and consoles us as we carry new crosses in the aftermath of my son's brain cancer diagnosis and ongoing recovery.

The reason I remain faithful to my spouse and the reason I stand for our marriage is because I said I would. I didn't say, "I do until he doesn't!" Rather, I promised that I would "do" even in the worst of times. I vowed this because I entered into a sacramental union in which my spouse and I cleaved together. Yes, I grieve the loss of companionship and physical intimacy that has been ripped from our one flesh, but those things do not comprise the entirety of marriage. Consider a spouse in a coma or one plagued by dementia or any other condition or season that bears the cross of sexual abstinence.

Furthermore, the details I have shared here, along with the unwritten testimonies of those who have been deeply and sincerely impacted by our marriage, point to a reality that I simply cannot deny. Some well-intended on-lookers might suggest that the initial period of fruitfulness and joy might have been a farce, that my spouse perhaps did not bring all of himself to marriage with sincerity, and that he is now showing his true self. To them I say no, on the basis that it rejects a Christian anthropology of how the human person is created and called. In that spirit, I believe that every person is made for goodness, and that the practice of the virtues sustains him in strength, not necessarily perfectly, but sufficiently. Our true selves are rooted in this calling and integration. That means my husband was *more* true to his natural identity during the time he practiced the virtues and sacrificed for his wife and children than when he walked away from those integrations as a self-proclaimed secular humanist. Consider also the fact that my spouse has claimed adamantly that he was faithful in marriage until the time of his faith crisis. His admission inadvertently reveals his capacity for fidelity and his ability to choose freely and with virtue. It also substantiates his intention to do so from the moment he professed his vows at the altar.

Finally, I remain faithful to my husband and to our marriage because it is just. It is just that I offer our children what I am capable of offering and what is due them as heirs to the grace of the sacrament. Since motherhood flows from my vocation to marriage, fidelity provides consistency in their faith formation, confirms the priority of their best interests, and assures stability and safety in a predictable home environment. Fidelity is also just because it dignifies my spouse on both a human and spiritual level, independent of whether or not he accepts it. This is sometimes hard to grapple with, but at some point between here and eternity, the veil will be lifted. When I imagine it, I feel like a child with giddy anticipation of the gift that awaits my spouse on Christmas morning. As for now, the long-sounding nature of my offering is but a speck of time against the backdrop of heaven. Since I believe marriage is about getting my spouse to heaven with my children in tow, my consolation and hope is in the merciful gift of indissolubility. [51]

I met my husband over 30 years ago in our parish's young adult group. He told me that he'd broken up with his last girlfriend because she didn't want marriage or children, and we started dating when we each saw in the other someone who had the same values and goals. We both came from practicing Catholic families, and both sets of parents were happily married after many years.

Every Sunday night, we would go to Mass together and then to dinner at his parents' house with his siblings. We all got along very well.

After dating almost four years, my future husband proposed to me on the first day of our vacation with his family, and that night we all celebrated and called my parents to tell them the happy news, which was met with great approval.

We prepared for marriage with our dear pastor, and we went on a beautiful Engaged Encounter weekend together. Six months later, on a sunny June morning, we married in our home parish. We had a joyful nuptial Mass, and I couldn't have been happier—I was marrying my best friend.

On the first night of our honeymoon, my husband told me how very happy he was that I was his wife, and he apologized for pressuring me, before marriage, into unchastity. We soon moved into our new house and began our married life together.

Before long, we conceived our first child. We were both extremely excited to become parents, and my husband embraced fatherhood with exuberance; wherever he went, he would tell random strangers to get married and have babies!

Over the following years, when we encountered couples in struggling marriages, we gave our support to redeem the marriage. For example, together we helped a friend reconcile with his wife after he'd had an affair and repented. Also, my husband told his sibling not to leave his marriage when it was at a low point, but to commit to working out their problems.

About 12 years into our marriage, we attended Marriage Encounter as a happy couple, and, though our marriage was already strong, we both recommitted to prioritizing our relationship.

My husband had done quite well financially with his business, and I had become a stay-at-home mom. I assisted him with his business and enjoyed raising our children.

I watched my father go through a debilitating illness, and I saw my mom care for him—honoring him in sickness, as she lived out her vow. On the day my father died, my husband promised my mother that he would be there for her.

The following year, we went away on a romantic anniversary weekend. We enjoyed each other's intimate company, far away from the pressures of life. On the drive home, my husband talked about how wonderful our time had been and that we should regularly set aside time to get away, just the two of us.

The following month—unbeknownst to me—he met someone and became infatuated with her.

I noticed him becoming more distant, and we began to argue more often. Then one day, after 17 years of marriage, he told me that he didn't want to be married to me anymore. He claimed that it had all been a big mistake, that he had never loved me, that we were not compatible, that we were not "soulmates"—and that he wanted to go out there and "find" that person.

My heart was crushed, and I struggled to breathe. He agreed to see a priest, and I was hopeful that this nightmare would soon be over. But it wasn't. The priest he met with eventually told him that it would be okay for him to leave me and "be happy" with someone "more compatible." I felt betrayed not only by my husband, but by the

Church. My husband continued to be distant and cold toward me. I felt so abandoned. I heard a quiet voice telling me that I was not alone—that God was there.

I sought refuge in prayer. Late at night, and during the day, I cried out to God. I began to attend daily Mass, and confession became a regular occurrence. (Sadly, while raising our children, confession had become a once- or twice-a-year thing, before Easter or Christmas.)

One day, my husband's best friend sent me a link to the EWTN site on the topic of marriage. I began to read all that I could on the sacrament of matrimony. I became convinced that I could not "move on" as some of my secular friends and even my husband told me to do; I could not see myself in good conscience "dating," as I was still a married woman. Even fellow Catholics—my sisters, several friends, my niece—did not understand.

I eventually left my old parish, because the current pastor assumed that because my husband was dating, I must be dating, too! I left that day in tears. Scandalously, he wasn't the only priest who encouraged me—a married woman—to date and/or divorce and "move on." After all, the priest said, everyone can get an annulment (and my diocese has a 100% affirmative rate on granting declarations of nullity, so he was not entirely wrong).

One day, my niece told me that she didn't respect me, and that I had to accept that my husband didn't want to be with me. I had realized by then that being a strong woman didn't mean doing what comes easiest or is most "liberating," but in doing what is hard and what is right, even when others disapprove. I realized that by not dating, by continuing to wear my wedding ring, and by acting as a married woman, I was remaining faithful to a sacred promise that I had made to God, regardless of my husband's choices. My husband had chosen to break his promise; I didn't want to give my children that example, too.

I remembered what it felt like in my younger days, when I had been living in mortal sin and was trying to convince my guilty conscience otherwise. The truth is that I never had inner peace before God. I did not want to live like that ever again.

I made a choice that instead of going out or dating (and I declined several invitations from men), I would focus on my two teenagers and be there for them. They needed at least one sane, responsible parent—and that became me. I focused on growing in the Faith by studying it and going deeper into the interior life of prayer. Christ became my

Spouse when my earthly spouse abandoned me.

It has been over ten years since that day when my husband shattered our family and subsequently left our home. I have left out most of the horror and sorrow and anguish that was caused—physically, emotionally, and mentally—to me and to our children. Along the path of tears, I gained a deeper faith, one that is still growing. I learned to trust God in ways I never had before, and I became aware of how very much He had always been there with me, guiding and protecting me. I truly am a different person than I was on that first day of abandonment, when I thought my heart would explode from the pain.

It still hurts.

But I understand now that suffering can be *redemptive*—that every suffering a Christian humbly offers up in union with Christ's suffering on the Cross can unleash untold graces for ourselves and others—helping souls get to heaven. The joy and peace that I have experienced in my life are so wonderful, even in the pain. God really is close to the brokenhearted. And I truly believe and understand that I have been blessed with the better part.

I am His, and that is where I want to stay. [52]

Unknown to us, as Joseph and I prepared to marry, there were lawyers meeting across the country, preparing to make it very easy for one person to destroy what we were trying to put together. Even as we spoke our sacred vows in June of 1970, "no-fault" divorce had already been successfully sold to California's then-Governor Ronald Reagan, and the laws were being changed across the nation.

In our extended family, the first evidence of these legal changes was felt as Joseph's father announced to his mother that he was done. "It's nothing you did, nothing you said, I just don't love you anymore." And with that, the poison of divorce entered our family. Its effects on the children, from adults on down, have been wreaking havoc ever since.

As I watched my husband hurt so badly, I felt confident that he would never do this to his own family; his anger at his father was palpable. Yet, just barely eight years later, he suddenly "had to talk to Dad," and a few weeks later, he used the *exact same words* to tell me that he, also, did not love me anymore and wanted out. A second generation now victim to the new no-fault, unilateral divorce laws.

We had worked together through infertility, had adopted two children, and then agreed to try one more time to conceive a child under the care of a different doctor. The son who was born to us as a result was not even ten months old at the time of my husband's bombshell. Our oldest had just turned seven. I could not believe this was happening, and I fell apart, begging him to stay. He did agree to counseling, and we stayed with the counselor through the diagnosis of alcoholism and beyond. He also saw a second counselor alone, who confirmed the diagnosis. And then a third, who said he saw many "red flags," but that "until he admits there is a problem, there is no problem...." Joseph heard only the last four words.

The first signs of that very real drinking problem could easily be traced to the time of his parents' separation, after which he had gradually begun to drink daily, then more each day, with many changes resulting in both of us.

After my husband's decision to go forward with the divorce, I went to our pastor, who was beside himself and overwhelmed with the sudden number of his actively involved parishioners (whom he described as "good, practicing Catholics") coming to him with their marriages falling apart. He told me that, at that moment, there were twelve other families from our side of town alone who were going through this. He was supportive, and he even helped financially with a loan to tide us over when car repairs and such came up unexpectedly. But he had no words of hope, no way to help us, and he did not offer to speak to Joseph, either alone or with me. He knew from the others that it would not make any difference. He reassured me of *my* good-standing in the Church, however.

When scouting for a good attorney, I had two lawyers tell me to "leave your religion at the door" when I made clear that I was Catholic and did not want this divorce. My godfather, also a Catholic lawyer, told me the same thing.

The man I ultimately hired was Catholic and understood me, but he told me, clearly, that there was nothing I could do to stop the divorce. However, he did advise that I could say whatever I wanted to say in court.

When last-minute changes were requested by my husband's attorney regarding the custody of the children, my attorney replied that I could easily be convinced to agree to them if Joseph simply called off the hearing that very day and checked into a treatment center of his choosing, sticking with it and the after care. Instead, the papers were signed "as is," granting me sole custody. I don't think Joseph understands even now that on that day, he chose the current beer over his marriage, his wife, and even his children.

The judge had already stated that he *was* going to grant divorce that day, as "this has gone on long enough." He'd heard not one word of testimony. Later, when asked under oath, I clearly stated that this marriage was *not* irreconcilable, and that I did not want a divorce.

The strongest Catholics I knew were praying for marriage healing, all the while also telling me that "it takes two," that "God may have something better in store" for me, that "God never closes a door without opening a window," and that "God forgives even divorce." And there were many who told me that if I really loved Joseph, I would let him go and get on with my life, because I would want *him* to be happy, no matter where he was, or with whom.

Some told me that, when it came to their own divorces, they had sought counsel with spiritual directors and prayed—resulting in "God told me I could get a divorce!" My response to them, after doing word searches with a *Catechism*, a Bible, and a concordance (*love; marriage; divorce; covenant; faith; forgiveness*), was the following:

"But God hates divorce! He is a witness to our covenant, and remarriage is adultery! God doesn't change; He isn't man, who lies. And He tells us to remain single or be reconciled!"

They would come back with, "Well, God may have called *you* to that, but He told *me* I could get a divorce!"

Yet, it was the Lord who said it, not I.

I watched as one after another of our friends and acquaintances divorced and then married someone else. I was slowly becoming an enigma, and many thought that I was, indeed, nuts.

When a relative married outside of the Church to a man divorced several times already, another relative assured me, "But this one will last." Some were upset with me for not attending the illicit ceremony and for telling her that she should not be receiving the Eucharist. I say it in love, out of concern for her salvation, but they believe that I am rigid, unhappy, and unforgiving.

I believe in marriage and stand for my vow, because *God has not changed!*

I have been counseled by many priests over the years to seek an annulment and "trust the Holy Spirit," but that did not seem to be what God would have me do. One priest told several of us that if our spouse suddenly, after five or ten years, became mentally ill, we probably could not get an annulment, as we had vowed "in sickness and health." *But*, he told us, if our spouse became an alcoholic, we *would* be able to obtain one, because an alcoholic cannot love or commit to anyone! I asked him if he accepted the concept of AA, and when he said, "Yes! Good group," I asked him how my vows were any different from those of the wife of a mentally ill person. "We are in sickness, poorer, and worse right now, but my vows are still binding, aren't they?" He said he'd never quite thought of it that way. I neither saw nor heard from him again.

A few years ago, again, three different priests in a week encouraged me to seek an annulment and "be free." I have very good and strong Christians and Catholics telling me all the time that I need to "get on with my life," that "God does not call us to be unhappy," and that perhaps I have peace in *my* decisions, but someone else who does *not* have peace has the right to marry again. They now tell me that I fit under Jesus' supposed "adultery exception" (which is a Protestant mistranslation), since my husband married again civilly.

Yet they ignore the beautiful truths of Pope St. John Paul II on this very issue (emphasis added):

> [It is] proper to recognize the value of the witness of those spouses who, even when abandoned by their partner, with the strength of faith and of Christian hope have not entered a new union: [These spouses] give an authentic witness to fidelity, of which the world today has a great need. For this reason **they must be encouraged and helped by the pastors and the faithful of the church**. —*Familiaris Consortio* (20)

According to canon law, my marriage is to be *presumed valid*, until proof of the contrary is found. Joseph is my spouse to this day, in the eyes of the Church—and in the eyes of God, to whom I must answer someday.

Where do we stand now? Joseph's civil marriage ended in divorce. For the past several years, we have spent holidays together as a family, including his daughter from the civil marriage. Together, we help out with the youngest grandchildren, and there is peaceful interaction between us. I still pray for his full return to the Church and to our marriage.

"For I hate divorce, says the LORD the God of Israel....So take heed

to yourselves and do not be faithless."
I, Theresa, take you, Joseph, as my lawful husband.
I promise to be true to you in good times and in bad,
in sickness and in health.
I will love you and honor you,
all the days of my life. [53]

Writing this story has loomed large in my life. I have had no rest since you asked for "a few words," so here goes. In a nutshell, regarding my abandonment and divorce: I thought I would die; I wanted to die from the pain; then I didn't die, but I turned around and had six angry and confused kids to deal with. So I dealt with it all. And we are thriving.

But looking back, my divorce almost killed me. It was so sudden and so awful. My anger at God and the whole situation was massive. Why did I have to suffer—truly suffer—with the pain of living? I fleetingly thought of suicide. In a flash, we had gone from a loving, stable home to utter, paralyzing chaos that almost crushed my six kids and me.

My husband of 17 years offered me a cup of coffee. It was a normal Saturday morning, and I had just returned from morning Mass. He calmly said to me, "I don't want to be married anymore. There are things I want to do with my life. And I can't do them with you and the kids." In my gut—immediately—I knew every word was true.

Life stopped and chaos reigned.

All of the cliché things that destroy families of divorce happened. Loss of income and terrifying financial situations, disappearing friends, and the total destruction of the safe, secure life that my kids had known.

The cliché and obvious stuff with the kids specifically was that their grades fell, their personalties changed, their friends started to exclude them, they became irritated with each other, and they began acting out. But the biggest hurt to me was how they started to treat me. If their dad didn't like me anymore, then they could begin to find fault, too. If you are a child in an intact, well-functioning family, your folks are like furniture; they are there and you take them for granted. Suddenly, because they saw the loss of the respect their dad had always shown me, I was fair game to be hated and yelled at. It was so hurtful. I understand now that I was a "safe target," but at the time, it just shredded my heart.

The kids were ages one to 12 when their father left. He literally slammed the door and left to begin his new, unencumbered life. He left me to deal with the consequences. I had to handle so many things on so many levels. I felt totally inadequate.

What I was, more than anything, was angry. At God. I was furious, because I had tried to be a good Catholic wife and mother and it didn't matter. After my husband abandoned us, I never stopped going to church or taking the kids with me, although none of us wanted to be there because the divorce was so public. We all felt exposed. There was lots of bad behavior from the kids when Mass was over.

I always let God know just how furious I was. At church I would say, "Here I am. I don't know why I'm here, but here I am." Then I would just numbly sit there. Over and over. With time, it changed to, "Please, help me. Please. Don't let this destroy my kids. Please."

I would also collect all of the hurts and slights and save them for when I was alone. Then I would let myself feel them, and cry and wail for an hour or so. That gave me sanity, and that was the only time when I let myself feel sorry for myself. It gave me the strength to cope.

When the kids realized the normal was gone, which happened pretty quickly, I sat them down and said we were only going to have the basics—food, clothing, shelter—and just barely. Our whole lifestyle changed. They were forced to grow up in a hurry. The one thing I would not compromise, however, was school. They all went to Catholic schools. I felt the only thing I could give them was an education, and I wanted the best. I also let my children know I was there for them no matter what, and that I was praying hard for them (in between yelling at God).

For the first time in my life, I knew I had to take care of myself. I found a weekly support group that was for dumpers and dumpees. I heard things that I needed to hear, listening to how others were dealing with the chaos. In the aftermath of an abandonment, friends and family either rush to help or totally ignore you. Some crazy stuff is said. Two of my sisters said they would each take a kid and give them a great life. They wanted to make my life easier, but it felt like they were ripping my heart out. I let them know that these were my kids and that I would raise them. (That is just one example of how family means to be helpful but really can't be. You have to find people you trust and who understand you, without getting emotional about the situation. Luckily, I also had two dear friends who were there for me.)

Helping my kids was harder. I steeled myself not to react to all of the things that they said when they returned from seeing their father. They had new people in their life and were exposed to so much that was unhealthy and immoral. The emotions and anger would just flow out of them. It was agonizing to give them the freedom just to vent—and for me not to say anything. One of the worst things was that my precious children didn't rate much with their dad anymore. New kids did. There was a lot of pain and confusion and bewilderment.

Unfortunately, my parish didn't have too much to offer. But for the first time, my pastor and I had more than a superficial relationship. He couldn't ignore the changes in my family because it was so public. My husband converted to Catholicism after our first child was born, and we were involved in everything. Then, suddenly, the kids and I were still there and my husband was gone. At the school, there were subtle changes in how the teachers started to treat my kids; they weren't as nice or supportive as they had been before the divorce. I never knew how to stand up for myself, but I learned to fight for my kids and to be there for them in a more visible way.

What helped to heal? There was a program for kids of divorce that was just getting started here when my kids needed it. My pastor helped me bring the program to the parish, and I trained the teachers and volunteers. Kids met during lunch once a week and shared their pain, things like: *I waited two hours and dad didn't show up; I don't like where he lives; his girlfriend is mean to me; no one remembered my birthday.* There was total confidentiality and trust. I would wince thinking about what my kids might be sharing in their group, but it was healing. This is truth: If you don't let kids get the emotions and pain and confusion out, they will act out. Either now or (as so often happens) when they get older. There is no getting around it.

There was another life-saving program that held long weekends for kids to share what their life is like with the divorce. There they found their strengths and got some perspective on their lives. Hope started to grow a little, and my kids were involved with that program for many years.

Here's another cliché fact. Kids lose respect for parents during a divorce. They don't want to hear anything from you. It is critical to find people who understand what the children are going through, with whom they feel comfortable and can be honest. Kids listen to each other, also, so encourage good and virtuous friendships.

As teens, my kids were involved in a solid parish youth group, and in my heart I know it made a difference in their faith. They met solid kids who paid attention to their spiritual life. One of the great blessings in my family is that five of my children, now all grown, attend Mass faithfully. One of my sons is a priest. I know his childhood has greatly influenced his ministry. My kids are strong, joyous, faithful people; they are funny and kind and loving. My grandchildren are precious and have good parents. I am eternally grateful for that.

Here is the most important part: I believe that my children's faith and stable lives have to do with the fact that I stood for my marriage. I never broke my vow and I kept the faith, even when their father didn't. I believe this made a huge impression on my kids, to witness one parent who would not be unfaithful. There is great grace that comes from staying true to your vows, "in good times and in bad," as I swore before God at His altar.

I knew when I got married that my vows were for life. I accept the hardship and suffering that comes with that promise. When I was young, I adopted two life mottos: "bloom where you are planted" and "actions speak louder than words." They are not always easy to live out, but my precious God, at whom I rarely get mad anymore, has blessed me more than I deserve. Someone once told me that if you do divorce right, you look back and bless that time. I feel very blessed. [54]

The court magistrate had just surprised my wife Marie by awarding me three overnights with our daughter. Soon after, when my wife was leaving our house after the drop-off, heading for her new apartment, our three-year-old daughter stunned us both by placing her mother's hand into mine. What an incredible way to communicate her primal need!

It was 23 years ago when Marie, my first and only bride, moved out without cause. She said she just didn't love me anymore. Neither of us was guilty of chemical dependency, infidelity, or abusive behavior.

Thirty years ago, we met at a Catholic young adult retreat that Marie co-led. We eventually took part in an engagement encounter, met with a counselor, and, after completing a Couple-to-Couple League class on Natural Family Planning, we married. The priest celebrant at our nuptial Mass was a friend of hers. After the wedding, Marie taught in our parish school while I continued my education and struggled with a middle-school teaching career.

In our third year of marriage, we were overjoyed when our doctor confirmed the life in Marie's womb. While our daughter was being delivered that summer, my mother-in-law commented how attentive I was to her daughter and said, "God must know what he is doing."

I was perplexed by Marie's subsequent unhappiness. Marie complained I wasn't providing an adequate income, even though we had purchased a new four-bedroom home. We endured some financial strain while Marie stayed home with our baby. We would mildly disagree on how to raise our precious daughter.

A year or so after our daughter was born, I spoke to Marie about conceiving a second child; she refused, saying I needed a more stable job. At my wife's suggestion, we went to both individual and joint psychotherapy. The second or third therapist was a priest/psychotherapist who later told me that Marie thought the sessions were a waste of time. Marie continued with a female psychotherapist who later told me that neither Marie nor I made much of an effort to work on our relationship. I agree. For example, when we discussed an issue at home for a few minutes, my wife would say, "We're not getting anywhere," and would go to bed early. Meanwhile, I was focused on finding a career and making more money. Truthfully, we each had gone to counseling not to change ourselves, but wanting to change the other.

Soon after, at a Marriage Encounter weekend, my wife announced that she did not like, love, or respect me. Devastated and shocked, I could barely finish the weekend. She later cancelled the Retrouvaille weekend that we had planned to attend.

At this point, I desperately sought help in our parish and diocesan communities. I wrote my diocesan marriage tribunal and pleaded for their assistance. A nun in the office said it was "silly" to contact the tribunal before the divorce was final. But what an opportune time to counsel us on marital validity, I thought.

Our parish priest/psychotherapist, according to Marie, had told her, "If you have done everything you can, you should divorce him." I later confronted him about what he had said, to no avail. Later, our pastor said, repeatedly, "It takes two to tango." He referred us to a psychologist who, within minutes of our only appointment, said essentially, "You guys are emotionally divorced anyway; you ought to just go ahead with it." I was stunned and shell-shocked. We had a very salvageable marriage, and my priests never mentioned the resulting trauma our daughter would face.[1]

When I was served with divorce papers a few months later, we still lived and dined together in our nice home, and we even attended Mass together on Sundays. I agreed to sell our house (something I regret now, but which would have been forced by the court anyway), and our realtor even commented how "civil" we seemed to be with each other in the middle of a divorce.

When the courtroom battle began, Marie insisted I should only have custody of our daughter for one overnight a week, even though I had always been very involved in our daughter's daily life and was not an abusive or dangerous father in any way. Marie, who was forcing me out of her life, was also forcing me out of our daughter's life. The stress was overwhelming.

That August, after we'd been married almost six years, I reluctantly signed our divorce papers, which stated, among other things, that Marie and I had "irreconcilable differences." It was a lie, but her attorney and mine conveyed to me that I might lose what custody I had with our daughter if I fought the system. It was such a painful dilemma. This is a poignant example of why the Church, acting only within the truths of Catholicism, should adjudicate such matters.

The following year, Marie began seeing another man and informed me that the same priest/psychotherapist had told her she was "free to date." I had to confront that priest, and he gave me his weak rationale, that "she needs to develop a social network." I reported this to the bishop, with no result. The priest/psychotherapist also told me to "emotionally detach from her" without ever stating the truth that we were still married in the eyes of the Church. The pain of Marie's rejection was agonizing enough, but to witness such dissent from Church teaching from other Catholics in authority….I was so devastated. How could any clergyman or layperson assume that God had not joined us together?

Eventually, the annulment petition and request for my testimony arrived. I asked the director of the tribunal to implement canon 1676 (reconciliation) and he refused, citing the fact that my wife was already dating. I sensed so much weakness in my clergy then—and, sadly, I still do. Why did he refer to me as Marie's "former spouse," and use her maiden name? This wording contradicted canon 1060, which states that validity of marital consent is assumed, unless proven otherwise. By exercising my right to a Roman Rota review of our case, Marie said to me, "You are in the way of my happiness." She withdrew her petition. (Thirteen years later, Marie asked me if I would continue to be an obstacle, and she re-petitioned, unsuccessfully, for nullity.)

At one point, my young daughter told me that Mom's boyfriend had spent the night. You can imagine what feelings that brings up in a husband and a father. Later, Marie's dad, a third order Franciscan, shockingly said he thought Marie would have a difficult time finding another husband since she now had a newly born son, out-of-wedlock. I was devastated when Marie informed me. I again confronted the psychotherapist priest who seemed to be maintaining a close friendship with her. I spoke to him of Marie's out-of-wedlock child on the heels of his previous counsel that she was "free to date." He retorted that I was "evil" and "malicious." I appealed to the diocesan Vicar General who counseled me to "get on with my life." How unbelievable!

Adding salt to an already deep wound, the civil court allowed Marie to move our daughter to another state. The courts respect the free movement of the custodial parent more than keeping a dad close to his child. I thought to myself: My number one job in life is to be a dad; so, I quit my stable and enjoyable job and reluctantly moved to the same Texas neighborhood as my wife and daughter. I now counsel dads to do the same, but I am always amazed that they won't. While living down there, where I didn't even want to live, Marie told me to take my ring off and stop appealing to the Roman Rota. Who influenced my spouse to think and say such things? I am at a loss for words to describe the pain I have felt. And, tragically, but not surprisingly, our adult daughter no longer practices the Faith.

Virtually every Church leader I knew did not understand why I had appealed to the Rota. A deacon had considered me to be "obsessed" with my wife. A layman said I was too "legalistic." An Army chaplain labeled me as "arrogant." A deacon told me that if mass murderers can be forgiven, why not divorcées who contract another union? When I thought I had heard it all, one of my pastors in Texas said I was "blackmailing" my wife. And yet, doesn't the "hardness of your hearts," sadly, still exist today?

I often meet attractive women. But if I date, I would be violating canon law and the *Catechism*, and I would be disobeying Jesus—who was so adamant against divorce (Matthew 19) that his disciples proclaimed it not expedient to get married. Dating would be a "near occasion of sin." How could I receive Holy Communion, if I do? And so, after all these years, I continue to stand for my marriage, just as I vowed to do so many years ago at the altar. I do so only by His grace, as I could never do this on my own strength, without Him and His Church. I pray that our daughter will one day see me and her mother walking hand-in-hand. [55]

I am standing for my marriage. As heart-wrenching as this ordeal has been, it has become a unique journey towards eternal glory. Years after the initial trauma of abandonment, the story of my fidelity in utter destruction can be told with perspective.

They say time heals all wounds, but I have found that time has simply and graciously placed a distance between myself and my husband's abandonment. Dealing with a loss is not a race to the finish line or even a clean, step-by-step process. Grief will take you two steps forward, one step back...and just when you think you've progressed enough, you'll be back where you started. This grief is distinctive—one cannot fully mourn an abandoner-spouse because his body continues to live. The emotional roller coaster of ever-changing circumstances affects the grieving process.

How we perceive our marriage, and the choice to truly love, will greatly depend on which side of the story we're living.

On the morning of yet another wedding anniversary, as the sun arose after the darkest of nights, I turned towards my husband's side of the bed in the desperate hope that he would be there—that this nightmare would be over. But, alas, this nightmare was still in the beginning stages. Where once stood a commitment to our marriage vows, there was now a sense of insistent disposal, a rejection of me as his spouse.

The trauma of being a discarded wife instigated the fight-or-flight reflex. Early on, I was given the grace to realize that, as unnatural as this division was, I could not fight my husband or force his will. Even though he chose to actively destroy our marriage, I had to find another way to react. My goal was not only possibly to keep him from leaving, but it was *most* importantly to keep me—and our children—intact as we survived through this period. Flight, to a degree, was also not an option; I cannot run from myself, and this man is my other half, my one and only. To run away from our marriage would be to abandon my partner in a fire. In birth, a similar dilemma occurs: Fighting the contractions makes the pain worse and can cause a longer labor; there are medications to distract from the pain, but nothing aside from birth ends the contractions.

During this process, one can *accept, detach,* and *appreciate* that which cannot be controlled. God is in charge. Applying these concepts have allowed me to survive and grow.

To *accept* what is happening is to consent to acknowledge my sheer lack of control—my inability to change what is occurring. If he stays, it is by the grace of God; if he leaves, I trust that God has a plan. How difficult it is to give God the steering wheel to your life! Especially because you don't just humble yourself once, you must do it daily!

To *detach* is a choice to let go, to choose not to be attached to consequences you can't control. To choose not to carry the burden of sin that your spouse has chosen. That is your spouse's story, *not* yours. Do not allow yourself to use your precious energy carrying a load that will not be fruitful. For example, the intimate details of your husband's (or wife's) sins are truly none of your business. It is easy to feel entitled to all sorts of information without considering its effects on yourself and others. Scripture clearly illustrates the folly of this grasping entitlement, in the choice that Eve made when she took that fateful bite. Once you choose knowledge of that which is not yours to know, its effects on you will be limitless. What if, instead, we choose to reject that which will not edify our lives? For example, my attorney could focus on the evidence for a legal case without my reading the details; I could ask that certain names and faces be covered so as to keep me focused on my goals. Such is a practice of self-discipline that not only will help with survival, but also offer a sense of peace that one might only find in the Garden of Eden.

Lastly, the *appreciation* step is the most crucial, and it is the one you will recall the most as you heal. My choice was to give myself over completely in love for my husband during this time. Many widows do not receive the privilege of knowing when they are about to lose their spouse. In my trauma of abandonment, I was gifted a very special opportunity to know that my time to love and serve my husband directly was coming to an end. I treated each day like it would be my last with him. I did not focus on the painful sin, but rather on this favor I was granted. And for that time, I'm eternally grateful. I remember vividly our last hug, telling him I'd love him forever, and the tears that fell as I laid out his clothes one last time, knowing full well he might not ever come back home. Everything that I might have taken for granted, I chose to cherish deeply. Why waste such pain on fighting?

Allow this suffering to bring out a purpose. There is nothing greater than to love and to lay down one's life for another, especially the one to whom we have made our exclusive promises before God.

The time to process emotions in this journey comes *after* the certainty that we have survived the initial trauma. That is when we build the foundation of our resilience and find the tools, through God's grace, to tackle what is to come. To process our emotions properly for healing to occur we must do so in view of heaven and with the use of our God-given reason. Through reason inspired by faith, we know that moving forward in life is not the same as the cultural idea of "moving on" with a new partner. Society would like us to believe that adding more distraction to our life will make coping easier. We are vulnerable and faced with the temptation to find fulfillment and comfort in life with another individual—but the fact is that we were created to be fulfilled by God.

Our union with our spouse, through the sacrament of marriage, is our *duty* not our fulfillment. Through reason, it is clear that "moving on" is a deception and a distraction. It also cultivates a lack of trust in God to believe that He can no longer work through the sacrament of your marriage. As Job learned in his trials, who are we to decide that? Through the tools we gain in processing what has happened, we are able to build the life that God intends for us to live right now. We cannot control others—nor should we wish to—but we can choose to keep proper perspective on our lives. A strong lesson I have learned in all this is to practice "Servitude in Gratitude not Bad Attitude." Grief, properly understood, will cause one to understand the limitations of time and this passing world. To bring purpose to our suffering is to reduce the waste and despair to which grief tempts us.

Live your life for the day that you will be brought Home and be told, "Well done, good and faithful servant; now enter into the joy of your master." [56]

My parents' story is not finalized yet, and I still have hope for them. I'm not sure if it's the kind of story you would like to include in this book, but I figured I would share it anyway.

My parents first separated when I was 11, reunited when I was 13, then separated again when I was 20. The first separation came as a complete shock to me and my younger brother and sister. Our parents sat us down in the living room and told us my dad would be moving out of the house. They told us they were doing this for our own sake, because they wanted what was best for us. I did not understand then what they meant, and I still don't understand today. All I wanted to say was, "Don't do it! If you love us, stay!"

Up until that moment, I remember my childhood as being "perfect." We lived in my parents' hometown with both extended families nearby, and we went on holidays with our aunts, uncles, and cousins. I am so happy we enjoyed those times, and I truly believe that I was later saved by the memories I have of those innocent, carefree years.

But for the next two years, I became isolated. I withdrew to a world of books. I refused to make friends. I felt so insecure, unworthy, and anxious. My mother was so depressed that she hardly had any energy left for us kids. I felt completely abandoned. As the eldest, I felt that I was in charge of my siblings. But I was only 11 years old, and I could not do much; this frustrated me greatly. I wished that I could alleviate their pain somehow, but of course I couldn't. At that young age, I decided that I would never get married, and that I would absolutely never have children. I was determined never to put a child through the misery of conditional love.

After being separated for two years, my parents reunited. On the first morning after our dad moved back in, my siblings and I woke up with great joy, and, as we were all having breakfast together, we said this was "the best day of our life!" Then, the next day at the breakfast table, we declared, "No, *this* is the best day of our life!" We were so happy to see them together, and we were thrilled when my father could visit my maternal grandparents' house again—even if it was awkward between him and my grandfather. I always appreciated my grandmother's ability to forgive and to be courteous with my dad. I resented my grandfather a little for not making it easier on all of us.

At some point after my parents' reunion, we all realized that something had been broken during the time they were separated. After the initial thrill subsided, everything got worse. While there was never any physical (or even verbal) abuse, they became experts at ignoring and blaming each other. As I got older, my mother started confiding in me, telling me everything about my father and his sins. My father himself openly told me detailed stories about women he'd been with prior to meeting my mom. The stories he revealed were a huge shock to me.

Around that time, my sister developed a serious eating disorder.

When I was 17, we all traveled to a rehabilitation center and left her there. I remember her being carried away, as she cried and stretched her thin arms out to me asking me to help her. It broke my heart to see my family in pieces again. My father openly blamed my mother for my sister's disease, and all of this reaffirmed my desire never to marry or have children.

Things went steadily downhill from there, and, two years later, my mother gathered us and told us that she had asked my father to leave. At that point, I was a 20-year-old college student and dating the man who is now my husband; he was a devout Catholic man, and I had returned to the Church. Even though I was an adult, I still wept like a small child when my mother told us the news. I was afraid that my boyfriend, who came from a very stable and loving family, would leave me. Around that time, it became evident that my brother had developed a serious drug and alcohol problem. And, during this second separation, my father began dating another woman (whom we have all refused to meet).

Throughout this second tearing apart of my family, I was truly blessed to have the support of my boyfriend. Instead of leaving me as I feared he would, he suggested that we pray the rosary every Saturday for my parents' marriage. It felt like such a hopeless endeavor at the time, but seven years later, I can see that it has borne fruit.

Little by little, everyone in my family has returned to the Church. Even my father, who had never been religious, now goes to Mass every single Sunday. My parents thank my husband and me for being a good example for my brother and sister, who have both overcome their disorders. Now that I have children—their grandchildren—my parents have grown closer together. In the past year, we all traveled together as a family for the first time. And while my father is still seeing his girlfriend, he tells us he will never be married again and that he's realized he will never be able to love someone as he loved my mother. My mother tells us she will never marry again and sees my father as her husband, until death parts them. They have even purchased burial plots next to each other; I could not believe it when they told me!

My father has started visiting my mother's home, and he offers to help fix things that are broken. He reassures her and us that he will take care of her forever. When I asked him why he never divorced my mother, he said he could not bring himself to do it. And, my mother has lately shared that she deeply regrets asking my father to leave seven years ago. Both of them, I think, have come to regret having separated. They regret not fighting for their marriage.

To this day, I offer every sacrifice and every Mass for their marriage. And while they still have a long way to go, and there is still suffering, it is my deep and long-held hope that one day soon they will be reunited for good. After so many years, I think the Lord is giving all of us reasons to hope, too. [57]

This is my story of standing loyally for the sacrament of matrimony.

I met my husband in high school, and we had been dating for two years when we decided to get married. We both came from strong Catholic families, and both sets of parents ended up being married for 50+ years. There was no hesitation in marrying my husband; I knew without doubt that he was the man I wanted to spend the rest of my life with. We were inseparable almost from the time we met.

We got married in college in 1986, and our first years together consisted of building a foundation for our future together. After graduation, my husband went on to complete his law degree. We were married for 19 years before the divorce, and we have six children together.

There were some years that were very difficult for us, most notably the year our third child, a son, was born and died. His death changed each of us in very different ways. The years after his death were difficult, but we survived and we grew in the journey of grief.

At Christmas 2003, my husband came up to me and said, "I know this doesn't make any sense, but I'm not happy and I'm leaving." Our living children were two, three, five, eight, and 12 years old at the time. I was shocked. I never thought he would break up our family, the family we had worked so hard to create. Yes, we were going through a rough patch in our relationship, and yes, life was so busy that we didn't take enough time to focus on us. But I never imagined he would leave us.

We spent the next four months in marriage counseling. My husband moved back in our home, and we tried to repair our relationship; however, he had already emotionally moved on. He was in a relationship with his secretary—a relationship that I did not know about at the time. He moved out for good in April 2004 and filed for divorce.

After lengthy deliberation and a court trial, the divorce was finalized in 2005 on the exact date we had buried our son years earlier. The death of our son, and now the death of our marriage.

My husband went on to live with several women, and he ultimately "married" one of them in a civil ceremony. Having to send our children to my husband's new house with his new lover was very hard for me. Exposing our children to adultery was so wrong, but I was forced by the court to send them to his house for visitation.

In 2012, my husband filed for an annulment. The annulment process, like the divorce process, was long and difficult. The tribunal's decision (negative) led to my husband's appeal to the Roman Rota, the highest tribunal in the Church. In 2019, we received the final decision from the Roman Rota—negative. Our marriage was and is valid.

I had always felt in my heart that our marriage was valid. I've never felt it was right to consider another relationship, and I have always kept myself open to the possibility of reconciliation—and I always will.

I am a "stander" because I know it's the right thing to do. It's the right thing for my husband, my children, and my grandchildren, and it's the right thing for my eternal life. [58]

This is the story of my mother standing for her marriage.

I am the youngest of ten children. When I was seven years old, my dad left my mother with five children still at home. They were married for 25 years.

My dad was an alcoholic who quit drinking before I was born. He spent decades attending Alcoholics Anonymous. My parents emigrated from Canada in the 1950s to escape the alcoholism in my dad's family, but he could not escape the dysfunction.

We were poor. My father worked hard outside the home, and my mother worked hard caring for us and making very little go a long way. She always had dinner on the table when Dad came home from work, and she always made sure that he had the best plate. They were faithful Catholics, and we attended Mass regularly and went to Catholic school. It was a normal thing to have priests over for dinner.

My parents lost two boys—one at age six and one at two weeks old —and I don't think they ever recovered from these traumatic losses.

We all had a different experience when my father left, and this is still obvious today, almost 45 years later. I was the "baby" and had been very protected when I was young. With four older sisters, I had a few "mothers." When Dad left, however, the bottom dropped out, and it was mayhem. My mother cried all the time, and I promised her that I would never make her cry like some of my older siblings did. I decided that it was my job to make her happy, and, ultimately, to protect her.

Unfortunately, there wasn't anyone to protect me after a while. I needed a mom and a dad, but that structure was gone. I had to figure out a lot of things for myself. Thankfully, my mother's prayers and my Catholic faith saved me. My faith is vital to my emotional health, my marriage, and every aspect of my life.

My dad "married" a woman who was an alcoholic. They did not stay married for long. After that second civil divorce, he sought an annulment for the marriage to my mother, telling my mother that he wanted to remarry in the Church. He was granted that annulment and was married to his third wife in the Catholic Church in the early 1980s. He asked me to be in his wedding, and I wanted to please him; I didn't feel I could refuse him. This event, however, threw me over the edge. It would take me ten more years to decide to forgive him for everything. Staying angry had made me sick. Forgiving him was the beginning of my healing, and it may have saved my own marriage.

My mother has never been one to speak poorly of my dad, but instead tended to defend him because of his terribly abusive and neglectful upbringing. Before my dad passed, he met with my mom to apologize for the pain that he had caused her, as he carried a tremendous amount of guilt. (His favorite saint was St. Jude, the patron of impossible causes.) She continued to remain faithful to the vows she made to him so many years before.[2] She never dated anyone after he left. She had to pick herself up and keep going for our sake. Mom worked very hard to keep me in Catholic school for as long as she could, and she went to college to better support us. My mother is a brave lady, and it is thanks to her strong faith and commitment that I am a Catholic today.

Divorce is a terrible legacy to leave one's family, and I will fight to avoid it at all costs. [59]

My husband and I met on a popular Catholic dating website in 1999. He wrote me a charming note, but I wasn't initially interested (and I noticed he had a "divorced, received Church annulment" by his profile). Still, we wrote back and forth and eventually met about a month after our first correspondence. The relationship progressed faster than I was comfortable with, but at the same time, I was eager to get married and have a family—a natural and normal desire placed in us by God.

He came home with me for Thanksgiving, proposed in December, and, as I wanted a long engagement, we set the date for October 14. Due to a job layoff and having to relocate the wedding to my husband's home town, the date was changed to October 13. This, of course, is the anniversary of the Miracle of the Sun at Fatima, and the apparition of Our Lady. When another Catholic friend mentioned the significance of the date, I simply thought, "Cool!" I had no idea that, later on, this date and Fatima itself would be full of meaning for me.

Our marriage was rocky from the start. My husband had a very broken and tragic childhood, and divorce, alcoholism, and suicide had all impacted his young life. He never had the model of a loving marriage nor a father who could teach him how to be a man. He had a broken and sinful past, a failed attempted marriage (he had a defect of form annulment because his first wedding was outside the Church), and, although baptized Catholic, he was raised Protestant and had never received First Communion or Confirmation.

He was a new Catholic convert, ready to be on-fire for the Lord, and I was a stubborn and independent woman, not ready to be submissive or let go of control (especially of finances, as I saw the recklessness of his past expenditures). There were many fights. He had a bad temper and punched a hole in the wall, which scared me. We went on a Marriage Encounter weekend and were in marriage counseling before the end of our first year. Nothing really helped.

But vows are vows, and eventually we had children, who brought us joy and a new focus. Things weren't great, but they became routine, and life was simply busy with children.

Over the years, I noticed he started drinking more often. Our fights became more frequent, and although we went on a Retrouvaille retreat out of town, we were unable to complete the aftercare program. I have learned that there are precious few solid Catholic resources or counselors to help couples in crisis.

At that point, we moved to a new state, as my restless husband found a new job with what he thought were greener pastures. The move, the new job, and a new pregnancy helped sweep the problems under the rug for a while.

Shortly after the birth of our third child, my mother had a stroke. I took the kids and traveled out of state to care for her for three months while my husband stayed home to work. When we were gone, he became like a bachelor again, drinking, staying up late playing online games, taking advantage of his "freedom." It was an adjustment for him when we came back home, especially because my mother moved into our basement (which needed renovation; that added stress). My husband gradually began spending more time at work, and I'd find alcohol stashed in his trunk, his tool box, and other odd places. Our fighting increased, and, eventually, we were living in the same house but leading two separate lives.

It all came to a head when I was planning an intervention for his drinking. Unbeknownst to me, he was planning to leave. He filed for divorce on May 13, the feast of Our Lady of Fatima, 13 years after we said "I do" on another Fatima anniversary. I searched for meaning in everything so that, as my world crashed around me, I could discern what this Fatima connection might mean for me. What was God trying to tell me? Why was this happening?

At first, I thought for sure I'd go through an annulment and seek happiness and marriage with another man. There was a nice Catholic widower in our circle of friends who had lost his wife to cancer. Surely God wanted me to marry him—how perfect! Her funeral had been October 13, two years prior. That's a sign, right? I wanted to be loved, and I was tired of the fighting, the alcoholism, and what I felt was a miserable marriage.

My world definitely crashed as a result of divorce. I was forced to leave my own home while he had his parenting time; I had to give up homeschooling; I had no money and had to seek employment; I received no alimony (educated women can work and support themselves, according to the system); I had to go to court to fight for the right to send my girls to Catholic schools—which I won by the skin of my teeth, but I had to foot the bill.

Around this time, the Vatican's "Synod on the Family" was happening, and I started to have a glimpse of God's purpose in all of this. During the divorce proceedings, I obtained a statue of Our Lady of Fatima at a Catholic store, and I asked the cashier where I might go to confession. She suggested St. Agnes parish, and I went. On the way out of the church, I grabbed a bulletin, and, lo and behold, there was an announcement for a "Faithful Spouses" support group for those who were separated or divorced.

That group became my lifeline. The witness of some of those ladies helped me to determine that God's will was not for me to pursue annulment, but to remain faithful. Four or five women from that group are still my close friends and confidantes to this day. Sadly, the group no longer exists, but the Lord brought it into my life when I needed it most. In March of that year, the civil divorce was finalized on—you guessed it—the 13th.

Fast forward to today, and it's been about six years since my husband filed for divorce. Two months after the divorce, he remarried civilly. Turns out, he had reconnected with an old flame on Facebook a year or so before he filed, and so he'd been pursuing an adulterous relationship. He has moved out of state and has mostly cut off contact with our children—an occasional email or gift card on a birthday is all they get—and he's also estranged from his family. It's safe to say he is spiritually blind (or in a "spiritual coma," to use Bai Macfarlane's words).[3]

My children are suffering with loss of faith, depression, anxiety, and eating disorders/body dysmorphia. They have a father who rejected them and moved on with another woman; the pain and wounds are deep. As for me, the stress of life now is hard, and my own relationship with my children can be strained. I cling to the Lord and try to keep up my prayer life while balancing work and family. It is a daily struggle, a daily battle.

I wish I had a happily-ever-after story, or a story of reconciliation; I know they have happened. All I know is that God wants me to stay faithful, and not to date or remarry. Recently was our 19th anniversary. I stayed and prayed in the Marian chapel of our church, and I asked for a sign. If we truly had a sacramental marriage, if all of this is not in vain, please, Lord, give me a sign. Immediately when I stood up to leave the church, I saw a rainbow outside the window. Talk about an immediate answer to prayer! Thank you, Lord.

In the notes from our Marriage Encounter so long ago, my husband wrote to me: "I want to be able to look at you and know, as I know the sky is blue, as I know the earth is round, as I know that God exists, that you will *never* give up on our sacrament...."

And I won't.

No, I don't understand all the whys. I have a lot of trials, and there is hardship, tears, suffering. But God is there, and He provides for all of our needs, even if not for all of our wants and desires. He has not abandoned us. All I'm doing is carrying the cross He gave me—to whom shall I go? This faithfulness to my sacred promise is His will. Happiness is not for this world, but for the next, says Our Lady of Lourdes. So, each morning, it is my duty to pray for the graces to live another day and to entrust my children's faith and life into God's hands. Our story is not finished. I don't know what lies ahead. But I know Who will win. [60]

Five years ago, the Lord allowed me to bear the cross of being betrayed by my husband of 20 years. I was shocked to learn that he was having a same-sex affair. I had no clue he had a same-sex attraction. None. He did not disclose this to me before we got married (he'd had same-sex relationships before we met), so I could have easily gotten an annulment and moved on. I didn't. Very clearly, one day, in the midst of my grief, I heard the Lord say, "Stay, stay, stay, stay." So, I stayed.

I continue to wear my ring and welcome him when he comes to see the kids. Our kids have been protected from knowing his secret—he doesn't want them to know. Nor do I. He is a very wounded and confused soul. He's chosen a false identity that has more to do with his wounds than his same-sex attraction. The kids live with me, and they do not go to his house, ever. They did nothing wrong. They deserve to have as much of their lives remain the same as possible. By shielding them from all of this, we give them a decent shot at having a much less complicated and messy life. It's not perfect, but it's a lot better than the alternative.

Only by the grace of God has my mental health remained intact through all of this. By the grace of God, we avoided a divorce. By the grace of God, hope is alive in my heart, as I continue to pray for his conversion and for God's will to be done in our marriage.

The battle for our marriage and family is still being fought. I intend to keep fighting by being faithful to my vows and frequenting the sacraments, which have quite literally sustained me. With God's help, I stand for marriage. I stand for my kids. They are most definitely worth the sacrifice. [61]

My husband proposed to me after I finished praying before Our Lady at the grotto in Notre Dame. It was a little miracle, because I had done countless novenas to the Blessed Mother, praying that we would one day marry. The wedding took place the following year, on the Feast of St. Rita—ironically, the patron saint of troubled marriages.

We were married for 15 years and had three children when my husband filed for civil divorce, and my life has been a living nightmare ever since.

My husband and I argued a lot over various things. Looking back, I can see many reasons for our problems. We used natural family planning to an extreme because of my fear of getting pregnant in my forties; we should have trusted God. We argued over disciplining the kids, and I argued with my teen, which caused stress. I wanted the kids in Catholic high school, and he said I was too controlling. I felt threatened by his tight-knit family when I should have been more accepting of them. I modeled my mom, who argued with my dad all the time. My husband said I did not do my duty in keeping a clean house and meals on the table, but I did my best. The kids were in too many activities, which was another big mistake. *I should have put my husband and my marriage first*, but the culture tells us otherwise. We also spent too much on our two homes and were not good financial stewards. I know now that I should have let so much stuff go. I should have let him lead. And, in retrospect, I now see that the hormonal shifts of peri-menopause also affected my thinking, factoring into my reactions.

But despite our problems, I always considered him my soulmate. My parents fought all the time, but they truly loved one another and were one. I was devastated when I found out, when he filed, that he had been having an affair for two or three years.

In civil divorce court, I was ordered to go to an employability expert. I had been a stay-at-home mom since giving up my career as a practicing civil lawyer to care for my children. The expert's report concluded that I could earn a certain dollar amount a year, and the courts took that number and put it into a formula to determine alimony and child support. The court then granted me alimony in an amount that would not allow me to afford even a three-bedroom apartment after taxes. Our marital home was located in a beautiful, safe neighborhood, and I did not want my kids to go back and forth; I did not want them to lose that stability on top of everything else.

And of course, the reality is that no one wants to hire a lawyer who has not practiced for 20 years, so today I work a service job, making

$18 an hour. Since I cannot afford a home for my children, the kids live with their dad; despite his high salary, I pay him child support. None of this can possibly be in conformity with Divine Law, but this is how no-fault divorce works in our nation. I do stay at the original family home with our children when my husband is at his vacation home or working in the city. Through all the injustice, all I can do is run to the Lord. I can truly say I have never been closer to Jesus—how could I not be? I am right on the cross with Him. My only consolation is that this life is temporary. It will pass.

Before the divorce, we were a church-going family. Our kids were in Catholic school, we attended Sunday Mass, and we prayed the rosary. After the divorce, our children were pulled out of Catholic school, and all three now reject the Catholic faith. My husband has not sought an annulment yet, but he openly dates women in front of our children. Before the civil divorce was finalized, he even took them on a vacation with a girl he was dating and her children.

Despite this, my husband considers himself a good Catholic—although, thank God, his conscience still won't allow him to approach for Communion. I went to my diocese hoping for some pastoral care for myself and fraternal correction for my husband. They refused to do anything, and simply expressed that they were concerned about my "healing." We both received letters stating that the Church was here for us, to support us during this difficult time—as if this divorce was inflicted by some mysterious outside force!

My husband's friend, a deacon, taught a Theology of the Body class that my 13-year-old daughter (unfortunately) attended. She told me that my husband's deacon friend wanted the class to know that divorce is not a sin, that a divorced person is always able to receive Communion if a remarriage has not happened (making no distinction between the abandoned and the abandoner), and that sometimes marriages just don't work out. He went on to say that if you are going to cheat, do your spouse a favor and divorce him or her first. My daughter said that she learned annulments were okay, because if you don't honor and respect your spouse, the marriage was invalid to begin with. There is no end to the scandal of divorce in our Church, and it has been inflicted on my children.

Why am I choosing to remain faithful to my marriage? Like I told the Superior Court judge during the divorce proceedings: "A court cannot break the bonds of marriage any more than it can declare the State of Pennsylvania does not exist." Civil divorce is a forced separation of spouses and the distribution of assets—but the sacrament remains. In marriage, I vowed to hand down the Catholic faith to our children, not a watered-down version of it. Someone needs to witness to my poor kids. It's not going to be my husband, and, sadly, it will not be the diocese, nor even friends in our faith community.

In a strange way, I feel blessed that our dear Lord has found me worthy to follow the path of St. Thomas More in this day and time. There is no doubt in my mind that by remaining faithful to the sacrament, graces from that sacrament will be transmitted to my husband and our three children. How could a wife and mother ever pass that up? I keep before my mind my husband's salvation. I was not always the wife that my husband deserved and that God wanted me to be. Like every sinner, I cannot change the past. However, it is a comfort knowing that by offering my prayers and sufferings for my husband, that may be what it takes to bring about his conversion and bring him back to the sacraments. If he is ultimately saved because of this, then "mission accomplished!" In the end, then, "in God's eyes," I will have proven to be a good and true wife. [62]

I have been married to a beautiful woman for over 24 years, and we have four children, ages 22 down to seven. Over the years, we have had our issues. As an engineer, I am more of a "fixer" than a listener, and I have battled with anxiety; my wife has struggled with financial overspending and has been treated for depression for about 20 years. The death of her mom and dad brought on a midlife crisis and resurrected family-of-origin issues.

My wife and I met at a Catholic university, and I asked her out after Mass one day. We dated for a year, got engaged, then married a year-and-a-half later. Our first child soon arrived, along with the first bout of the "baby blues" and depression for my wife. Our second child was born about four years after the first, and my wife became a homeschooling mom. Eight years after our second child, our third child was born. Our first, brief separation happened at that point, which lasted about six weeks. She said she wanted more "spark" or "us time," and I suspect postpartum depression played a part. After we reconciled, she renewed her love for me and said she did not want to get to that place again.

About two years later, we had our fourth and last child. Right around that time, her father died suddenly, and her mom developed cancer. Her dad's death was hard on everyone, and a lot of time was spent with her mom, trying to keep things organized.

My wife's brother had an extramarital affair within a year of their father's death, which greatly saddened my wife. To add to the overwhelming stress, my wife's mom had a stroke, which afterwards required therapy and constant care. Her mother lived two hours away from us, and I took many days off work to care for our children so that my wife could travel to help with her mom's many healthcare needs.

My wife's depression combined with traveling to care for her mother was impacting our marriage and family. In addition to the mental illness, stress of separation, and care-taking burdens, there were extra financial burdens on our family, as we didn't have the funds to cover all the costs of travel and being away. I continued to provide for the family as best I could, while trying to cover the day-to-day family things my wife was unable to do. Her coming and going from home was unpredictable, which made planning with the kids and their activities very difficult.

When my mother-in-law's cancer recurred, she decided not to fight medically any longer, and she died six months later. This was hard on all of us, but especially on my wife. She became very distant and started sleeping on the couch more and more. She'd had issues in the past with gastroesophageal reflux disease (GERD), and sleeping on the couch was one way she dealt with that. I had a secret fear that her mom's death might impact my wife the way her dad's death had impacted her brother (i.e., being tempted to an affair), but I shook it off, thinking that could never happen to us.

A few months after her mom's death, we got word that my wife would be receiving a sizable inheritance. She decided to use it on a "mommy makeover"—tummy tuck and breast reduction—at the same time as our daughter's tonsil removal. She wanted me to take the other kids out of town for Christmas at my parents' house, which would have left her home without post-surgical care for both herself and our daughter. About this same time, I found out that my wife was having emotional affairs via Facebook and texting. I was devastated.

I started to see a counselor to talk about this. My anxiety was going up, and I sought help for it. For the next nine months, my wife told me she loved me but was not "in love" with me anymore. She did not want to work on our marriage and would not talk to the counselor; she only wanted to talk about a divorce all the time, and how to do it.

We took a weekend away where our discussions included a deeper revelation of her emotional affair, which she told me a lot about. I would try to steer the discussion toward reconciliation, but that never worked, and a couple of times I mentioned that by seeking a divorce, she was being hypocritical—we are both cradle Catholics, and we should not have been talking about divorce at all.

The cross of living day-to-day in a house with someone who had checked out of our marriage was hard. She started being more secretive in her illicit conversations and locked her phone so no one else could use it.

I talked to our local priest, and he stated that it would be difficult for my wife to get to heaven without me, and that the chances of her going to hell would increase if she abandoned the marriage. So, one night after that conversation, I told my wife that I was not going to participate in any discussion about divorce anymore, and that I was not going to hell for her.

My wife waited until the school year, Father's Day, and my birthday were over (she was cold and disrespectful during those two events), and then at about this time, she transferred money from our joint bank account to an account of her own. I was served divorce papers at work at 4:15 on Friday. The locks to our house had been changed, and she and the kids had gone to her brother's for a few days. My stuff was on the back porch in bags. Since filing, my wife bought a motorcycle (she'd never had one before), got a new car, and got her nose pierced—all of which seems tied to a midlife crisis.

Becoming closer to Christ has given me some wisdom and understanding as to what is going on, and God has told me to stand for my marriage until death, which I plan to do, just as I promised the day I made my wedding vow. [63]

For our 25th wedding anniversary, Frank and I renewed our wedding vows in Rome. Four years later, he said he wanted to move out because he needed time alone. He told me that he was willing to go to counseling, but only as long as I understood that his purpose was simply to help me accept my new situation peacefully; he was not interested in working to keep our marriage together.

My husband had always seemed to be the kind of man who cared about his Catholic faith and Church teaching. Prior to his leaving our low-conflict marriage, he frequently attended daily Mass and had a subscription to *Magnificat*. Our daughter is a religious sister who wears a full traditional habit, and when she took her final vows, my husband posted on Facebook, "I expect to get along well with my new son-in-law." My husband knew that Jesus was our daughter's Spouse.

After he left our home, I searched the internet and found an organization, Mary's Advocates, that upholds marriage and fights against no-fault divorce. Although it was affirming, I had no desire to join with "divorced people," because I didn't want to be divorced and my husband hadn't even filed. However, I downloaded a canon-law-based petition from Mary's Advocates[4] so that I could write to my bishop, asking him to instruct my spouse that he had an obligation to try to reconcile, reminding him that marriage is permanent.

To my shock, rather than upholding marriage, the diocese stabbed me in the heart and chastised *me*, and not my husband. In a stunningly condescending letter, the monsignor essentially told me to accept the death of my marriage and move on. He was very clear that if I did not move on, I would be causing harm to myself and others, and setting a bad example of marriage for those around me. I still can't fathom why a representative from the diocese would respond like this, but I've come to understand that it's not uncommon.

Around the same time that I wrote the bishop, my husband filed for divorce. I naïvely thought that both parties had to apply for or consent to the divorce. I did not realize that no-fault divorce could be obtained even if the other party—an innocent party—didn't want it.

Annulment was suggested by some, but after doing my own research, I am even more confident that we have a valid marriage. At the time of our marriage preparation, the diocese had us take a compatibility test, and Frank and I each scored 100%, to our mutual delight. Our diocese had a stringent premarital investigation in which the priest had us answer questions, under oath, to affirm our understanding of marriage. In our marriage prep records, our signed oaths tell the truth that we knew what we were doing: "With God as your witness, do you swear to tell the truth in answering the questions that I shall now ask you?" Frank swore that he believed marriage was permanent and requires fidelity. We married when Frank was 23 years old and a successful career man. Early on in our marriage, he got a Ph.D. at an Ivy League university and thereafter became a professor. I know he was very capable of understanding what he was doing for something as natural and universal as marriage.

After my husband's divorce petition was granted, I started to become sensitive to the way our culture undermines marriage when it uses terminology such as, "I'm single again." I'll never say, "I'm single." I'll admit that we are *civilly* divorced, then clarify that I *am* married but my husband separated from me. I now participate in monthly support phone conference calls with Mary's Advocates, and I learned a great way to explain my situation from another caller: "The state didn't marry me; it can't un-marry me." During the calls, we use the book, *The Gift of Self: A Spiritual Companion for Separated and Divorced Faithful to the Sacrament of Marriage*, by Maria Pia Campanella, to help us carry our unique and lonely cross. Unlike in times past, even most priests today have never met someone wanting to remain faithful to a spouse after being abandoned.

My husband is in a spiritual coma. My children are confused, wanting each of us to be happy. I tell them that I know love is a choice, and that feelings come and go. They don't understand why I don't "move on." I believe that my husband has been grooming my children for the secular path, introducing my children to his paramour, and then civilly marrying her a couple of months ago. Frank contacted me via email to tell me that he was engaged, and that he didn't want the children to have to keep it a secret. I responded in truth: "How can you be engaged if you are still married to me?" I asked him not to invite our young adult children to this ceremony legalizing his adultery. Our children, having been put into an impossible position and one which requires them to ignore Christ's teaching, seem to have accepted the paramour, because they want their father to be happy.

Many women my age who have been forcibly divorced are out in the field looking for a new boyfriend. I can empathize with why someone would do that; after all, I don't like being alone, and I don't want this cross—but I will accept this cross. Some days are better than others, and my faith is the only thing upon which I know I can rely. However, I feel like I have been given an ultimatum: either accept the truth of my reality as a married separated woman, or embrace the post-Christian culture's perspective that I am single again and free to find a new partner. I can't embrace the post-Christian lies. My children are watching, and I need to give them a good example of marital love so that, if they ever find themselves getting married, they recognize that marriage is permanent and that it doesn't end just because one is unhappy.

If Frank had cooperated with the counselors that I was seeing who are pro-family, we could still be together today. When all of this was happening, I had discovered catholictherapists.com, where all of the therapists are committed to an authentically Catholic understanding of marriage (including permanence and fidelity), and we had attended Retrouvaille, a program for marriages on the brink of divorce. Sadly, Frank's heart was already hardened. I believe he had decided on a civil divorce months before he even told me he was moving out. To illustrate how disastrous many Catholic responses to troubled marriages are, one "Catholic" counselor who worked with us (before I found catholictherapists.com) suggested a separation plan as follows: 1) continue to go to counseling, and 2) agree to let the other spouse know if you start dating. I pondered, "How can we work on our marriage if one spouse is breaking the sixth commandment, and why didn't the counselor object to a married man dating someone else?"

I know that Christ will never abandon me. I know that God hates divorce (Malachi 2:16) and that it is never His will. My spouse has a free will and has used it to perpetrate an evil upon me and upon our family. My continued prayer is that Frank's heart will soften, and that he will return to the sacraments and his true wife. I trust in the Lord, and I hope to pray my spouse into heaven. My faith has gotten me through this, and I shall stay faithful to my vows and never withdraw my unconditional love for my husband. [64]

I end with a most transcendent story, originally written as a Facebook post by Regina Vivanco, the sister of a new widow, Denise Jordan, whose husband Sean had just died. I've edited for clarity and more details, but the point-of-view stands. Here we see what miracles of grace can occur when a spouse remains faithful to the very end. When we remain patient and prayerful, when we rely solely on the Lord and carry the cross we are given, and when we don't end the story in the middle, God shows forth His most beautiful plan.[5]

I had the privilege of witnessing, firsthand, God's love and mercy given to one who remained faithful and prayerful for many, many years. For those who know my sister Denise, they know she has worn her wedding ring for the past 29 years, faithfully committed to the covenant she made with her husband and God. Even though she has really been a single mother for the past 13+ years (as Sean left her for a life of sin and addiction), she has always prayed for him and believed that one day, if God willed it, her husband's soul would be saved. On her 20th wedding anniversary, I asked her what she did that day. She said she went to Adoration and prayed to Our Lord, asking Him to be "Spouse" enough for her...to fill that void that her husband had left.

Her estranged husband, who chose to have no contact with his wife and child, lived a dissolute life of drugs, drinking, and adultery, and was beset by depression and ultimately cancer. My sister feared getting the call that he had passed, and that she wouldn't be able to do anything about it.

Well, this past week she got a call from one of Sean's siblings saying that he was sick in the hospital—pneumonia and cancer—and that there was nothing else they could do. My sister went to his side without hesitation, bringing a priest, a scapular, and her rosary. She was introduced to medical staff as his wife (thankfully, there had never been a civil divorce), and she was able to care for him as such...just as she had prayed for.

He received the sacrament of anointing, wore the scapular, heard a few of us praying the rosary, the Divine Mercy Chaplet, and Memorares. And, he went to eternity hearing his long-faithful wife say, "I love you," "All is forgiven," "Go in peace," and "Go give Dad and Fr. Joe [our brother who had died] a big hug from us!"

To witness my sister, my role model—the one whose heart I had seen be pierced by many swords during her marriage—give her husband a wet sponge to his dry lips, to see her hold his hand and whisper in his ear comforting words, was something beautiful beyond expression. She is nothing short of heroic. She showed me, time and time again, what it means to fulfill one's vows and covenant with God: "For better, for worse, in sickness and health, until death do us part."

Many told her along the way, "Why don't you get divorced? You need to be taken care of! Go find happiness with a new man." They didn't understand what the marriage vow meant. She never took off her rings.

Because she remained faithful, she was able to bring her husband's soul back to God on his deathbed and to be by his side in the end.

Her text to me today sums it all up:

> I am truly at awe over God's mercy and love. I will forever praise Him with gratitude for His answer to my years of prayer for Sean's soul. I have an overwhelming desire to tell the world, never stop praying for a person's soul! God is

always at work, and He not only hears your prayers but He is behind the scenes orchestrating His triumphal victory over the return of that one soul.

May I follow in her footsteps. May we all shoot for sainthood. May we all be as faithful. Marriage vows *mean something*. [65]

The cross, therefore, is always ready; it awaits you everywhere. No matter where you may go, you cannot escape it, for wherever you go you take yourself with you and shall always find yourself. Turn where you will—above, below, without, or within—you will find a cross in everything, and everywhere you must have patience if you would have peace within and merit an eternal crown. If you carry the cross willingly, it will carry and lead you to the desired goal where indeed there shall be no more suffering, but here there shall be. If you carry it unwillingly, you create a burden for yourself and increase the load, though still you have to bear it. If you cast away one cross, you will find another and perhaps a heavier one. Do you expect to escape what no mortal man can ever avoid? Which of the saints was without a cross or trial on this earth? Not even Jesus Christ, our Lord, Whose every hour on earth knew the pain of His passion. "It behooveth Christ to suffer, and to rise again from the dead, . . . and so enter into his glory." How is it that you look for another way than this, the royal way of the holy cross?

—Thomas à Kempis, *The Imitation of Christ*, II., xii.

PRAYERS FOR MARRIAGES IN CRISIS

For the Couple or Individual to Pray When Experiencing Marital Strife, or When Facing Separation or Divorce

Almighty God, we place before You our marriage and family, requesting Your urgent and divine assistance.

We humbly pray that You bring healing, calm, peace, and clarity of thinking to all involved in our current situation. In some ways, our hearts have hardened and the desire to heal our marriage may at times have wavered. We pray for softened hearts that can listen to one another. We pray for an openness to rehabilitation of our relationship, whether or not we feel hope or even if at times we fear it long over or decayed beyond repair. Help us make a new beginning, putting the past behind. We may have done things we regret, but with humility, we approach one another again.

Please heal the wounds we brought into our marriage through childhood and other life experiences. Help us recognize how those wounds can affect how we relate to one another now. Please assist us in seeking and accepting help and healing where needed.

We pray for a recommitment to the health of the relationship. Lead us on the path to trusting one another again. We ask You to drive away fear and pride, and to give us courage for the road ahead.

We pray You will infuse us with hope in all aspects of this relationship, even the deepest and darkest corners. Please help us turn away from any temptations and addictions. Where necessary, lead us to experts in healing from these addictions and give us the humility to accept assistance.

Please help us focus on You and one another. Give us wisdom regarding the sacrificial love needed in our marriage. Intervene in any areas of injustice, infidelity, and impurity. Help us to forgive, and, as we process past hurts, help us to forgive again and again. Help us build a strong disposition of good will toward one another and help us remember the qualities in one another that initially drew us together. Give us patience as we await Your beautiful work in this marriage. May Your healing lead to deep reconciliation.

Since marriage is a covenant for life, may any false promise of counterfeit happiness with anyone else now lose its appeal. We beg You to remove any forces that separate us. We pray for Your guidance back to a strong marital commitment and ask for You to rekindle in us the beauty of the marital embrace.

We know that many children of divorce face anxiety, hidden and unspoken pain, lack of confidence, feelings of abandonment, lack of protection, and anger. Please help us care for and protect our children. Help us strengthen our intact family structure which was created for their security, mental and emotional development, and moral education. May that motivate us to try harder and surrender to Your loving guidance. Knowing that divorce causes suffering in the immediate family, the extended family, the circle of friends, the generations to come, and society as a whole, help us sustain our marriage as a witness to overcoming difficulties and honoring the marital bond.

Please send with haste solid and faithful friends to stand by us, to share the truth in charity, and to be listening ears and advocates for our marriage. Send people who are faithful to true teachings of marriage, family, and life. May no one in our circle of friends or family contribute to the disintegration of this marriage. Help us to reject and stand against any false support from others who try to convince us that our marriage is irredeemable, hopeless, or too difficult. Protect us from believing that abandoning our vows will lead us to happiness. We call the angels, archangels, and saints to duty, to strengthen and encourage our hearts, and to quiet the voices and influence of any people who drive a wedge between us or who feed the fire of discontent.

Help us embrace sacrifice and suffering as a path to holiness. We know this is how saints are made and how long-married couples overcome periods of difficulty in order to finish their story together, not quitting before the last beautiful chapters are written.

St. Joseph, pray for us.
St. Rita of Cascia, pray for us.
St. Monica, pray for us.
St. Thomas More, pray for us.
St. Priscilla, pray for us.
St. Valentine, pray for us.
St. Adelaide of Burgundy, pray for us.
St. Gengulphus of Burgundy, pray for us.
Sts. Louis and Zelie Martin, pray for us.
St. Raphael the Archangel, pray for us.
Amen.

Shorter Version of the Above Prayer:

Dear Lord, please hear this prayer for our marriage, which needs Your divine assistance. Intervene to remove any sinfulness that separates us. We pray for peace, joy, and sacrificial love to renew this relationship for us and our entire family. Guide us to the help our relationship requires and give us the humility to accept that help. May we continually turn to You in times of need. Let no one contribute to the disintegration of this union. We trust that You know our needs, and that Your will can be done for our marriage and for all marriages needing Your urgent assistance.
　　Amen.

For Friends and Family to Pray Upon Hearing of a Couple Contemplating Separation or Divorce

Almighty God, hear our prayer for [Name of Family] and for all families who have marriages in need of Your urgent and divine assistance. In all things, may Your will be done.

We humbly pray that You bring healing, calm, understanding, joy, peace, and clarity of thinking to all involved in this current situation. We pray that You will remove the pain and hurt in their hearts and strengthen them if they have wavered or lost the desire to heal their marriage. Please instill in them an openness to rehabilitate the relationship, whether or not they feel hope or even if at times they fear that their relationship is long over or decayed beyond repair. Please help them make a new beginning.

Heal the wounds each of the spouses brought into the marriage through their childhoods and through other life experiences. Send others to help them recognize how those wounds can affect their marriage now, and aid them in accepting that help.

Help them recommit to the health of the relationship and begin trusting one another. Drive away fear and pride and give them courage for the road ahead. Give them softened hearts that can listen to one another.

We pray for a mighty introduction and maintenance of hope for all aspects of this relationship, even the deepest and darkest corners. Help them turn away from any temptations and addictions. Where necessary, lead them to experts to help them heal from any addictions, and give them the humility to accept assistance.

Help them focus on You and one another. Infuse them with wisdom about the sacrificial love and suffering needed in marriage. Intervene in any areas of injustice, infidelity, impurity, or any other sins. Help them to forgive, and, as they process past hurts, help them to forgive, again and again.

Help them build a strong disposition of goodwill for all involved and a patience to await Your beautiful work in their marriage. Remind them of the qualities in one another that initially drew them together.

Give anyone who is in danger a respite of safety from which to allow Your work of healing. May all involved receive from You an infusion of knowledge regarding licit options to take, which lead to safety, sobriety, mental health, and protection of provision. May Your healing lead to reconciliation wherever possible.

Remove any forces that separate the couple. May any false promise of counterfeit happiness with anyone else now lose its appeal. Guide them back to a strong marital commitment and rekindle in them the beauty of the marital embrace if it has faded.

We know that many children of divorce face anxiety, hidden and unspoken pain, lack of confidence, lack of protection, and feelings of abandonment and anger. Please help them care for and protect any children, whether unborn, young, or older. Help them strengthen their intact family structure, which was created for the children's security, mental and emotional development, and moral education. May their children's well-being motivate them to try even harder and surrender to Your loving guidance. Knowing that divorce causes suffering in the immediate family, the extended family, the circle of friends, the familial generations to come, and society as a whole, help them sustain their marriage as a witness to overcoming difficulties and honoring the marital bond.

Please send with haste solid and faithful friends to stand by them, to share the truth in charity, and to be listening ears and advocates for their marriage. Send people who are faithful to true teachings of marriage, family, and life. May no one in their circle of friends or family contribute to the disintegration of this marriage. Help them to reject and stand against any false support from others who try to convince them that their marriage is irredeemable, hopeless, or too difficult. Help them embrace their marriage, which is a covenant for life. Protect them from believing that abandoning their vows will lead to happiness.

We call the angels, archangels, and saints to duty, to help them. Strengthen and encourage their hearts, and quiet the voices and influence of any people who would drive a wedge between them or who feed the fire of discontent.

May they never surrender to the challenges they encounter. Help them embrace sacrifice and suffering as a path to holiness. We know this is how saints are made and how long-married couples overcome periods of even great difficulty in order to finish their story together, not quitting before the last beautiful chapters are written.

St. Joseph, pray for us.

St. Rita of Cascia, pray for us.

St. Monica, pray for us.

St. Thomas More, pray for us.

St. Priscilla, pray for us.

St. Valentine, pray for us.

St. Adelaide of Burgundy, pray for us.

St. Gengulphus of Burgundy, pray for us.

Sts. Louis and Zelie Martin, pray for us.

St. Raphael the Archangel, pray for us.

Amen.

Shorter Version of the Above Prayer:

Dear Lord, please hear this prayer for [Name of Family], whose marriage needs Your divine assistance. We beg You to remove the pain and hurt in their hearts. Intervene to remove any forces, temptations, or sinfulness that separate the spouses. Infuse peace, joy, patience, understanding, and sacrificial love into the soul and heart of each spouse so as to renew their relationship, both for them and their family. May they turn to You in their time of need, and may they never surrender to the challenges they encounter. May Your mercy and blessing help them spend the rest of their lives together. Let no one contribute to the disintegration of their union. Help both of them love one another anew, and please remove anything that has complicated their relationship. Knowing and trusting that You know what they need, may Your will be done for them and for all such marriages needing Your urgent assistance.

Amen.

RESOURCES

For a regularly updated list of resources pertaining to marriage, divorce, and support for adult children of divorce, please visit:

LeilaMiller.net/imr

For those in need of immediate advice for a marriage on the brink, please email:

MarriageResponders@gmail.com

The title of this book was inspired by an Archbishop Fulton Sheen talk that I recommend routinely. Archbishop Sheen speaks of "impossible" marriages, asking: "Suppose the husband or the wife develops anti-social characteristics, becomes a drunkard, cruel, unfaithful, a tyrant....What are we to do?" His recommendations, which constitute a truly Christian response, are here:

https://www.youtube.com/watch?v=KBckoWr2Vs8
"Fulton Sheen ~ Marriage Problems"
on the *Sensus Fidelium* YouTube channel

ACKNOWLEDGMENTS

I would like to thank:

My husband Dean, who has been my rock for 30 years. I love you!

My children and their spouses, for endless support.

Pauline Zaro, my sister, who was instrumental in getting this book to print.

Dirk Dykstra, my son-in-law, for his help and admirable patience.

LeeAnne Abel, whom I call my "partner in crime" for good reason. And, oh, by the way, she wrote the beautiful "Prayers for Marriages in Crisis" that you saw at the end of the book.

Megan Stout, proofreader, and Beth Pack, photographer, my talented friends who have been with me from the first book.

Andrew Centrella, my friend, fellow author, and book designer.

Philip and Leila Lawler, for their kind encouragement.

The Posse (you know who you are), for keeping me inspired and fighting.

Dr. Farouk and Mary Habra, my parents, who have always been my biggest cheerleaders. They were married for almost 55 years when my dad passed away last August; I am so grateful for their strong witness to their children, grandchildren, and great-grandchildren.

The contributors to this book, whose recounted sufferings *will* save marriages and families. God bless you.

Leila Miller
March 19, 2020
Feast of St. Joseph

ENDNOTES

Introduction

[1] Even sources I consider to be "divorce friendly" admit as much: https://www.divorcesource.com/ds/considering/most-marriages-and-divorces-are-low-conflict-483.shtml

[2] To my knowledge, not a single US bishop follows this canon, much to the confusion and embarrassment of those spouses requesting separation and approaching the Church in the canonically indicated manner.

[3] See *Catechism*, 2383.

[4] I wrote an explanation for Catholic Answers, which was vetted by a tribunal judge: https://www.catholic.com/magazine/online-edition/when-does-the-church-tolerate-divorce

[5] It should go without saying, but for clarity's sake, we must state that an innocent, abandoned spouse is not guilty of the sin of divorce. Many people are divorced against their will, and, just as with the children of divorce, they are the *victims* of divorce. These victims are not culpable for the evil that was imposed upon them by an abandoner. From the *Catechism* (2386): "It can happen that one of the spouses is the innocent victim of a divorce decreed by civil law; this spouse therefore has not contravened the moral law."

[6] *Catechism* 2384 (emphasis mine): "Contracting a new union, even if it is recognized by civil law, *adds to the gravity* of the rupture: the remarried spouse is then in a situation of public and permanent adultery." The illicit "re-marriage" is the second offense, not the first.

[7] https://www.leilamiller.net/blog/2019/12/18/tribunal-psychologist-could-make-every-marriage-null

[8] To find out how to be a "divorce first-responder," discerning what to say and not say to a suffering spouse, go here: https://www.catholic.com/magazine/online-edition/be-a-divorce-first-responder

[9] https://www.leilamiller.net/blog/2019/3/27/husband-wife-and-other-woman-with-whom-will-you-stand

10 From the Rite of Christian Marriage from 1962, this includes the Instruction on the Day of Marriage and the Exhortation Before Marriage: https://sanctamissa.org/en/resources/books-1962/rituale-romanum/66-matrimony-instruction.html

11 For a free PDF copy of *Primal Loss: The Now-Adult Children of Divorce Speak*, go here: LeilaMiller.net/digitalbook. To join a secret Facebook group only for the adult children of divorce, go here: LeilaMiller.net/secretfbgroups. And, for teens and young adults coping with parental separation or divorce, go here: restoredministry.com

How To Read This Book

1 More on the idea that those who "stand" for their marriage make us very uncomfortable: https://catholicphilly.com/2017/01/commentaries/why-catholics-uncomfortable-with-amoris-arent-dissenters/ and https://www.ncregister.com/daily-news/are-the-churchs-teachings-on-sexuality-still-good-news-for-the-divorced

Section One

1 If this had happened today, the woman would simply have gone to the diocesan website, searched for "tribunal" or "annulment," and she would have seen pages of "grounds" for nullity, read about how "healing" the process was, and had all the encouragement she needed to go forward with a petition. She would have had advocates standing ready to help her get that declaration of nullity, along with the example of myriad other Catholics who had gotten theirs and "moved on" to the next romance.

2 I know Julie and Greg Alexander personally, and I highly recommend their apostolate. As of this writing, their services are free of charge: https://www.thealexanderhouse.org

3 A "90/90" in the 12-step programs means attending 90 meetings in 90 days.

4 RCIA, the Rite of Christian Initiation of Adults, is the process by which those above the age of reason are brought into full communion with the Catholic Church.

5 Retrouvaille is a program designed to save very troubled marriages: https://retrouvaille.com or https://www.helpourmarriage.org

6 Pre-Cana is a term commonly used for the Catholic marriage preparation process.

7 As noted in the Introduction: According to canon law, in cases of unrepentant adultery, "grave mental or physical danger," or unlivable situations, the physical separation of spouses is allowed (with the bishop's permission), but: "In all cases, when the cause for the separation ceases, conjugal living must be restored...." (cf. canons 1151-1155). Even should circumstances require continued or even permanent separation, the marriage bond remains.

8   https://www.thepublicdiscourse.com/2017/03/18600/

9   https://www.catholiceducation.org/en/controversy/marriage/culture-of-divorce-culture-of-death.html Copyright © 2008 Inside Catholic

Section Two

1   This is no exaggeration. The *Catechism* (2385) indeeds speaks of "children traumatized by the separation of their parents."

2   To understand why a spouse would choose to remain faithful to marriage vows even after annulment, go here: https://marysadvocates.org/cardinal-raymond-burke-to-separated-faithful/

3   Bai Macfarlane is an abandoned spouse who founded Mary's Advocates, an apostolate to "strengthen marriage against unilateral no-fault divorce and support those who have been unjustly abandoned." Website: https://marysadvocates.org

4   https://marysadvocates.org/resources/defending-marriage/petition-bishop/

5   For more information on the incredible story of Denise and Sean (and a photo), please go to LeilaMiller.net/imr

Made in the USA
Las Vegas, NV
27 September 2021

31184627R10142